Invisible Barriers

# Invisible Barriers

## Understanding and Overcoming Discrimination in the Workplace

Stéphane Carcillo and Marie-Anne Valfort

The MIT Press
Cambridge, Massachusetts
London, England

The MIT Press
Massachusetts Institute of Technology
77 Massachusetts Avenue, Cambridge, MA 02139
mitpress.mit.edu



The MIT Press would like to thank the anonymous peer reviewers who provided comments on drafts of this book. The generous work of academic experts is essential for establishing the authority and quality of our publications. We acknowledge with gratitude the contributions of these otherwise uncredited readers.

This book was set in Stone Serif and Stone Sans by Westchester Publishing Services. Printed and bound in the United States of America.

Library of Congress Cataloging-in-Publication Data

Names: Carcillo, Stéphane, author. | Valfort, Marie-Anne, 1978– author.
Title: Invisible barriers : understanding and overcoming discrimination in the workplace / Stéphane Carcillo and Marie-Anne Valfort.
Description: Cambridge, Massachusetts : The MIT Press, [2025] | Includes bibliographical references and index.
Identifiers: LCCN 2024033327 (print) | LCCN 2024033328 (ebook) | ISBN 9780262552134 (paperback) | ISBN 9780262382670 (pdf) | ISBN 9780262382687 (epub)
Subjects: LCSH: Discrimination in employment. | Sex discrimination in employment. | Minorities—Employment.
Classification: LCC HD4903 .C37 2025 (print) | LCC HD4903 (ebook) | DDC 331.13/3—dc23/eng/20241212
LC record available at https://lccn.loc.gov/2024033327
LC ebook record available at https://lccn.loc.gov/2024033328

10 9 8 7 6 5 4 3 2 1

EU product safety and compliance information contact is: mitp-eu-gpsr@mit.edu

To our children, Antonin, Isaïe, Juliette, and Virgile. We hope that you will help build a world where barriers to success caused by discrimination have been removed.

# Contents

# Acknowledgments

We thank Pierre Cahuc and André Zylberberg as well as anonymous reviewers for their careful reading of the book. Our gratitude similarly goes to our editors, Caroline Helms, Laura Keeler, Emily Taber, and Catherine Woods, for their encouragements. The opinions expressed and arguments put forth in this book are those of the authors and do not reflect the official views of the OECD or its members.

We extend our thanks to Michael Westlake for the English translation of our book with Sciences Po, supported by funding from the Institut Louis Bachelier and the Chaire "Sécurisation des Parcours Professionnels" whose partners are also gratefully acknowledged for their valuable feedback on earlier versions of our work. We significantly rewrote and augmented Michael Westlake's translation, revising directly in English.

# Introduction

Discrimination against minorities is still felt acutely even in most economically and socially advanced countries. In the United States, according to a survey conducted in 2021 by the Pew Research Center, nearly half of Americans (46 percent) say there is "a lot" of discrimination against Black people. About three in ten see a lot of discrimination against Hispanic people and Asian people. But 80 percent of Black people declare perceiving a lot of discrimination against their group, and nearly half of Hispanic and Asian people say the same.[1] Europe is no exception. In 2023, six in ten EU residents believed that discrimination on the grounds of skin color and ethnic origin was widespread, and that share can be almost 80 percent in some countries (e.g., France, the Netherlands). Unfortunately, discrimination is not limited to racial/ethnic differences. A comparable share of Europeans perceive discrimination against LGBTIQ+ (lesbians, gay men, bisexual, transgender, intersex, and queer) individuals to be widespread, and four in ten also believe being old exposes people to frequent discrimination.[2] Compared to the findings of the survey carried out ten years earlier, the figures have barely changed. If anything, they are worse.

These findings are obviously difficult to interpret. What respondents perceive depends in part on the state of the local labor market. For instance, high and persistent levels of unemployment do not facilitate entry by minority groups. Variations between countries may also be influenced by cultural factors and policy efforts to raise awareness about discrimination, leading to systematically higher perceptions of discrimination in certain countries. Finally, and most important, declarative data offer only a very imperfect measure of discriminatory behavior.

Discrimination in the labor market consists of unequal treatment of people who are identical in terms of their employability and performance. However—and this is the difficulty—people who are potentially susceptible to being discriminated against may at the same time be less employable for other reasons: briefer professional experience, obsolete skills, lower educational levels, and so on. Consequently, the visible difficulties experienced by certain groups in entering or remaining in the labor market may partly result from factors that have nothing to do with discrimination.

Such considerations do not mean that statistics on discrimination should be dismissed. Indeed, quite the contrary: respondents' perceptions testify to the existence of a deep and visible problem that has very serious economic, human, and social implications. It is therefore essential to implement appropriate strategies so as to measure the extent of discrimination and understand what drives it.

Fortunately, there has been extensive research in economics, management, psychology, political science, and sociology on this topic over the last twenty years, and answers have emerged as to the degree of discrimination in employment. Discrimination rarely is explicit, and it can make its way into all aspects of working life, from job applications and recruitment through promotion opportunities and being made redundant. It can also come into play well in advance of the labor market, during the educational process, and can affect both the acquisition of key skills and career choices. In this book, we consider the main methods for detecting discrimination in a particular country, sector, or profession. The book also presents the results of research, some of it very recent, on a wide range of social groups: women, older people, LGBTIQ+ people, racial/ethnic and religious minorities, and those who are subject to discrimination because of their physical appearance.

The discrimination experienced by these groups is sometimes very pronounced. Racial/ethnic and religious minorities and LGBTIQ+ people face widespread discriminatory behavior in matters relating to the workplace, especially during recruitment. While attitudes toward them vary from one sector to another, women generally encounter discrimination in advancing to positions of responsibility when they are of childbearing age, not only after having had children but also before, with negative repercussions for their career advancement. Older job seekers also are markedly stereotyped with regard to their motivation and adaptability, resulting in unequal treatment, despite their equivalent skills, when they apply for jobs, especially in large cities. Physical appearance, whether it be a matter of attractiveness or height or weight, also strongly affects the chances of being recruited and the level of remuneration, especially in occupations characterized by frequent contact with customers.

These findings from research on the labor market are wholly consistent with the perceptions outlined above. For these various groups, the experimental approach—comparing each group potentially affected by discrimination with a majority "control" group, all other things being equal—is essential for advancing knowledge of the issue. It reveals the sources of discrimination and the reasons for its persistence, such as the existence of cognitive biases or lack of information on the part of employers.

This book proposes a broad array of public policies to combat discrimination in employment, going far beyond the strictly punitive approach. Drawing on hundreds of mainly economics research papers, but also bringing in insights from other disciplines, such as psychology or sociology, we find that, while it is important to punish discriminatory practices, doing so does little to prevent them since proving that discrimination has occurred in the labor market remains challenging. Regulations prohibiting discrimination thus need to be combined with other policies and mechanisms, such as monitoring employers' hiring practices and career management behaviors and complementing bias training with human resources strategies that make it difficult for conscious and unconscious bias to operate. Such measures should also be accompanied by efforts to combat prejudice and stereotypes at school and beyond the school years through communication campaigns, though their impact depends very much on the approach adopted. Finally, inequalities in access to employment often are rooted in factors that exist long before a person enters the labor market: school achievement, for example, may be influenced by overt or covert discrimination. An effective strategy must therefore also include an educational component that addresses contexts in which behaviors develop.

In the course of writing this book, we learned there is nothing inevitable about discrimination. Even in a country like the United States, where it is greatly in evidence, discrimination can be identified and combated. Cognitive biases, which are the source of prejudice and stereotyping, can be corrected or at least minimized in recruitment and career management processes if the right policies are adopted and effectively implemented. At a time when governments are looking for new ways to restore growth, and in light of the immense waste of talent attributable to discrimination, this objective may even be seen as an obligation.

The book opens with a methodological section that outlines the various forms of labor market discrimination, its primary sources, and its broader economic, human, and social impacts. Additionally, it presents the key strategies to measure and analyze these disparities (chapters 1 to 4). Readers wishing to skip the more technical aspects of this presentation can concentrate on the first two chapters. Part II summarizes the main research findings for five different groups: women, racial/ethnic and religious minorities, seniors, those whose physical appearance disadvantages them, and LGBTIQ+ people (chapters 5 to 9). Each chapter may be read independently. Part III examines the public policies needed to mitigate discrimination through a combination of regulatory frameworks and incentives. It also explores strategies to combat prejudice and stereotyping, alongside the development and adaptation of educational policies to foster inclusion (chapters 10 to 12). These different components are all essential for the development of a coherent action plan to reduce discrimination in the labor market.

# I Concepts and Methods

# 1 What Is Labor Market Discrimination?

Discrimination in the labor market occurs when individuals with equal skills, educational backgrounds, and cognitive or noncognitive competencies are treated differently by employers solely because they belong to distinct groups, such as groups defined by gender, race/ethnicity, religion, age, or sexual orientation. Of course, not every difference in employment status or wage between persons from different groups indicates discrimination. Discriminatory treatment arises only when these people are, as the law says, "in a comparable situation," and in particular when they are equally productive on the job. Such *behaviors* on the part of employers are deeply rooted in *cognitive biases*—patterned thought processes that replace logical thinking when confronted with objective information—that emerge from stereotyping and prejudice.

Stereotyping entails the application of generalized, automatic beliefs about certain groups or categories. Stereotypes are simplifications that people tend to apply without distinction, whether consciously or not, to all individuals in a given group. Some examples are "women show more empathy than men but are less assertive," or "older people are less adaptable," or "ethnic minorities are less skilled." These beliefs and simplifications may concern how people behave or their preferences or abilities. They can be false or inaccurate. But they may also, on occasion, contain a kernel of truth.[1] Wrong or right, stereotypes save considerable cognitive resources in everyday life and allow people to act swiftly, which is why they are so pervasive. They also tend to be adopted early in life, to be resistant to new information, and to be ingrained in cultures. Discrimination may arise when employers apply stereotypes to make human resources decisions. In doing so, they tend to pass over the actual characteristics of individuals to retain only overly general beliefs about their group. Economists call such behaviors "statistical discrimination." As we will see, stereotypes can also affect the behavior of those so targeted in a self-fulfilling way. For instance, people in a class stereotyped as "lazy" may end up working less because their self-esteem has been undermined.

Another form of group-based automatic responses is sheer prejudice, that is, an instinctive *emotional* attitude, such as disgust or hate of (or liking for) certain groups. Differing from stereotypes, prejudices have a strong affective component. They are gutlike, strong reactions to outgroup members. Their origins may lie in perceived threats to one's group or oneself.[2] For instance, some people cannot live close to homosexuals, let alone work with them, for they deem homosexuality to be "against nature." Others might prefer not to interact with racial minorities, let alone hire them, thinking that they lack capacity or are unpredictable or dangerous; they would surely also consider interracial dating an abomination. Yet others hate having women as their boss because they view women as "unable to lead" and think they would prefer to stay home. Such attitudes can lead to discriminatory behaviors in the labor market, as when they lead to the exclusion of gay men from male-dominated occupations, bar women from accessing managerial positions, or confine ethnic and racial minorities to unemployment or unstable and entry-level jobs. Economists call such behaviors "taste-based discrimination."

## Taste-Based Discrimination

According to Daniel Kahneman, winner of the Nobel Memorial Prize in Economic Sciences in 2002, human thinking combines two systems.[3] System 1 corresponds to commonsense thinking—instinctive, approximate, but requiring little effort. System 2, in contrast, corresponds to scientific thinking, which is carefully considered and more accurate, but also requires more energy.

System 1 leads us to view favorably people who resemble us even before we know them, and to "prejudge" others negatively. This liking for those similar to us is evident in the most trivial decisions in day-to-day life. Numerous studies in social psychology have shown that when people arrive at a meeting, they do not seat themselves haphazardly. Instead, often unconsciously, they sit next to people who have as many physical features as possible in common with them. They are, for example, more likely to sit next to same-sex individuals with the same skin color. This "pairing" is also based on less overt similarities, such as wearing glasses or having the same hairstyle.[4]

Liking what is familiar is a very powerful force and is expressed even when the criterion of belonging to a group is created from scratch. In a famous experiment, the psychologist Henri Tajfel presented participants with pairs of paintings, one by Klee, the other by Kandinsky, and asked them to say, for each of these pairs, which painting they preferred. He divided the participants into two groups: the "Klee" group, made up of individuals who preferred the Klee painting in most of the Klee/Kandinsky pairings, and the "Kandinsky" group, composed of those who opted for the Kandinsky. Tajfel then handed out money to some individuals in the Klee group and to some in the Kandinsky group, asking them to share it between a member of their group and a member of the other group. The results speak for themselves: participants favored their own group to the detriment of the other group.[5] Tajfel obtained similar results when, a few years later, he conducted the same type of experiment with individuals whom he had previously randomly distributed into different groups, thus generating a belonging criterion that was even more arbitrary than a preference for Klee or Kandinsky.[6]

Individuals are even willing to incur a cost in order to be matched with similar others, as strikingly shown by Morten Størling Hedegaard and Jean-Robert Tyran.[7] These authors hired students with Danish-sounding and Muslim-sounding names in Copenhagen to prepare letters for a large mailing. This real job was paid at a piece rate. The hires were requested to show up for work twice in two consecutive weeks. In the first round, they worked by themselves. Before they came back for the second round, they were informed that they would be paid the same piece rate as in round 1 but that this time they would have to share earnings from the team output with a coworker. They were also given the opportunity to choose their coworker, depending on his or her ethnic background (conveyed by a Danish-sounding name or a Muslim-sounding name) and his or her productivity, as measured by the number of letters they prepared in round 1. The authors show that a significant share of students (38 percent) deliberately decided to discriminate: they chose a less productive coworker of the same ethnic type rather than a more productive coworker of a different ethnic type. The price they agreed to pay to indulge in this prejudiced behavior was substantial: on average, discriminators were willing to forgo 8 percent of their earnings in round 2 to avoid a coworker of the other ethnic type.

In view of these findings, it would not be surprising if certain employers, as well as some of their employees and customers, preferred interacting with people who resembled them.[8] Such a hypothesis was put forward by Gary Becker, another winner of the Nobel Memorial Prize in Economic Sciences, in his 1957 book, *The Economics of Discrimination*.

Yet it could be supposed that these preferences are not necessarily vectors of disparities in employment rates and labor earnings between different groups in society. As shown by Becker, these disparities should progressively disappear, provided market competition is sufficiently high. In the simplest version of Becker's canonical model of discrimination, prejudiced employers dislike hiring Black workers and require a fixed level of compensation to hire a Black worker rather than a white one. However, their prejudice puts them at a disadvantage compared to unprejudiced employers: they pay more for preferred-race workers (or hire less-qualified workers), which decreases their profits. Unprejudiced employers expand, prejudiced employers contract. This process increases the demand for Black workers, and their relative wages rise. If there are sufficient unprejudiced employers able to enter the market, they will eventually drive the wage differential to zero. In this setting, although a few prejudiced employers hiring only white workers may survive, Black and white workers will be equally well off.[9]

Evidence confirms that employers who discriminate are more likely to go out of business. Relying on the results of an "audit study" (see chapter 4) that she conducted in 2004, Devah Pager investigated whether employers who then discriminated against Black applicants (relative to non-Black applicants) were more likely, six years later, to be wiped out by the "cleansing effect" of the 2008 financial crisis—that is, by the fact that economic downturns heighten the costs of inefficient practices.[10] Pager found that the likelihood of going out of business in 2010 for an employer who was identified in 2004 as one that discriminates was more than twice that of its nondiscriminating counterpart: 36 percent of discriminatory employers had failed by 2010, versus 17 percent of nondiscriminatory employers.[11] However, these findings do not allow us to conclude that the lower survival rate of discriminatory employers is entirely the result of their discriminatory hiring practices. It may also flow from the fact that in other areas of business management, these employers overly rely on intuition, hence on Kahneman's system 1, rather than on evidence or on more sophisticated forms of decision-making. Relying more on intuition ultimately leads them astray not only in their hiring decisions but also in their capital investments, financial management, and numerous other domains. More generally, although the literature investigating the effect of increased market competition on labor market discrimination concludes that discrimination should eventually disappear,[12] we do not often see that effect in practice. This may be because no market ever gets competitive enough for discriminating employers to leave it or change their behaviors in such high numbers that labor market gaps between discriminated-against and nondiscriminated-against groups disappear.[13]

Some may argue that, even when markets are not perfectly competitive, individuals' preference for those who resemble them may *not* generate disparities in employment rates and labor earnings across groups. After all, for job applicants—say, African Americans in the United States—not to be discriminated against in the labor market, they would simply need to approach companies that are not unfavorably disposed toward them. However, there are reasons to believe that this strategy is largely out of reach. First, opting for nondiscriminating companies when applying for a job assumes that the applicants know which companies discriminate. This assumption is unrealistic: observation of the facts suggests that applicants, especially those at risk of being discriminated against, do not generally respond selectively to job vacancies but instead apply indiscriminately to job offers as long as they match their profile.[14] Moreover, it is not certain that companies whose employers, employees, and customers do not show distaste for interacting with Blacks offer sufficient jobs to recruit all African American candidates. For instance, one-fourth of employers examined in Devah Pager's aforementioned audit study were identified as discriminating against Black applicants—a significant share. The share of discriminators has proved to be significant in other contexts as well. Felipe Goncalves and Steven Mello tested whether police officers treat white drivers caught speeding more leniently than they do Black drivers. Because the punishment for speeding increases discontinuously with the speed of the driver, some officers may be tempted to reduce the penalty by lowering the driver's speed to just under a threshold. The authors show that Black drivers are less likely than white drivers to have a reported speed just below the threshold and that this gap is unlikely to reflect differences in true speeding behavior.

They show that 40 percent of officers account for the racial discrepancy, suggesting that not just "a few bad apples" drive racial bias in policing.[15]

All in all, it is likely that people's tendency to be biased in favor of their in-group (the social group with which they identify as a member of) or to be biased against their outgroup (the social group with which they do not identify) does cause significant and persistent inequalities in employment and wage rates between groups in society. These disparities are all the more plausible in light of the existence of what sociologists call "institutional discrimination"[16] and what legal frameworks refer to as "indirect discrimination."[17] This type of discrimination refers to an organization's institutional practices that do not depend on any particular individual (in the sense that they may be stable even as people enter and leave the organization) but still lead to treating equally skilled individuals differently simply because they belong to different groups. In the labor market, one such institutional practice is the common hiring norm whereby employers fill job vacancies through referral networks. Many studies have documented that employees are often asked to recommend candidates for positions.[18] Yet, given individuals' preferences for resemblance, social networks are very homogeneous, meaning that they are mainly composed of people from the same group. In this setting, even an organization composed of nondiscriminating individuals belonging to the same group would still tend to hire relatively few people from other groups if referral-based employment is the rule.

### Statistical Discrimination

Statistical discrimination is based on risk analysis by employers, which they rely on when they are unable to fully determine people's productivity. This is usually the case during recruitment since the applicant's CV and the job interview allow potential employers to gain only a very imprecise impression of the applicant's strengths and weaknesses. Employers are therefore inclined to supplement the information on the CV with information at their disposal regarding the group to which the applicant belongs. As a result, people belonging to groups that employers believe to be less productive *on average* may be excluded. This situation, which stems from statistical reasoning, is termed statistical discrimination.

Statistical discrimination is often perceived as based on beliefs that reflect real differences in *average* productivity between groups. But even in this case, statistical discrimination is unacceptable, as explained by Steven Pinker,[19] because it violates moral justice and thus the logic of impartiality, that is, refusing to do to others what is hateful to oneself.[20] None of us wants to be treated differently on the basis of gender, race, ethnic origin, or other aspect, and according to the logic of impartiality, we must extend this right to everyone.

Another reason why statistical discrimination is unacceptable flows from the fact that it relies on beliefs that are often inaccurate. Let us not forget that system 1 always threatens to take over: our representation of reality is rarely fully objective. In particular, we tend to overestimate other people's flaws so that we can entertain the illusion of being better than they are.[21]

Employers from a given group are thus likely to focus only on the possible defects of other groups and ignore their strengths. They also tend to greatly exaggerate the perceived weaknesses of other groups. This cognitive bias has been widely documented.[22] One of its most striking manifestations was identified by two American economists, Amanda Agan and Sonja Starr, following the implementation of "ban the box" (BTB) policies in some U.S. states and cities.[23] These regulations prohibit employers from asking questions about jobseekers' criminal record, usually disclosed by asking the applicant to check a box. BTB is presented as a way of reducing unemployment among African American men, who are disproportionately convicted compared to the population as a whole. But BTB can also have unwanted effects. The suppression of information on criminal records may encourage statistical discrimination against African American men. Since they are unable to request this information, employers are more inclined to make assumptions about the criminal background of applicants—assumptions that, given the cognitive bias described above, may be much more damaging to most African Americans than the objective information in their criminal record.

To test this mechanism, Amanda Agan and Sonja Starr sent some 15,000 applications from fictitious young men to employers in New Jersey and New York before and after the adoption of BTB policies. The applications varied according to the applicant's name (distinctively African American or distinctively white) and criminal record. The results confirm the suspicion that BTB policies actually encourage racial statistical discrimination. The response rate gap between African American and white candidates increased dramatically as a result of these policies: white applicants had a response rate that was 7 percent higher before the introduction of BTB but 43 percent higher after.[24]

The beliefs on which statistical discrimination is based are rarely fully accurate. Yet it is possible to replace inaccurate beliefs with accurate ones by providing information to employers on the actual productivity of individuals from different groups. Aislinn Bohren, Kareem Haggag, Alex Imas, and Devin Pope conducted an experiment on Amazon Mechanical Turk in which participants were recruited for the purpose of completing either a work task (performing mathematical calculations) or a hiring task (making wage offers to potential hires).[25] Participants assigned the role of "worker" differed along several characteristics, including their country of origin (United States versus India) and their gender. In the absence of information on past performance, participants assigned the role of "employer" made substantially higher wage offers to Indians than to Americans, and somewhat higher wage offers to males than to females. Elicitation of their beliefs revealed that they predicted that American workers would perform much worse than their Indian counterparts, and that female workers would only slightly underperform relative to males. However, these beliefs are mistaken. Observation of workers' actual performance shows that Americans and Indians perform equally well on a task, while females underperform relative to males to a greater extent than anticipated by employers. When employers are given information by the experimenters about the average actual performance of the different groups, they update their beliefs, which therefore become more accurate: employers' wage offers to workers from different groups better reflect these groups' average productivity.

It is worth noting that the extent to which employers' beliefs can be influenced by additional information depends on the extent to which they trust or understand this information. For instance, if employers are unaware of the quality of the educational establishments attended by individuals with a minority background, more detailed information on these studies will have little impact on the assessment of their actual skills. Similarly, employers may find it difficult to interpret the quality of minority applicants' career paths and the extent to which this may reveal or affect their actual productivity. In that case, revealing more information on the CV or during an interview is less likely to change employers' assessments for minority workers than for majority workers. This is what is often called variance-based statistical discrimination, as opposed to level-based discrimination, discussed above.[26] Joanna Lahey and Douglas Oxley have identified both types of discrimination based on a laboratory experiment in which they used eye tracking of fictitious recruiters over six thousand résumés signaling comparable skills and productivity but randomized over race to identify the impact of stereotypes on hiring chances.[27] Not only did they find that recruiters spend less time on the résumés of young Black candidates relative to those of comparable young white ones, they also found that recruiters believe young Black candidates have worse computer skills and worse training and are more likely to hide gaps in their work experience, since adding additional positive signals on Black résumés improved their rating (level-based statistical discrimination). Lahey and Oxley also found that adding positive signals did not have the same effects for white and Black candidates. White candidates received higher rating increases from recruiters than Black candidates on producing high-quality signals, including details on job history and high school curriculum (variance-based statistical discrimination).

In real-life labor markets, employers typically are not provided additional information by a third party of the actual average performance of different groups on the type of jobs for which they recruit. In this setting, inaccurate beliefs may persist. Imagine that an employer discriminates against a candidate because of the mistaken belief that the group to which the candidate belongs is on average less productive than other groups. Because the employer does not hire individuals from this group, the employer cannot observe the group's actual productivity and therefore cannot come to the realization that the belief is ill-founded.

But the persistence of initially erroneous stereotypes can also flow from a self-fulfilling process by which these stereotypes ultimately end up describing reality. Members of a group that an employer mistakenly perceives as unproductive and thus refuses to hire do not have an incentive to invest in maintaining their skills. This lack of investment can lead to confirmation of the employer's beliefs. This self-fulfilling process can also occur on the job: managers who invest less in developing the potential of employees who belong to groups for which managers have low expectations will indeed cause their underperformance. If, on top of entertaining negative stereotypes, managers are also prejudiced against these employees, then the gap in productivity relative to the rest of the workforce will widen further: managers' distaste for interacting with these employees will lead to a series of management mistakes, from lack of supervision to derogatory comments, whose effects will be strongly demotivating. As an illustration, the economists Dylan Glover, Amanda Pallais, and William Pariente conducted an experiment in a large French retail company in 2011–2012.[28] Their aim was to measure the impact of managers' prejudice and negative stereotypes regarding people of African descent (North African or sub-Saharan) on the performance of the check-out staff they were supervising. The authors compared the productivity of check-out staff according to their French or African origin and whether their manager was "biased," that is, displayed prejudice and negative stereotyping with regard to individuals of African descent. The findings are edifying. Being assigned to a biased (rather than unbiased) manager decreased the productivity of check-out staff of African descent, as measured by the number of articles scanned per minute, whereas, as might be expected, managers' prejudice and stereotypes regarding individuals of African descent had no effect on check-out staff of French origin. Combining these findings leads to an unexpected conclusion. With an unbiased manager, employees of African descent perform better than those of French origin, having a scan rate of almost one additional item per minute. This productive advantage disappears, however, when they are supervised by a biased manager. A further survey of check-out staff revealed that the negative impact of biased managers on the productivity of employees of African descent did not involve open hostility on the part of managers but simply lack of supervision: biased managers limited their contact with check-out staff of African descent.

### The Pervasiveness of Bias

Individuals most exposed to prejudice and negative stereotypes in a given society are, by construction, those most likely to be rejected by the majority; hence they are "minority" individuals. By "minority," we mean members of groups that constitute a minority in the total population, such as racial/ethnic or religious minorities, LGBTIQ+ individuals, people with disabilities, seniors, and so on.

But minority groups are not the only ones who face obstacles in the labor market. So do women. Women suffer from gender stereotypes, deeply rooted in history and culture, according to which men are destined to engage in paid work and women to take up domestic and family work. An important strand of interdisciplinary literature traces the emergence of the unequal sharing of paid and unpaid work to the agricultural revolution.[29] Unlike hunter-gatherer societies, in which women contributed a significant share of the food supply through gathering (and also hunting), women in agricultural societies were economically dependent on men because the physical strength required to clear the land and prepare it for sowing made these tasks a man's job. The gendered division of labor thus became particularly unequal with the emergence of agricultural societies. As an illustration, economists have shown that the longer the agricultural history of a country, the fewer women are present in the labor market.[30] Moreover, economists have revealed that this relationship is particularly strong in societies characterized by plow agriculture.[31] Unlike the hoe or digging stick, the plow requires significant upper-body strength, grip strength, and a burst of power either to pull the plow or to control the animal that pulls it. As a result, regions with a tradition of plowing developed the belief that the natural place for women was in the home.

This gendered division of labor ultimately evolved into deeply ingrained restrictive social expectations about the roles of men and women, and thus heralded the emergence of a patriarchal culture. This transformation explains why, despite the steady decrease in the economic advantage conferred by physical strength, particularly over the past century, a significant share (nearly half) of citizens in EU countries still express traditional views on gender roles: they endorse the view that "the most important role of a man is to earn money" and that "the most important role of a woman is to take care of her home and family."[32] What is more, the emergence of a patriarchal culture induced the dissemination and persistence of additional gendered stereotypes detrimental to creating a level playing field for men and women, including the stereotypic belief that men and women are unequal not only in terms of ability to deal with paid and unpaid work but also in terms of intellectual skills. Compared to men, so the stereotype goes, women are governed more by emotions than by reason, whereas decades of work in neuroscience have not succeeded in confirming clear differences between the brains of men and women, let alone differences that would allow affirming the intellectual superiority of one gender over the other. Unfortunately, these beliefs are still pervasive in public opinion, even in countries considered advanced in terms of gender equality. As an illustration, in all EU countries but one, Sweden, a majority of people surveyed agreed with the statement that "women are more likely than men to make decisions based on emotions," thereby suggesting that men are more rational than women.[33]

Implicit association test (IAT) results confirm that minority individuals are victims of prejudice and negative stereotypes. IATs are designed to make it impossible for test takers to hide their automatic association of ideas. For example, to measure bias against persons of North African descent in France, the IAT displays a series of given names and descriptive words on the computer screen. The first names are of either French (Michel) or North African origin (Mohammed), and the words are positive (e.g., "good," "pleasant," "hardworking") or negative (e.g., "bad," "unpleasant," "lazy"). In the first IAT session, the participants are asked to place the first names of French origin and positive words on one side of the screen and first names of North African origin and negative words on the other side. In a second IAT session, first names of French origin and negative words are to be placed on one side of the screen and first names of North African origin and positive words on the other. The IAT is based on the assumption that people with prejudice and negative stereotypes about people of North African origin will be faster in the first session (where the names are associated with negative words) than in the second session. Bias against people of North African origin is thus measured by the difference between the time taken to associate given names of North African origin with positive words and the time taken to associate these given names with negative words (while bias in favor of people of French origin is measured by the difference between the time taken to associate given names of French origin with negative words and the time taken to associate these given names with positive words).

Thousands of IATs have been and are still being administered online through Project Implicit, started in 1998 by the creators of the IAT.[34] The tests reveal that most participants have an automatic preference for light skin as opposed to dark skin, for young as opposed to old people, and for heterosexual as opposed to gay people. The IATs also reveal an automatic association between "women"/"family" and "men"/"career," on the one hand, and between "women"/"liberal arts" and "men"/"science" on the other hand.[35]

Of course, IATs do not constitute perfect measures of actual discriminatory behaviors since bias leads to discrimination only if people act on it. Moreover, IATs may capture not only individual prejudice and stereotypes but also individuals' perception of the prevalent culture and social norms. For instance, if a person identifies women with domestic and family work more than with career on an IAT, the test taker's automatic association may simply reflect a fact of life rather than personal bias. However, although the correlation between IAT results and actual behavior may be below expectations, studies by and large reveal that IAT results still constitute better predictors of discriminatory acts than explicit self-reports, which are often biased by social desirability.[36] For example, recruiters' bias against ethnic minorities or obese people measured by the IAT is positively correlated with the probability that they will discriminate against individuals belonging to these groups. More explicit measures of negative prejudices and stereotypes, such as expressing hostility toward ethnic minorities and obese people, are not, however, correlated with recruiters' behavior, possibly because it is very easy for them to falsify their response on surveys where they are asked to self-report their attitudes and behaviors.[37] A striking illustration of the unreliability of more explicit measures of prejudice and negative stereotypes was recently provided by Redzo Mujcic and Paul Frijters.[38] These authors ran a field experiment in Australia that entailed randomly assigning test customers to board public buses with no money to purchase a fare, leaving the bus driver to voluntarily decide whether to offer them a free ride. Based on 1,552 transactions, Mujcic and Frijters uncovered strong evidence of racial bias: bus drivers were twice as willing to let white testers ride free as they were Black testers (72 percent versus 36 percent of instances). Moreover, the authors provide new insight into the methodological weaknesses associated with explicit self-reports. Rather than showing that these explicit self-reports correlate poorly or do not correlate at all with actual behaviors, they go a step further by documenting that explicit self-reports are in fact negatively correlated with actual behaviors: bus drivers who responded to a hypothetical survey on whether they would accommodate random customers shown on a photograph reported that they would favor Blacks, which is in complete contradiction to their actual behavior in the field.

It is interesting to note that repeated exposure of minority groups to discrimination may make them less inclined to prefer individuals who resemble them. The discrimination they experience is also likely to change their tendency to perceive their own group in positive terms. Indeed, IAT participants who belong to a minority do not always express a preference for their group. This ability to internalize the disparaging norms to which they are subject is a phenomenon well known to social psychologists. As early as 1947, Kenneth Clark and Mamie Clark showed that the majority of African American children prefer to play with a white doll than with a Black doll indistinguishable from the first apart from its color.[39] Some years later, Steven Asher and Vernon Allen replicated this experiment by also involving white children.[40] They showed that regardless of their ethnic background, children tend to prefer the white doll to the Black doll. In other words, while the majority group does express a "pro-in-group" bias, the minority group is tempted by a reverse, "pro-outgroup" bias.[41]

The particular vulnerability of women and minorities explains why the EU, the most active international organization in the fight against unequal treatment since its directives of the year 2000, prohibits discrimination on the basis of the following criteria: gender (to protect women but also transgender people),[42] race or ethnicity, age, sexual orientation, and disability. These directives oblige the twenty-seven EU member states to create and implement legal standards to combat discrimination and ensure the application of the principle of equal treatment in accordance with these criteria.[43] Several countries outside Europe also prohibit discrimination based on the aforementioned criteria, especially when discrimination is perpetrated in the labor market (see chapter 10). This is notably the case of the United States since June 15, 2020, when the U.S. Supreme Court ruled, in a groundbreaking and historic decision, that sexual orientation and gender identity are included under "sex" as a prohibited ground of employment discrimination in the Civil Rights Act of 1964.

# 2 Why Fight Discrimination?

Tidjane Thiam was born in Côte d'Ivoire in 1962, into two influential West African families. At the age of twenty, he was the first Ivorian to pass the entrance exam to the prestigious École Polytechnique, one of France's most respected elite universities. In 1986, he was offered a scholarship to do his MBA at INSEAD, consistently ranked among the world's leading business schools, from which he graduated on the dean's list. But this outstanding track record did not yield any job offer from top French companies, and Thiam quickly turned to U.S. and British companies to find a position that matched his ambitions—first McKinsey in Paris, then, following a ministerial interlude in the Ivorian government, Aviva and Prudential in London. Then, in 2015, he was appointed CEO of Credit Suisse, one of the top banks worldwide at the time, thanks to his expertise in risk management. In this position, he was able to steer the bank away from its risky investments, clean up the mess of the subprime crisis, and return the company to profitability. For that achievement he was named by *Euromoney* "banker of the year" in 2018. In 2020, he had to leave the company abruptly. It is true that the spying on an employee at the end of 2019, which Mr. Thiam repeatedly said he knew nothing about, badly tarnished the company's image. This seems minor in comparison with other multibillion-dollar scandals in the banking sector following the subprime crisis, which did not really threaten the position of many of the CEOs in charge. But the treatment of Mr. Thiam was different, and his origins are likely to have played a significant role.

In October 2020 the *New York Times* devoted a long article to the "short tenure" of Tidjane Thiam as the head of Credit Suisse.[1] The article opens with an account of the sixtieth birthday celebration of Urs Rohner, then chairman of the board of Credit Suisse, in November 2019. The only Black guest, Tidjane Thiam, attended a performance that proved to be in questionable taste: a Black man, dressed as a janitor, danced while sweeping the floor. Leaving the room, Tidjane Thiam returned later to be astonished again: several friends of Urs Rohner had taken the stage to perform their own musical number, all wearing Afro wigs. According to the *New York Times,* this event was just one of a series of incidents that marked Tidjane Thiam's five years at the head of Credit Suisse. The *New York Times* concluded that, had he been white, Tidjane Thiam might have had more luck in seeing his mandate survive the spying scandal.

If this interpretation is correct, it would not have been the first time that Tidjane Thiam was treated as someone who did not belong, a mess given his extraordinary potential and achievements. In a collected work published in 2009 and titled *Qu'est-ce qu'être français?* (What does it mean to be French?), Tidjane Thiam speaks of his attachment to France, despite the many rebuffs he has suffered:

> Frustration sometimes. Faced with policemen with French citizenship like me, who use the familiar "tu" when addressing me. Frustration at having to go into exile in London, tired of banging my head against a glass ceiling that is invisible but so very real.
>
> Tired of seeing less competent colleagues get promoted and advance their careers when mine stagnated. . . . Frustration when one of my schoolmates turned head-hunter confessed to me with embarrassment that he stopped including my profile in his replies to his French clients, because the answer invariably was: "An interesting and impressive profile, but you do understand . . ."
>
> Everything was always left unsaid, in the form of those three suspension points.
>
> Only my faith in the ideals defended and represented by France allowed me when it was necessary to put into perspective the narrow-mindedness with which we, all of us who are visibly different, are so often confronted.[2]

Discrimination must be combated because it is a denial of equality between equal people. But that is not the only reason. In addition to being ethically unacceptable, discrimination imposes a huge economic cost on society, both directly and indirectly. It prevents some people from getting jobs while leading others to being underpaid. It hinders societies from reaping the advantages diversity can bring to them. The human cost of discrimination includes psychological suffering which negatively affects people's ability to fulfill their potential. In addition, discrimination generates a social cost because prejudice and stereotypes undermine a community's capacity to build a society.

## The Direct Economic Cost of Discrimination

### Standard Mechanisms

The standard labor market mechanisms through which discrimination imposes a direct cost on society are well-known. Whether stemming from employers' preferences or from their beliefs about the lower productivity of certain groups, discrimination reduces demand for labor of the discriminated groups, which reduces their wages and their access to employment and confines them to less-qualified positions than they might otherwise occupy. These negative consequences are magnified by reactions of the labor supply. Reduced wages undermine incentives to work. The discrimination-induced decrease in the demand for labor also reduces the productivity of those who are discriminated against because they invest less in education and lifelong learning since they anticipate low returns. Broadly speaking, discrimination hurts the economy by annihilating incentives: disfavored groups see no point to becoming more engaged, while favored groups take their position for granted and thus do not put in as much effort as they could. This negative spiral results in production losses that in turn affect public finances. Lower production and wage levels reduce state revenue from income tax, corporation tax, and social security contributions. At the same time, discrimination in access to employment increases public expenditure as a result of unemployment benefits and social transfers to those who are discriminated against.

Few studies have evaluated the direct economic cost of discrimination in the labor market because it is a difficult exercise. But available estimates suggest that this cost is considerable. In the United States, the reduction in discrimination against women and African Americans between 1960 and 2010 is estimated to be responsible for 20–40 percent of the increase in GDP per capita over this period, thanks to a better allocation of talents, as reflected in a remarkable convergence in the occupational distribution among white men, women, and Black men.[3] For example, 94 percent of doctors and lawyers in 1960 were white men. By 2010, the fraction was just over 60 percent. Similar changes occurred throughout the economy, particularly in high-skill occupations. Since the innate talent for a profession among members of a group is unlikely to change over time, the change in the occupational distribution since 1960 suggests that a substantial pool of innately talented women and Black men in 1960 were not pursuing their comparative advantage because of discrimination. Consider the world that Supreme Court justice Ruth Bader Ginsburg faced when she graduated from Columbia Law School in 1959. Despite being ranked first in her class, she was rejected by Supreme Court justice Felix Frankfurter for a clerkship position because of her gender.[4]

Focusing on anti-LGBTIQ+ discrimination, the Organization for Economic Cooperation and Development (OECD) has recently taken advantage of a unique set of nationally representative U.S. microdata.[5] The data reveal that LGBTIQ+ individuals continue to face considerable disparities in areas critical to individual and societal well-being, including education, employment, and health. The economic consequences of achieving LGBTIQ+ equality appear substantial.[6] Should the United States succeed in closing the unexplained LGBTIQ+ gaps in employment and labor productivity by 2050, an increase in GDP equal to 2.6 percent of the baseline GDP could be expected. This corresponds to a yearly increase in GDP of 0.1 percent. A more ambitious goal of closing the gaps by 2030 would lead to a higher yearly GDP increase, representing not 5 percent but about 10 percent of the average annual U.S. GDP growth observed between 2013 and 2023. If the United States were to achieve full LGBTIQ+ equality in the labor market now, U.S. GDP would increase by 1 percent, equivalent to more than 250 billion dollars.

Attempts to evaluate the direct economic cost of discrimination in other national contexts have yielded similarly huge estimates. A report published in 2016 by France Stratégie, an institution attached to the French prime minister's office, assessed the impact of a modest reduction in *unexplained* differences in employment rates and wages between two populations: men aged twenty-five to fifty-nine years and without a recent migration history (who enjoy an advantageous position in the labor market) and men and women of working age from North Africa and sub-Saharan Africa.[7] France Stratégie found that the modest reduction in unexplained differences in employment and wage rates would bring in €150 billion, or nearly 7 percent of French GDP.[8]

In the same vein, Kilian Huber, Volker Lindenthal, and Fabian Waldinger show that discriminatory dismissals of Jewish managers in Nazi Germany, caused by surging antisemitism, harmed large corporations.[9] Firms that lost Jewish managers experienced considerable and persistent reductions in stock prices, dividends, and returns on assets. A back-of-the-envelope calculation suggests that the aggregate market valuation fell by 1.8 percent of German GNP because of the expulsion of Jewish managers.

### Taking Other Mechanisms into Account: The Untapped Diversity Dividend

Although they highlight a considerable negative impact, the aforementioned figures remain an imperfect assessment of the economic cost of discrimination. Namely, on top of restricting their attention to only one or two grounds of discrimination, gender and ethnicity, they do not factor in that discrimination prevents the economy from harnessing the economic potential of diversity. This incapacity constitutes a major loss of opportunity because in many countries, the population is getting more and more diverse.[10] The size of groups defined by individual characteristics such as gender, age, disability, sexual orientation, nationality, ethnicity, or race is on the rise. Over the past decades, the labor market participation of women has soared; the population shares of migrants and their children are increasing in almost all OECD countries; and more LGBTIQ+ people are open about their sexual orientation and gender identity. These societal changes are occurring against the backdrop of aging societies, meaning that the proportion of older workers is also growing.

The business case for diversity is not clear-cut. This is because diversity can have both positive and negative consequences on economic performance and brings a net advantage only in a nondiscriminatory environment where everyone feels welcomed and valued irrespective of their gender, age, skin color, ethnic background, disability, sexual orientation, or religious or political views. On the one hand, enhanced diversity increases the prospect for complementarities between different skills, experiences, and ideas: research finds that teams higher in cognitive diversity, defined as differences in perspective or information-processing style, solve problems faster than teams where everyone has the same thinking approach.[11] On the other hand, enhanced diversity drives communication costs up because of animosity and lack of trust; differences in social and work norms, which may lead to different interpretations and understandings of concepts and goals; disparities in cognitive frameworks, which may also trigger gaps in how the same information is processed; language differences, and so on.

Against this backdrop, empirical evidence shows that diversity is a performance factor, but only in a work environment open to difference, since it allows the pooling of a greater wealth of skills and experience, the benefit of which more than outweighs the higher cost of communicating and coordinating with people from different backgrounds. Provided the organization has inclusive practices, diverse teams challenge individuals to alter their patterned ways of thinking and hence enhance their creativity and ability to generate value.

This finding has been confirmed by Dutch researchers who studied a sample of 550 students from Amsterdam University of Applied Sciences, known for seeking to attract a diverse mix of profiles, each eager to interact with others of different backgrounds.[12] Consistent with this mission, the pool of students analyzed is nearly equally split by gender and foreign versus nonforeign status. More precisely, students of foreign origin account for no less than 55 percent of the sample, and a high proportion of these are of non-European origin (excluding North America, Australia, and New Zealand). As part of their training, the students have the task of creating and managing a real company in groups of ten to twelve over a period of a year. Each team is responsible for raising funds, producing and marketing goods or services, keeping the accounts, paying corporation tax and social contributions, and so on. To test the impact of diversity, the researchers defined the composition of each team. They varied not only the proportion of women (from 20 percent to 60 percent) but also the mix of students from different national origins. The researchers found that not only gender diversity but also ethnic diversity significantly improved the turnover and profit of the startups created by the students, a result presumably flowing from the inclusive mindset in which the students from a diverse set of backgrounds interact.[13]

By contrast, in a setting composed of more standard coworkers, that is, those not selected based on their capacity to value different others, communication costs can rise to the point that gains from knowledge sharing can no longer compensate for these costs. Based on a field experiment conducted in an international online market for contract labor, Elizabeth Lyons showed that teams whose workers come from the same country outperform teams whose workers are nationally diverse, despite focusing on countries that once belonged to the same national entity (e.g., India, Pakistan, and Bangladesh).[14] Similarly, analyzing the performance of entrepreneurial teams composed of MBA students in the United States who participated in a business course to build startups, a group of economists did not identify a positive effect of gender mix or ethnic diversity.[15] Quite the contrary: regarding the latter, they found that greater racial/ethnic diversity led to significantly worse performance, even holding national origin constant.

That said, it is possible to unlock the potential of diverse teams, even when they are made up of coworkers who are not particularly open to different others to start with, if these coworkers are overseen and managed by an employer who helps to facilitate coordination. Empirical evidence confirms that diversity brings a net benefit under inclusive management. Using a unique data set consisting of the gender of venture capital partners' children, Sophie Calder-Wang and Paul Gompers found strong evidence that when partners have more daughters, they are more prone to hire female candidates and to see the deals and fund performance of their team rise with this enhanced gender diversity.[16] This finding suggests that, while implementing a blunt gender quota may not bring any economic dividend, gender diversity is likely to be performance enhancing if introduced in an unbiased or debiased environment.

Of course, diversity can also be documented as an underperformance factor in a context of intergroup rivalry. As an illustration, the economist Jonas Hjort observed the performance of a production line in Kenya during a period of severe interethnic tensions.[17] Each team comprised three people: a worker upstream of the production provided flowers to two downstream workers, who were responsible for arranging them in a bouquet. The plant carried out regular staff rotations, leading to three types of teams: ethnically homogeneous teams, and teams in which one or both downstream workers belonged to an ethnic group that was in conflict with the ethnic group of the worker upstream. Hjort showed that in this last configuration, upstream workers undersupplied flowers to workers who did not belong to the same ethnic group but oversupplied the others, thus generating congestion effects.[18]

## The Indirect Economic Cost of Discrimination

The lost diversity dividend is only one of several reasons why current estimates of the economic cost of discrimination are understated. Notably, these estimates overlook the human and social costs of discrimination. These costs have a significant financial counterpart, which deprives the economy of a substantial share of its potential resources.

**The Human Cost of Discrimination**

Discrimination undermines performance through psychological processes. A natural experiment induced by the COVID-19 pandemic provided a unique opportunity to test this phenomenon. A group of economists examined how the sudden absence of fans at football games had an impact on player performance in Italy.[19] Their findings revealed that African players, who are frequently subjected to racial harassment, performed better when fans were no longer present in the stadiums. The study, which utilized official records of racist behavior by fans, demonstrated that performance improvements were most pronounced on teams that had experienced the highest levels of abuse before the lockdown.

Social psychologists have long suspected that individuals may feel threatened by the possibility that their behavior confirms a negative stereotype about their group's abilities. By undermining their self-confidence and self-esteem, this "stereotype threat" ultimately does impair their performance and hinder the realization of their potential.[20] In a famous experiment, Jeff Stone and his coauthors confirmed that it is indeed possible to make people lose their bearings when reference is made to a known negative stereotype pertaining to their group.[21] Based on the finding that African Americans in the United States are perceived as more athletically talented but less intellectually gifted than whites, the researchers randomly assigned Princeton students to three groups. In the first group, students took part in a sporting exercise described as "a measure of people's natural athletic ability." In the second group, this exercise was described as "a measure of the ability to develop a strategy during a sporting performance"—or, without spelling it out, an intelligence test. In the third group, the control group, the exercise was described more neutrally as "sports performance measurement." The results confirmed what the researchers suspected. The performance of African Americans was lower in group 2 (sports intelligence) than in group 1 (natural athletic ability), where their performance was "normal" in that it coincided with the control group's performance. Conversely, the opposite occurred among whites. They performed significantly worse than African Americans in group 1 but significantly better than African Americans in group 2. The performance of African Americans and whites was the same in the control group. In other words, neither African Americans nor whites can achieve their full potential when placed in a stigmatizing context.

Another experiment pointed out the detrimental impact on girls' performance of the stereotypical view that boys have more developmental resources in mathematics than girls: when asked to study a complex figure and later to reproduce the figure from memory, girls outperformed boys if the task was described as testing drawing ability, but they underperformed boys if the task was described as testing geometry ability.[22]

The stereotype threat effect is in fact a more general phenomenon. All that is needed to trigger it is to stress that a person is a member of a discriminated group, as became evident from an experiment carried out in India by two World Bank economists, Karla Hoff and Priyanka Pandey.[23] The experiment involved asking children of low and high caste to find their way out of mazes drawn on paper. The children's performances were unrelated to their caste when their anonymity was preserved. On the other hand, the performance of the low caste children fell significantly, by 20 percent, when their caste was publicly revealed, while the performance of the high-caste children was unchanged.[24] These conclusions are not specific to India. When replicated in China, the experiment produced the exact same results.[25]

In this context, it can be expected that the repeated experience of microaggressions, that is, daily discriminations that may seem trivial when considered individually, will end up generating chronic stress that undermines people's mental health.[26] Lower mental health in turn has the potential to impair people's physical health by providing a fertile ground for other pathologies to grow, such as cardiovascular disease. This health penalty for groups at risk of being discriminated against may be compounded by the fact that minority individuals are less likely to be matched with a health practitioner of the same group. Whereas Blacks make up approximately 13 percent of the U.S. population, they make up only 4 percent of physicians and fewer than 7 percent of recent medical school graduates.[27] Yet, in a context of preference for similar others, being able to meet with a physician of the same group could be a key ingredient of a good patient-doctor relationship that ultimately helps correct false beliefs, increase demand for preventive care (which is typically low owing to understatement of the benefits), and hence improve health status. Marcella Alsan, Owen Garrick, and Grant Graziani confirmed that a common racial background facilitates communication and interpersonal trust between patient and physician, and therefore boosts the demand for preventive care among African American men.[28] Their findings suggest that assigning Black men to Black rather than non-Black male medical doctors could reduce the Black-white male gap in cardiovascular mortality by 19 percent.

Survey data confirm that minorities are more likely to report being discriminated against and more likely to face mental health issues, as has been shown to be the case globally for racial/ethnic minorities[29] and LGBTIQ+ populations.[30] It can be argued, however, that these linkages are pure correlations that do not necessarily imply that discrimination has a causal effect on people's psychological well-being. It could be that the cause-and-effect relationship goes in the opposite direction, that is, the minorities might have a predisposition to mental illness that would incline them to paranoia.

Empirical evidence shows, however, that living in a discriminatory environment does have a negative impact on mental health.[31] A study compared suicide rates among the heterosexual population, on the one hand, and among the homosexual and bisexual population on the other in two types of U.S. states, those that allowed same-sex marriage before its legalization by the Supreme Court in June 2015 and those that did not. The authors showed that the difference in suicide rates between LGB and heterosexual populations decreased much faster in states that had introduced same-sex marriage prior to the Supreme Court decision—a trend that was not at work before these states embarked on more LGB-inclusive policies. The authors estimate that the legalization of same-sex marriage caused a reduction by nearly 15 percent of suicide attempts among adolescents who self-identify as gay, lesbian, or bisexual while leaving suicide attempts among heterosexual adolescents unaffected.

More recently, groundbreaking research provided the first comprehensive analysis of the impact of anti-LGBTIQ+ laws implemented by provincial, county, and municipal governments in Poland between 2019 and 2020 on the mental health of the population.[32] Using county-level data from 2017–2020, the authors estimated difference-in-differences models to compare changes in suicide attempts, suicides, and overall mortality in areas that adopted anti-LGBTIQ+ laws to changes in these outcomes in areas that did not pass such laws. The study found that annual suicide attempts increased by 16 percent, or by five attempts per 100,000 people, after the enactment of anti-LGBTIQ+ statutes. Additionally, the authors uncovered an increase in suicide attempts in areas that deliberated but ultimately rejected anti-LGBTIQ+ resolutions, providing evidence that even the stigmatization of minority groups leads to declines in population mental health.

Compelling evidence shows that living in a discriminatory environment adversely affects the mental health not only of LGBTIQ+ individuals but also of other marginalized groups. In the United States, researchers have examined the impact of police killings of unarmed Black Americans and their spillover effects on the mental health of African Americans.[33] Annually, over three hundred Black Americans—at least a quarter of them unarmed—are killed by police in the United States. Using a nationally representative health survey, researchers analyzed differences in reported mental health issues among Black and white respondents exposed to one or more police killings of unarmed Black Americans in their state in the three months prior to the survey. The study found that each additional police killing of an unarmed Black American was associated with 0.14 additional poor mental health days among Black respondents, while no mental health impacts were observed among white respondents. The most significant effects on mental health occurred within one to two months after exposure. Further evidence of a causal effect was demonstrated by the fact that mental health impacts were observed only after police killings of unarmed Black Americans, not after police killings of unarmed white Americans or armed Black Americans.

These findings thus confirm the magnitude of the human cost of discrimination. The financial counterpart is equally substantial. Assessment of the average cost of managing depression by health systems in EU countries reveals an expenditure per patient of €2,000 a year.[34] But this figure does not take into account a range of other indirect economic costs, such as the effect of a parent's depression on the cognitive development of her or his children or the loss of human capital arising from suicide by individuals whose mental health was undermined by discrimination.

These findings regarding the human cost of discrimination also show how taste-based and statistical discrimination can be mutually reinforcing. Prejudice against a group can undermine its members' mental health. This shortfall can in turn feed into negative stereotypes about the psychological state and thus productivity of people from this group. In other words, indefensible prejudices have the power to gradually evolve into self-fulfilling prophecies.

**The Social Cost of Discrimination**

Prejudice and stereotypes undermine the capacity of members of a population to live together. It is only when a system is perceived as fair—when people know that they will be treated fairly and will not be prejudged on the basis of features of their biology or history that are beyond their control—that it can gain the trust of citizens. By contrast, discrimination instills the poison of mistrust: mistrust on the part of discriminators directed toward those who are discriminated against induces a sense of general mistrust on the part of the latter. This mechanism explains the negative correlation between ethnic diversity and trust, first identified in the United States by political scientist Robert Putnam.[35] The degree of the correlation depends strongly on the level of racism among whites: it is strong if whites are very hostile to ethnic minorities but weak otherwise.[36]

Discrimination can create deep divisions. While it crushes some of those who are discriminated against, it induces in others feelings of resentment and a determination to break with social norms (see chapter 6). One example in the United States of this often self-destructive temptation is hostility toward "acting white." This phenomenon refers to the rejection by African Americans of those who adopt behaviors that are considered characteristic of whites, such as doing well in school. Studies suggest that this low-grade culture developed as a result of school desegregation, especially in institutions that became integrated by force.[37] In these institutions, fraught with interracial tensions, African American high school students who excel are much less likely to have African American friends. By contrast, in schools where the student body is more predominantly African American, students' circles of friends are unrelated to their academic performance.[38]

Discrimination undermines social cohesion and compromises the emergence of a "society of trust," defined by Alain Peyrefitte as "an expanding win-win society, a society of solidarity, common endeavor, openness, exchange and communication."[39] The shortfall is staggering. In his speech on being awarded the 1972 Nobel Prize in Economics, Kenneth Arrow surprised his audience. Urged to account for the origin of the wealth of nations, he did not mention any traditional economic factors such as the accumulation of physical and human capital. Instead, he suggested that the indispensable ingredient for prosperity is trust: "Virtually every commercial transaction has within itself an element of trust, certainly any transaction conducted over a period of time. It can be plausibly argued that much of the economic backwardness in the world can be explained by the lack of mutual confidence."[40] These intuitions have since been confirmed by the economists Yann Algan and Pierre Cahuc. Their measurement of the impact of trust on economic development reveals that GDP per capita in France could be 15 percent higher were French people as trusting as the Swedes.[41]

Assessing to what extent discrimination might undermine trust and social cohesion requires first identifying and quantifying discrimination. This is not an easy task since employment, wage, and careers are influenced by so many other factors. Spotting discrimination in labor market performance gaps requires implementing fine-tuned identification methods.

# 3 The Challenge of Identifying Discrimination with Representative Surveys

Measuring the extent of existing discrimination is a necessary prelude to combating discrimination through targeted and effective policies. For this purpose, there are two possible approaches: using survey or administrative data and conducting field experiments. This chapter takes up survey data, which, along with administrative data (see chapter 5), make up observational data, or data collected without manipulating the study environment, as opposed to experimental data.

The use of survey data is unavoidable if the goal is to measure the differences in employment or wages between a "majority" group and a "minority" group, the latter of which may be discriminated against. Indeed, survey data have the advantage of measuring the average performance gap in a representative sample of individuals from different groups in a given economy. More specifically, survey data can be used to subdivide this gap into two components: one that is accounted for by differences in productive characteristics between these groups and another that cannot be explained by these differences. The "unexplained" component is often interpreted as reflecting the discrimination suffered by the minority group. Indeed, if there remain gaps in terms of employment or wage once all differences in age, abilities, experience, and so forth—that is, all characteristics that determine productivity—are netted out, this means that the two groups are being treated differently for other reasons.

But it is difficult to know whether this interpretation is correct. Once the impact of observed characteristics that can influence employment or wages is taken into account, such as education, work experience, occupation, sector, and the like, the remaining gap does not necessarily reflect the impact of discrimination. In fact, certain characteristics that influence workers' productivity and therefore their labor market performance are not always observed in surveys. Unless their effect is neutralized, one runs the risk of overestimating the share of labor market gaps that persist when every productive characteristic is held constant and that therefore can be attributed to discrimination. This chapter describes the main methods for identifying employment or wage gaps from survey data and discusses the difficulties in interpreting them. Despite these limitations, many studies continue to use what are called "wage equations" because of the representativeness of the survey data they exploit. Wage equations are discussed in more detail below.

## Estimating the Relationship between Wages and Belonging to a Minority Group: "Wage Equations"

Indictment for discrimination is still unusual because it remains a challenge, when a wage gap is observed, to distinguish the impact of productivity factors from the effect of deliberately discriminatory behavior by employers. In principle, wages should be determined primarily by productivity—that of the firm and of the individual.

Against this backdrop, discrimination would be identifiable if wage comparisons could be conducted between individuals exhibiting the exact same productivity but belonging to different groups, defined according to a legally protected ground such as gender, ethnic origin, or sexual orientation. Traditionally, much of the evidence for labor market discrimination therefore came from ordinary least squares regressions in which wages were treated as the dependent variable while a dummy variable for a legally protected ground, such as race, along with a set of control variables, such as age and educational attainment, were treated as explanatory variables. The working assumption behind such "wage equations" was that if the coefficient for the dummy variable for the legally protected ground was significant, this was evidence of discrimination.[1] Unfortunately, productivity is not easily observable. What is observed are various characteristics thought to strongly influence it, such as those pertaining to the job (e.g., sector, occupation) and to the individual (e.g., educational attainment, work experience). However, a number of important additional determinants of productivity, such as noncognitive skills (conscientiousness, openness to new experience, extraversion, agreeableness, emotional stability),[2] are also likely to actively enter into wage formation, despite not being measured (or at least rarely measured) in representative surveys. In this context, estimates of discrimination obtained from wage equations are doomed to be biased unless, after observable characteristics are accounted for, there are good reasons to believe that the unobservable determinants of wages are on average the same for the two groups studied.

Yet this assumption is implausible. For example, individuals belonging to a racial/ethnic minority often grow up in poorer households characterized by lower parental investment in children's education and greater barriers to the development of their noncognitive skills. Unless these noncognitive skills are observed, the wage penalty for the racial/ethnic minority will be interpreted as attributable to labor market discrimination, while at least part of it results from differences in noncognitive skills that emerge upstream from the labor market.

To further complicate the analysis, individual characteristics may themselves be influenced by discrimination. For instance, it has been shown that gay men and lesbians avoid applying for jobs in occupations where they expect higher discrimination (i.e., male-dominated occupations for gay men and female-dominated occupations for lesbians), meaning that the type of sector in which LGBTIQ+ individuals work at least partly flows from their anticipation of discrimination.[3] Similarly, women's maternity decisions may be influenced by their wage prospects, which themselves depend on discrimination. In such cases it is difficult to separate the determinants of wages related to belonging to a minority group from those that are not. Yet, unless the set of control variables includes only factors orthogonal to being a member of the minority, estimation of the wage equation yields a coefficient on the dummy variable for the legally protected criterion that is biased; that is, it inaccurately measures discrimination in the labor market based on this ground.

Some studies have therefore attempted to better identify the effect of belonging to a vulnerable group, by including among the control variables more precise measures of people's productivity, such as skills tests' results. However, even this approach is not devoid of weaknesses.

## The Case of African Americans

A good example of this approach is the analysis performed by the economists Derek Neal and William Johnson of the pay gap between whites and

African Americans in the United States.[4] The researchers used the National Longitudinal Survey of Youth (NLSY), which for nearly forty years has been tracking the lives of a sample of 10,000 Americans born between 1957 and 1964. Aged from fourteen to twenty-two at their first interview in 1979, the participants are now at, or approaching, retirement age. They were regularly interviewed to ascertain their situation in the labor market, as well as their educational attainment, training, social benefits, family life, health status, income, and wealth. The first survey also included many questions about their ethnic and family background. A panel of this kind that tracks individuals over the long run is extremely unusual and of great value. Furthermore, in 1980, participants were given a battery of aptitude tests regularly used in the Armed Forces Qualifying Test (AFQT). These tests enabled a wide range of skills to be measured for all the participants, including their reading and writing ability and mathematical reasoning.

The authors estimated the wage equation for years 1990 and 1991 among the subsample of respondents who were eighteen at the time they passed the AFQT in 1980. The findings show that the wages of young African American men and women are respectively 24 percent and 19 percent lower than those of their white counterparts. These gross differences are substantial. Yet these estimates are plagued by two main issues.

First, their validity is threatened by so-called selection bias: to the extent that a significant share of African Americans are deprived of employment owing to discrimination, they would probably be paid lower wages relative to whites should they be employed. Ignoring this selection bias would probably lead to underestimating the pay gap between groups that is attributable to discrimination. A way to solve this issue consists in assigning a notional minimum wage to all individuals who are not in employment. Relying on this approach, Neal and Johnson computed a wage gap between white and African American men equal to 35 percent.

Second, producing an unbiased estimate of the pay gap that flows from discrimination entails controlling for skills in an accurate way, which is hardly possible if one uses education as a proxy. For instance, it is likely that the quality of educational institutions varies greatly between whites and African Americans, which can result in differences in ability between groups, including among young people having the same level of education. In addition, the educational attainment of African Americans is likely to be lower because of the anticipation of hiring discrimination on entry into the labor market. For why invest in education when it brings nothing in return? Consequently, taking education into account in the wage equation may lead to underestimating discrimination: the wage gap is wrongly attributed to the education deficit, whereas in fact the deficit is due to anticipated discrimination.

In this context, the AFQT is probably a much better measure of skills. This test has proved its worth since over the years it has been a good predictor of people's performance once they enter employment, both for ethnic minorities and for whites (in contradistinction to other standardized tests, which often end up being biased in favor of white people). The problem, once again, is that the results of this test may be influenced by discrimination, for example if the tests are passed after entry into the labor market, because skills may also be acquired on the job. For this reason, Neal and Johnson focused only on those who took the test no later than age eighteen. They found that differences in test performance accounted for almost three quarters of the gross wage gap among young men and all of it among young women. This result suggests that wage differences are mainly the result of differences in skills acquired prior to entry into the labor market rather than to actual discrimination once in this market. Neal and Johnson confirmed that these skills are strongly influenced by factors acting upstream of the labor market, such as family background, for example the employment status of parents, the number of siblings, and how many books were in the home.

These conclusions sparked controversy, however, and prompted two other American economists, Kevin Lang and Michael Manove of Boston University, to revisit them.[5] Like Neal and Johnson, they began by ignoring differences in educational attainment in their wage equation, not only because these differences only imperfectly reflect differences in skills but also because educational attainment after the end of compulsory schooling may be influenced by discrimination, in which case a self-fulfilling prophecy could be at work: people educate themselves less when they expect that their prospects will be disappointing, and ultimately their prospects are poor because they are not sufficiently qualified.

But the solution to use skills tests is not perfect either since their results do not derive solely from innate skills but also are influenced by educational attainment: an extra year of school significantly increases test scores. Lang and Manove show that with equal results on the AFQT, African American youth had on average more, not less, education than whites—an additional year of schooling on average. This result may be interpreted in two ways. Either African Americans are disadvantaged by the quality of the schools they attend as well as by their family history, and must therefore make a greater effort to attain the same skill level, or young African Americans anticipate discrimination by employers and, rather than underinvest in education, overinvest in education to compensate for discrimination.

Lang and Manove show that with equal skills, quality of schools, and family history, but also with equal years of education, there is a significant wage gap of about 10–15 percent between whites and African Americans. This pay gap is twice as large as the one they get when education is absent from the wage equation. Lang and Manove argue that the year of education not recognized by employers—or the lower pay with equal years of education, which amounts to the same thing—is a form of discrimination in the labor market. If African Americans with equal skills have to overinvest in education to get the same wages as whites, ignoring the number of years of education in the wage equation would lead to understating the effect of discrimination.

These examples illustrate the difficulty of choosing the right control variables when comparing the wages of a majority group and a minority group. The same factor may be a "bad test" in some contexts but a "good test" in others, as illustrated by the example of education. When it is cut short in anticipation of discrimination in the labor market—that is, when the members of the minority group underinvest in their human capital—discrimination in employment is underestimated if education is included in the wage equation. But when the members of the minority group overinvest in education to compensate for the discrimination they expect to encounter, not including education in the wage equation also leads to understating discrimination. The previous examples also demonstrate the importance of taking into account factors that are at work upstream of the labor market: many of the inequalities that are observed may have their roots in people's childhood and adolescence, before individuals enter the workforce. Ignoring these determinants can also lead to a biased estimate, which this time overestimates discrimination in employment.

## Analyzing the Wage Gap in More Detail: The Blinder-Oaxaca Decomposition

The work of Lang and Manove shows that the effect of education on wages may vary from one group to another, a difference that conventional wage equations are unable to take into account. To get around this difficulty, an alternative, two-stage approach is available. In the first stage, the influence of wage determinants is estimated by estimating two wage equations: one for the minority group, the other for the majority group. In the second stage, the proportion of the wage gap resulting from differences in productive characteristics is identified, and the proportion that remains unexplained is therefore attributable to discrimination. This approach, inspired by the innovative work of Ronald Oaxaca and Alan Blinder, is known as the Blinder-Oaxaca decomposition method because it decomposes the influence of each factor into an explained part and an unexplained part.[6] But it proceeds to this decomposition in a finer way than classic wage equations.

To better understand how the method differs from the previous approach, it should be remembered that when we estimate the influence of productive characteristics—say, education—using a single wage equation, we assume that a year of education in terms of pay is the same for African Americans and whites. This is obviously a simplification because, as we have seen, it is quite possible, even likely, that a year of education yields less for some minorities. The advantage of separately estimating the effect of education on wages for each group is that we can vary the return depending on the group concerned.

The unexplained share of wage differences is then measured by comparing the return on productive characteristics across groups. To get back to the previous example, the wage gap between whites and African Americans is partly explained by the fact that African Americans on average have had less education than whites (or are less skilled, depending on the exact indicator used)—this is the explained part of the gap. But the gap also flows from the fact that, with equal education or skills, African Americans earn less—this is the unexplained part that is interpreted as discrimination.

It is thus possible to calculate differences in returns for all factors influencing wages other than racial/ethnic identity, such as work experience, education, and so on, and aggregate these differences to obtain a global measure of discrimination. Of course, any factor influencing wages that is not considered in this calculation would also be found in the unexplained part, even if it is not necessarily linked to discrimination in the labor market—for example, the quality of schools or the family background. It is therefore essential to take into account all possible determinants, at least when they are not affected by the anticipation of discrimination (or not negatively so), at the risk otherwise of obtaining a biased estimate of discrimination.

## The Case of Gender Equality

To understand the subtleties of the decomposition method, let us look at the analysis of wage differences between men and women in the United States carried out by the American economists June O'Neill and Dave O'Neill.[7] While a gender gap undeniably persists despite the convergence of wages and employment rates in recent decades (see also chapter 5), the extent to which discrimination contributes to this gap is subject to intense debate. To determine the share of the different factors influencing wages, O'Neill and O'Neill also base their analysis on the NLSY described above. With such a panel, it is possible to consider a wide range of individual characteristics that can influence career paths. The authors conducted their study on a subsample of 5,600 individuals aged from thirty-five to forty-three years and interviewed them every two years in the second half of the 1990s. They obtained a gross wage difference between men and women of 23 percent within this population.

O'Neill and O'Neill then estimated the wage equation separately for men and women, in each case taking into account the same factors likely to influence pay: age, ethnic origin, education, scores on AFQT proficiency tests, periods out of work, the number of years of labor market experience, economic sector, and type of job held—a very comprehensive set of explanatory variables. The authors then calculated the share of the wage gap attributable only to differences in these characteristics between the two groups. When an equal return from these characteristics in terms of wages is assigned to both men and women—for example, by taking the return observed for men as the basis of the calculation—it is possible to explain a percentage of the gross wage difference. This "explained" share corresponds to composition effects: women do not have the same work experience as men, do not occupy the same types of occupation, and so on. The authors also calculated the share of the wage gap that is strictly attributable to the differences in return from characteristics between men and women and found that age, education, work experience, and so forth do not impact wages equally in these two groups. When equal levels of characteristics are assigned to both men and women—for example, by taking the average of the characteristics among women as the basis of the calculation—the share of the wage gap that is attributable only to differences in return can be measured. This is the "unexplained" part, which is considered to flow from discrimination.

With this approach, O'Neill and O'Neill found that the objective differences in productive characteristics between men and women accounted for twenty percentage points of the 23 percent gross wage gap, or 87 percent of the difference. Work experience alone accounted for two-thirds of it, notably owing to the career interruptions influenced by societal expectations around women's roles (see chapter 5), while differences in educational attainment or skills accounted for only a very small share. The same is true for differences between economic sectors, which in any case are likely to be affected by discrimination (insofar as people choose the sector where they work to escape discriminatory behavior, this variable should therefore in principle be eliminated from the analysis).

The remaining three percentage points of the gap are unexplained and stem from the fact that the wage return from age, years of experience, the type of job held, and similar factors is a little lower for women than for men. In other words, the correlation coefficients between the wage and each explanatory variable are not the same when one examines the wage equation for men, on the one hand, and for women on the other. It is this unexplained gap, and only this, that can be interpreted as being the result of discrimination. Gender-based wage discrimination in this particular sample therefore turns out being low. However, as we will see in chapter 5, it should not be concluded that wage discrimination against women is negligible.

Unfortunately, the decomposition method is not devoid of weaknesses. First, it suffers from the same shortcoming as the simple wage equation approach: it assumes that unobservable components that influence wages are on average the same across groups. But this assumption is unrealistic. For example, it is uncertain that unobserved factors determining labor market participation, such as motivation, are the same for men and women. Second, the decomposition method considers that the set of variables relevant for accounting for wages is the same for men and women because decomposition of the differences would otherwise be impossible. This again is a questionable assumption. Another questionable feature is that the method assumes that the return from productive characteristics for men would remain unchanged if the returns for women were similar. To calculate the explained share of the wage gap, the same returns are indeed applied to both men and women. Finally, the choice of the reference group greatly influences the results of the decomposition. In the previous example, men were used as the reference group to calculate the explained share: if women had the same returns as men in terms of education, work experience, and so forth the wage gap would be no more than three percentage points. But if we take women as the reference group, the unexplained gap rises to ten percentage points. To solve this problem, instead of taking the output of one or other group as the benchmark, researchers use a weighted average of the output obtained for both groups, using the share of each group in the sample as the weighting. In this case, the unexplained magnitude of the pay gap is around seven percentage points.

Both of the methods discussed in this chapter have a major advantage: they use data that are representative of a given population and are easily accessible through national statistical institutes. However, the proportion of the gaps that they attribute to discrimination is open to question. To overcome this problem, researchers have turned to the experimental approach, the main advantage of which is that it is better able to compute gaps between groups that are comparable in terms of employability and productivity.

# 4 Measuring Discrimination with Experiments

Field experiments offer several advantages over survey data analysis, particularly with respect to internal validity. This refers to the ability to establish a causal relationship—in this case, whether the results are driven by belonging to a minority group rather than by other factors. Although survey data have the advantage of being representative of a given population, the gross differences in employment or wage rates they reveal may derive as much from discrimination as they do from factors that influence productivity but are difficult to measure. Distinguishing between the two can be very complicated, as illustrated in the previous chapter. The experimental approach tries to avoid this source of confusion. The three most common types of experiments are audit studies, correspondence studies, and laboratory studies. Each type of experiment has its own advantages and flaws, which we discuss in the rest of the chapter.

The best-known experimental method is embodied in correspondence studies. This field experiment involves sending out, in response to real job ads, the CVs and letters of application of fictitious candidates who are identical save a ground of discrimination that is prohibited by law. Unlike survey data, correspondence studies have the major advantage of ensuring that any difference in the rate at which these fictitious candidates are invited to a job interview by employers is the result of discrimination based on this ground. Sometimes these CVs are supplemented by real job interviews with actors playing the role of fictitious applicants and "auditing" the recruitment process at the interview stage. For that reason, such experiments are called audit studies. Certain mechanisms leading to discrimination may also be identified through laboratory experiments rather than in the field. Experiments of this kind can lead to a better understanding of the workings of discrimination and its underlying nature, whether taste-based or statistical.

But these experimental approaches are not without flaws. They have the disadvantage of giving only a partial view of the differences in treatment between the majority group and the minority group, since their findings are conditional on a specific period, location, or occupation. As such, their external validity, that is, the generalizability of their results, is questionable.

### Audit Studies of Job Interviews

Audit studies have long been used to identify discrimination. The idea is simple: it involves being present at job interviews to see how the employer behaves toward candidates belonging to different groups. For this end, people ("auditors") with fictitious identical CVs are asked to apply for a job and to go to the job interview when invited. They differ only with respect to a ground protected by law, such as gender, ethnic origin, or sexual orientation.

The main purpose of these studies is to determine whether the productivity revealed to employers through the CV and during the job interview is the same for candidates from different groups. Indeed, the candidates are not only similar with regard to their CVs, the actors who play them are trained to behave in a similar way during the job interview. In addition, the candidates (auditors, actors) are comparable in how they search for a job: their CVs are sent randomly to employers offering similar positions. Consequently, lower hiring rater or salary offers for the minority job candidate should be attributable to discrimination.

A well-known and seminal example of the audit method—although unrelated to labor—is the study conducted in 1995 by Ian Ayres and Peter Siegelman, professors at Yale University and the University of Connecticut, respectively, on the car market.[1] Teams of actors were trained to bargain for the price of a car in the same way. The actors, indifferently male or female, white or African American, were then sent at random to dealers in the Chicago area, who were also randomly selected. Their mission was to pretend that they wanted to buy a new car. This type of experiment is referred to as "random" because the assignment of buyer profiles to dealers is done by random draw, so as to avoid any selection bias and thus to ensure the comparability of results between groups. Each member of the pair of actors bargained for the same model of car and at the same dealership, usually a few days apart. A total of thirty-eight "buyers" bargained for 306 cars at 153 dealerships. Although the buyers used the same negotiating scenario learned during training, and although they all provided the dealers with proof of their creditworthiness, the dealers did not behave in the same way toward the different profiles. They offered lower prices to white males than to white females and to African Americans of both genders. However, determining the mechanisms behind this discrimination is not easy. It is possible that the price differences offered by dealers reflected differences in preferences (taste-based discrimination), which could happen if, say, dealers were naturally inclined to be more affable toward white men. But the price differences could also have resulted from different assessments of the limit price that each group was willing to pay (statistical discrimination). More precisely, it may be that dealers viewed white men as better negotiators and tougher in business than women or African Americans.

The 1996 study by David Neumark of the University of California at Irvine and colleagues Roy Bank and Kyle Van Nort is another well-known example of the audit approach, this time with regard to the labor market.[2] The researchers asked two male and two female students to apply for waiting staff jobs at sixty-five restaurants in Philadelphia. The study was designed so that each member of a male-female pair responding to the same job ad had equivalent CVs. The results were clear. Of the thirteen job offers from the most expensive restaurants in Philadelphia, eleven were made to men, whereas of the ten job offers from the most affordable restaurants in the city, eight were made to women. Additional findings suggested that the discrimination was not attributable to the employer but derived from customer preferences. While the gender of the recruiter or restaurant owner had no effect on the likelihood of a man or a woman being hired, discrimination against female candidates increased with the proportion of men in the restaurant's clientele. The restaurants whose customers were predominantly male were also the most expensive.

Despite the best intentions of experimenter, however, it is difficult to ensure that actors assigned to the different candidate profiles act in exactly the same way in the presence of the employers. This is the criticism that James Heckman and Peter Siegelman level at the audit method.[3] Studies using this method make a point of choosing actors with equivalent physical traits: same size, weight, same style of dress, same age. The actors must also follow a script written in advance. But it is unlikely that all the differences an employer may perceive can be controlled, such as greater self-confidence or extroversion, meaning that these factors can play a major role in employers' final choice—especially since the skills listed on their CVs are the same. In addition, if the actors involved in the experiment are aware of its purpose, namely, combating discrimination, it is not clear that they will manage to act alike during the interview. Consciously or unconsciously, they may be tempted to confirm or controvert the expected differences in callbacks between the majority and the minority candidates. This risk is all the greater as these actors are not really looking for a job: the cost for them not to behave as they would in a real job interview is in fact zero.

### Sending Out Fictitious Applications in Response to Real Job Ads: Correspondence Studies

To forestall the criticisms made by Heckman and Siegelman, most researchers now avoid sending actors to job interviews. They simply submit the similar applications of fictitious majority and minority job candidates to real job ads and compare the rates at which the candidates are invited to job interviews. This method also has the advantage of generating a larger number of tests (since there is no need to manage the interview processes), which enhances the researchers' capacity to detect discrimination.

For example, the economists Marianne Bertrand and Sendhil Mullainathan published an influential study in 2004 on discrimination against the African American population.[4] In response to ads published in Chicago and Boston newspapers, the authors submitted fictitious CVs that differed only in the name of the applicant, which was either distinctively white (Emily Walsh, Greg Baker) or distinctly African American (Lakisha Washington, Jamal Jones). In total, the authors responded to 1,300 ads in the areas of sales, administrative support jobs, and customer service, thereby sending out nearly five thousand CVs. The results were striking: an applicant with a distinctively white name needed to send out ten CVs to get a job interview, against fifteen CVs for an applicant with a distinctively African American name. This 50 percent difference in callback rate is statistically significant and stable across industries and occupations, a fact that may reveal taste discrimination against applicants perceived as African American. The relevance of this interpretation was confirmed when the authors investigated the effect of having a high-quality CV characterized by higher level of educational attainment, richer work experience, and fewer career breaks: while stronger CVs resulted in a 30 percent increase in the callback rate for white candidates, they had no effect on the probability that African American applicants would be invited to a job interview.

Unfortunately, correspondence studies have their drawbacks too. Like audit studies, correspondence studies usually identify discrimination that occurs not on the scale of the entire economy but in the inevitably more restricted confines of the experiment—a specific period, as well as a few regions or cities, economic sectors, or types of job. For instance, the results obtained from experiments at the local level (city, region) cannot easily be generalized to the whole country. When the experiment is very local or very specific to a given sector, we say that the external validity of the results is limited. Moreover, fictitious applicants are not necessarily representative of the average applicant. It is for this reason that the rates of discrimination obtained from experiments carried out in different countries are difficult to compare.

The external validity of correspondence studies also depends on how the job ads are selected. Ideally, one should focus on a representative set of employers. But employers who use press ads to recruit probably differ in terms of discriminatory behavior from those who use a public employment service, who in turn probably differ from employers who post job openings on private websites. Yet correspondence studies rarely focus on all these types of employers at the same time, meaning that their measurement of discriminatory behavior is likely biased.

It is also unclear whether the level of discrimination as measured by correspondence studies reflects employers' *potential* discriminatory behavior or whether it constitutes a good estimate of the discrimination that actually prevails in the labor market. If, for example, members of the discriminated-against group have acquired the capacity to target the least discriminating employers, then the real degree of discrimination in the labor market will be lower than that predicted by correspondence studies. Similarly, for candidates whose group affiliation is usually not included on their CV—LGBTIQ+ people, for instance—correspondence studies, which are precisely based on making this group's affiliation explicit, can lead to results that do not describe the reality of hiring discrimination so much as its potential.

Another difficulty highlighted by the Nobel Prize in Economics winner James Heckman concerns the interpretation of differences in response rates between different groups.[5] These differences do not necessarily reflect employers' different preferences (taste-based discrimination) or employers' different beliefs about the mean of applicants' unobserved productivity (statistical discrimination). This ambiguity arises as soon as employers perceive one of the groups as more heterogeneous, that is, as simultaneously comprising both more very weak and more very strong applicants (i.e., employers perceive a group difference in the variance of unobserved productivity). This can occur, for instance, when inequalities in the quality of education are greater in one group than in the other. In such a situation, the results of correspondence studies may depend on how the fictitious CVs are calibrated against the requirements of the job, meaning that the level of discrimination found may simply be an artifact of how the correspondence study is implemented.[6] As put by economist Dan-Olof Rooth: "If the variance of unobserved productivity characteristics differs across groups, even though there is no difference in the mean of those same characteristics, this implies that one group has a higher probability to go over, or fall under, the threshold used for hiring. In fact, in such a scenario, a standard correspondence study could find discrimination when it does not exist or find no discrimination when it does exist."[7] More specifically, if the average quality of the fictitious CVs is below the recruiter's minimum requirements, then he or she will favor applicants belonging to the more heterogeneous group—for the probability that applicants' productive characteristics lie above the bar is higher in the higher-variance group if the bar is high. Conversely, if the average quality of the fictitious CVs is above the recruiter's minimum requirements, then he or she will favor applicants belonging to the less heterogeneous group—for the probability that applicants' productive characteristics lie above the bar is higher in the lower-variance group if the bar is low. This mechanism can therefore generate differences in response rates between the majority group and the minority group that have nothing to do with taste-based or statistical discrimination. It is nonetheless possible to correct the bias, provided that the quality of the fictitious CVs in each group is sufficiently varied, as was shown by David Neumark.[8] When revisiting the correspondence studies data produced by Bertrand and Mullainathan, Neumark found that discrimination against African Americans is even greater when the effect of recruiters' beliefs about heterogeneity within the majority group and the minority group is taken into account.

One last major limitation of correspondence studies is that they provide only a partial measure of hiring discrimination since they do not allow measuring the outcome of the job interview. This experimental approach also says nothing about discrimination in wage or promotion that may occur should the fictitious applicants get hired. For instance, a model of hiring and interviewing behaviors reveals that, when interviewing costs are low, which may be the case in the public (nonmarket) sector, the rate at which applicants are invited to a job interview can fail to capture hiring discrimination as discrimination shifts to the postinterview stage.[9] Even in the private (market) sector, callbacks as a measure of hiring discrimination could miss a large share of discrimination that occurs later in the interview stage. Evidence from all available audit studies implemented to measure racial/ethnic discrimination (twelve studies overall) reveals considerable additional discrimination in hiring after the job interview: candidates representing the racial/ethnic majority not only receive approximately 50 percent more callbacks but also, if invited to an interview, secure roughly 50 percent more job offers than minority candidates. This pattern indicates that overall hiring discrimination against visible minorities is twice as large as what is measured at the callback stage alone.[10]

Despite all these limitations, correspondence studies remain the most widely used and reliable experimental method to detect hiring discrimination. The large number of observations that can be generated by multiplying the number of tests and signals on CVs can also help us understand which stereotypes drive discrimination and to what extent revealing additional information can mitigate them.[11] Nevertheless, like the wage equations presented in the previous chapter, this approach makes it difficult to distinguish whether discrimination is taste-based or statistical. Differences in response rates may reflect differences in beliefs about unobserved productivity within each group, over and beyond what individuals' CVs indicate, as much as differences in taste for working with this or that group. To distinguish the source of discrimination, it is helpful to turn to laboratory experiments.

## Laboratory Experiments

Laboratory experiments study the behavior of individuals within a particular environment—the "laboratory"—in which the researcher tries to control the parameters likely to influence their decisions. This approach allows better identification of the mechanisms that lead to discrimination.

For example, the economists Chaim Fershtman and Uri Gneezy relied on this method in 2001 to study ethnic discrimination in Israel.[12] They invited Ashkenazic Jewish students (descendants of European and American Jewish communities) and Sephardic Jewish students (descendants of Jewish communities in Asia and Africa) to participate in a so-called trust game. A trust game is a two-player game in which player A is given an amount of money and must decide how much to give to player B. The experimenter then triples the amount transferred and gives it all to player B, who then has to decide whether to hand over part or none of the gain to player A. The game is called "trust" because the amount transferred by player A to player B depends on player A's trust in player B, that is, player A's belief in player B's willingness to return an amount at least equal to the original donation. If player A trusts player B, she is more likely to transfer the entire amount she holds. But if player A anticipates that player B will keep everything to herself, she won't transfer anything.

The results revealed that player A transfers less to player B if player B is Sephardi rather than Ashkenazi. The outcome does not depend on player A's ethnic background: Sephardic Jews are as likely as Ashkenazic Jews to penalize player B if player B is Sephardi. This result may reflect statistical discrimination, that is, lower trust in Sephardic Jews. But it may also stem from taste-based discrimination, or lower altruism toward them. To test this hypothesis, the authors also invited students to play the so-called dictator game. This game involves giving player A an amount of money and letting her decide how much she wishes to transfer to player B, without player B being able to return part of the amount transferred. The dictator game is used in experimental economics to measure the altruism of player A toward player B. Fershtman and Gneezy found that players A transfer equivalent amounts to Sephardic and Ashkenazic Jews. Against this backdrop, the lower amount received by player B in the trust game when player B is Sephardi does not reflect lower altruism but lower trust. Discrimination against Sephardic Jews is therefore statistical in nature. Yet complementary findings indicate that this discrimination is based on erroneous beliefs (a possibility described in chapter 1). The authors show that the stereotyping of Sephardic Jews as less trustworthy is unfounded: the amount they return to player A in the trust game is strictly equivalent to that returned by Ashkenazic Jews.

Other laboratory experiments are more directly related to the study of behaviors in the labor market. For example, some invite participants to evaluate each other's management skills, after having observed them in a role-play situation. These experiments have notably been used to analyze perceptions of female managers. On average, these studies do not reveal any divergence in the assessment of men and women as managers.[13] But this finding does very much depend on the context. For example, when women adopt a style of management considered to be overly "masculine"—too authoritarian, not sufficiently participative—they are devalued by their assessors relative to their male counterparts, especially when these are men.

The main limitation of laboratory experiments clearly flows from the impossibility of knowing whether the players behave as they would have in the field. In the real world, individuals are subject to many influences that experimenters are unable to recreate. It is therefore likely that behaviors in the field are very different from those observed in the laboratory. These experiments can, however, identify sources of discrimination that field experiments will never be able to detect.

All these methods, whether observational or experimental, have their advantages and limitations. When applied repeatedly, across different circumstances and countries, they have enabled researchers to gain a better understanding of the prevalence of discrimination and its socioeconomic consequences. In the following chapters, we present their main findings, first concerning women and then for different minorities.

# II The Evidence for Discrimination

# 5 Gender Equality: A Difficult Battle to Win

When Ruth Bader Ginsburg started law school at Harvard, she was one of nine women in a class of 550 people. When she was invited to a dinner party hosted by the dean for the female students, she was asked why she was at the law school, potentially taking the place of a man. She could only say that she wanted to support her husband, who was also pursuing a legal career, because that was how life was at that time. As she could not find a suitable job in the United States after graduating, she accepted one in Sweden—a much more egalitarian country than the United States in the 1960s. That experience profoundly changed her views on the organization of society. Once back in the United States, she started championing equal rights among men and women. She started by showing that discrimination is harmful not only to women but also to men. In the 1970s she won a case in which a father whose wife had died in childbirth was declined child benefits to raise his child because the underlying assumption was that "wives are dependent on their husbands, husbands are not dependent on their wives"[1]. She not only became in 1996 the second female Supreme Court justice, she fought for gender equality her whole life, as exemplified by several emblematic cases, such as that requiring equal access to military school for men and women.[2]

Much career progress has taken place for women over the last few decades. Today about half the law school students in the United States and more than one-third of federal judges are women. Yet in the United States, women still earn nearly 20 percent less than men, and this gap has stopped narrowing since the mid-2000s. Men are 50 percent more likely to be employed as managers, and women make up only 16 percent of board members in the top five hundred multinational firms.[3] Some industries seem particularly difficult to access. Women are often discouraged from embarking on scientific, technological, or engineering careers because from an early age they hear they are not suited to such jobs. Thus, fewer than one-third of researchers in the world today are women.[4] Overall in the United States, about four in ten women say they have personally experienced discrimination or have been treated unfairly because of their gender, and most frequently this experience relates to hiring, pay, or promotion.[5]

Thanks to a wealth of statistical material on women, in particular flowing from nationally representative surveys in which the gender of the person interviewed is always documented, it is possible to follow closely the evolution of the employment and wage gaps between men and women and to analyze them in detail, with a view to taking appropriate measures.

This does not mean that the situation is easy to resolve. Men and women do not work the same number of hours in the course of a year, do not occupy the same positions, and are not represented in the same proportions in all sectors. All this gives rise to considerable selection bias that makes comparisons of employment and wage rates difficult to interpret. For example, those who work full-time throughout the year often have individual characteristics that favor employability, and these characteristics also influence their hourly wage.

It is not only a question of the level of education (which tends to be higher for young women than for young men) but also of factors that are unobservable in survey data, such as interpersonal skills, health status, and motivation. It is far from obvious what in the observed gaps is attributable to differences in productive characteristics (whether or not observable) and what is attributable to discrimination. It is nevertheless essential to distinguish the two if we are to combat discrimination. Once again, the experimental approach can more convincingly shed light on the issue than survey data.

## Employment and Wage Gaps Tend to Shrink over Time but Not over the Life Course

Let us start with an overview of the gross gap in access to employment and wages between men and women. Despite significant catching-up during the twentieth century, men are still significantly more likely to be employed than women. In the United States, there are about 10 percent more men of working age in employment compared to women, and about 7 percent on average in Europe (figure 5.1a). This gap is twice as high among those who have not completed high school and thus for whom there are fewer job opportunities, and it is lower among those with higher education qualifications, a cohort businesses increasingly need to access.

The availability of affordable childcare plays a major role in access to employment for mothers, especially among the low-skilled. In the OECD, the difference in the employment rate is only 5 percent between men and women without children. The level of access to childcare explains why the employment gap is almost zero in the Nordic countries, where childcare is a public service, but higher in Italy, Greece, or Japan, where childcare solutions are hard to come by and work schedules are not compatible with young children's schooling.

Once in employment, men and women do not earn the same wage. On average, in OECD countries women's earned income is about 30 percent less than men's. But among those who work full-time, the gap is more than half that figure, around 12 percent,[6] which shows the importance of differences in working time (figure 5.1b). About one in four women in employment work part-time, compared to only one in ten employed men.[7] Labor earnings gaps also reflect different employment sectors since eight of ten women work in services, as opposed to six out of ten men.

As with access to employment, the wage gap tends to be lower in the Nordic European countries and higher in Japan and Korea (where it is more than 20 percent). In addition, the gap usually increases with income bracket: the wage gap between men and women who have not obtained a high school diploma is lower than between those who have earned a higher education degree. Larger wage differentials at the top of the pay scale may suggest a glass ceiling effect that prevents women from accessing the highest-paid jobs in their sector.[8] In fact, one-third or fewer of managerial positions are held by women, on average, in OECD countries.

The existence of relatively low wage differences in some countries does not in itself constitute evidence of nondiscrimination. Observed performance in the labor market is the result of a selection process in which only the most productive women enter and remain in the market, especially at the top of the wage scale. Similarly, at the bottom of the wage scale, restricted access to the market for some women owing to a lack of affordable childcare creates a selection bias that also leads to underestimating the gender pay gap.

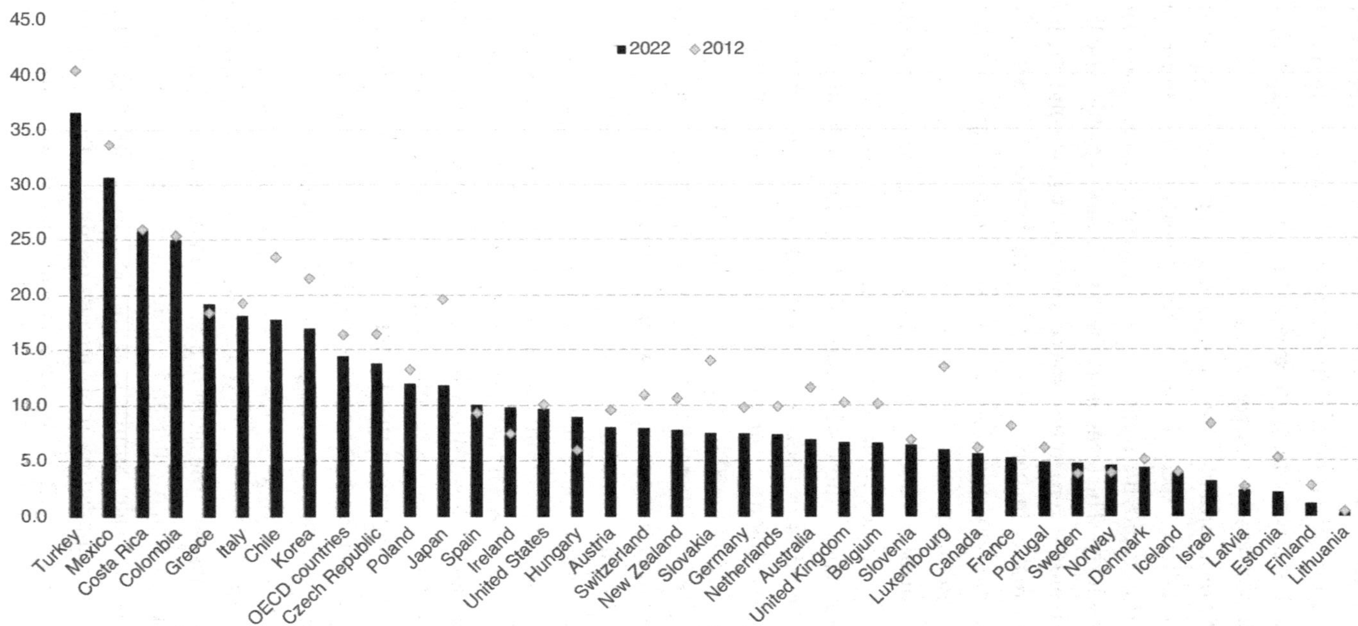


**Figure 5.1a**

Gender Gaps in the Labor Market. Employment rates gap between men and women in 2022, compared with 2012 or closest (percent). *Note:* The gender employment gap is the difference between the employment rate of men and that of women for the working-age population (fifteen to sixty-four years). Public and private sectors combined. *Source*: OECD, OECD Dashboard on Gender Gaps (https://www.oecd.org/en/data/dashboards/gender-dashboard.html).

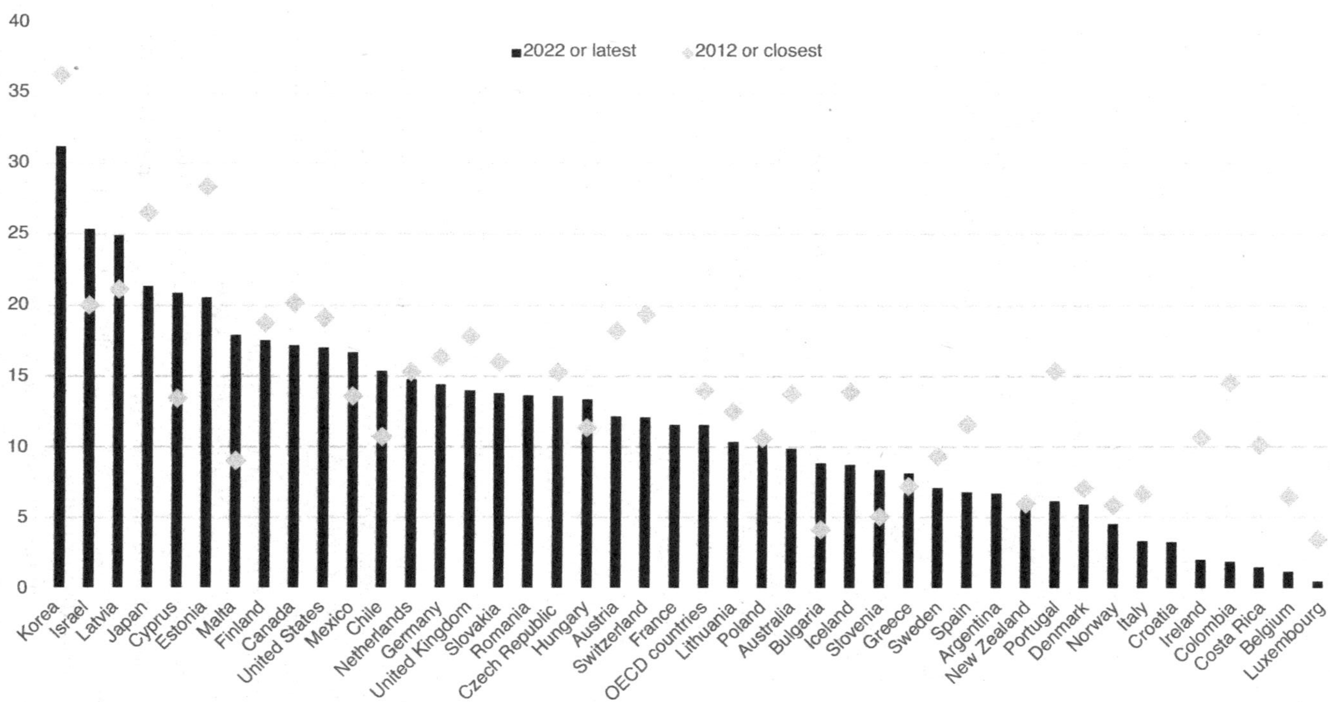


**Figure 5.1b**

Gender Gaps in the Labor Market. Wage gap between men and women working full time in 2022 or latest, compared with 2012 or closest (percent). *Note:* The gender wage gap is the difference between the median earnings of men and women as a proportion of the median earnings of men, for full-time employees. Public and private sectors combined. *Source*: OECD, OECD Dashboard on Gender Gaps (https://www.oecd.org/en/data/dashboards/gender-dashboard.html).

The widening of the gender pay gap with age is another salient fact. In all OECD countries, older women earn much less than men of the same age, compared to younger women and younger men. The reversal of the educational achievement gap between men and women in recent decades has undeniably led to a reduction in wage disparities in the younger generations. But the wage gap tends to grow over a lifetime, as is shown by longitudinal data. This situation could be accounted for by the accumulation over time of differences in professional experience, in particular because of unequal family responsibilities, which seriously hamper women's careers and frequently interrupt them. Another explanation could be women's relative immobility in employment, leading them to change jobs and companies less frequently than men, whereas mobility helps people move up the salary scale at the beginning of a career.[9]

Last, the wage gap between men and women has shrunk significantly over the past five decades. The reduction was particularly marked from the 1970s through the mid-1990s, when countries with the widest pay gap were tending to catch up. This trend toward a shrinking wage gap has continued in some countries, such as the United Kingdom (UK), but has stalled in others, such as the United States, and on average in OECD countries (figure 5.2). In the United States, the gender pay gap for full-time employees experienced only an 8 percent decrease between 2006 and 2020, from 19.2 percent to 17.7 percent (as compared to a 43 percent decrease in the UK, where it fell from 21.7 percent to 12.3 percent).

### A Significant Proportion of the Gender Pay Gap Remains Unexplained

What proportion of the pay gap between men and women is accounted for by differences in productive characteristics and what proportion by discrimination? The wage decomposition techniques presented in chapter 3 help to disentangle these different effects by breaking down the gender wage gap according to educational qualification, work experience, type of job held, economic sector, and number of hours worked. Marital status and number of children also play a role: fathers typically have higher incomes than men without children, while the opposite is true for women. Once all these factors are considered, the remaining wage gap may in principle stem, at least in part, from discrimination.

The OECD carried out this type of decomposition using survey data collected in 2014 in twenty-eight countries.[10] The higher levels of education

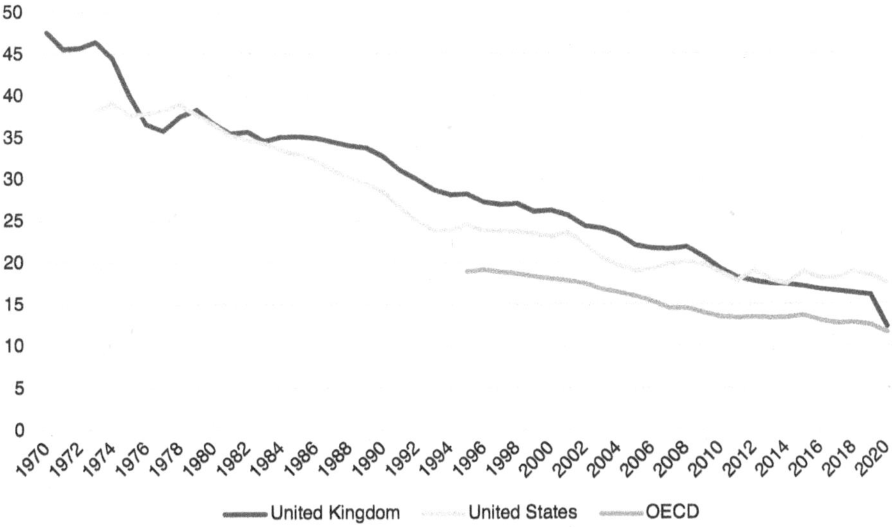


**Figure 5.2**
Evolution of the Gender Wage Gap in the OECD, the United Kingdom, and the United States for Full-Time Employees. *Note:* The gender wage gap is defined as the difference between median earnings of men and women as a proportion of median earnings of men, for full-time employees. *Source*: OECD, OECD Dashboard on Gender Gaps (https://www.oecd.org/en/data/dashboards/gender-dashboard.html).

now attained by women should in principle mean that they earn slightly more than men do. But, as the OECD study shows, the positive effects of education are largely offset by other factors, such as the characteristics of the job held (women working more often in less lucrative sectors and in less lucrative occupations within sectors), labor market experience, and, notably, the prevalence of part-time work. These factors account for one third of the 30 percent gender pay gap, while two-thirds of the gap remains unexplained.

Yet the unexplained component in this type of analysis is difficult to interpret. It can flow from discrimination against women, but also from unobserved individual characteristics, such as the frequency of career breaks, that most studies fail to accurately measure. Relying on long-term panel data provides a remedy that some authors, such as Francine Blau and Lawrence Kahn, have exploited in the context of the United States.[11] Once differences in work interruptions are accounted for, these authors compute that the unexplained gender wage gap declines from 60 percent to 40 percent. However, as they stress, it is unlikely that this residual can be entirely attributed to discrimination. It certainly also captures differences in soft skills that influence productivity, hence pay. In addition, when looking for a job, women around the age of maternity tend to be geographically less mobile, internalizing the norm that women must bear the brunt of family duties and need to stay close to home. This constraint limits their opportunities for salary progression and feeds the gender gap.[12]

### Gender Pay Gaps Are Closing at a Slower Pace Than Previously

Studies of wage differences between men and women have recently sought to understand why, on average, these gaps have been closing at a slower pace since the mid-1990s (figure 5.2). Catch-up was fast in the 1970s and 1980s but slowed during the 1990s. Convergence has been virtually nonexistent since the turn of the twenty-first century. Is this slowdown the result of an interruption in the improvement of certain factors favoring women's employability or of a slower decline in discrimination against women?

To address this question, Blau and Kahn used data on a panel of Michigan residents who had been followed for a number of years during the 1980s and 1990s in the Panel Study of Income Dynamics (PSID).[13] The authors showed that the reduction in the gender pay gap in the 1980s was mainly attributable to an improvement in the characteristics of women participating in the labor market, such as their level of education, work experience, type of job occupied, and motivation.[14] The "positive" selection effect became less marked at the end of 1990s because of slower growth in the female workforce, with the largest contingent of women having already joined the labor market. This then gave way to a reverse selection effect: women who had not yet participated in the labor market, and who were thus characterized by low employability, began to join it after the 1990s.

Overall, this negative selection effect could explain 25 percent of the slowdown in the reduction of the unexplained gender wage gap.[15] Though substantial, 25 percent still falls far short of the total. It is therefore possible that at least part of the remaining unexplained 75 percent results from a slower reduction in discrimination against women.

One way to test this hypothesis is to look at changes in attitudes regarding the distribution of roles between men and women. Indeed, the more traditional such attitudes are, the more likely it is that the level of discrimination against women in the labor market will be high. Studies on the topic confirm that differences in gender performance in the labor market are strongly correlated with the roles that social norms assign to each gender. In OECD countries, when 1 percentage point more men than women agree that "men should be given preference when jobs are scarce," the gender pay gap increases by almost half a point.[16] In the 1970s and 1980s, far more women than men expressed their disagreement with a traditional view of the division of paid and unpaid work within the household (e.g., "men work, women stay at home"). But this perception gap gradually diminished as men's attitudes became increasingly progressive. The trend continued until the mid-1990s, when it stabilized and eventually slightly reversed thereafter. This recent reversal is supposed to explain at least a third of the recent leveling off of women's participation in the labor force.

Distressingly, this reversal is currently worsening, as younger generations express less support for gender equality compared to older generations. A survey conducted by Ipsos across 31 countries for International Women's Day 2024 reveals concerning trends: 10 percent of baby boomers agree with the statement that "a man who stays home to look after his children is less of a man," compared to 25 percent of Gen Z.[17] Furthermore, the survey underscores a growing global gender divide in attitudes toward gender equality. While the gender gap in opinions on this statement is almost nonexistent among baby boomers, it widens to 11 percentage points within Gen Z, with 20 percent of Gen Z women and 31 percent of Gen Z men agreeing with the sentiment. The divide is even sharper on the question of whether gender equality has gone so far as to discriminate against men. Six in ten Gen Z men agree with this statement, compared to four in ten Gen Z women, highlighting a significant split in perspectives among younger generations.

## Stereotypes of How Men and Women (Should) Behave in the Workplace

Stereotypes can feed discrimination in the workplace. They are cultural constructs, shared at a social level, describing how individuals are known to behave.[18] Psychological studies based on laboratory experiments have shown that women are often *considered* to be nurturing and cooperative rather than aggressive and competitive, and to seek to avoid risk. They are *deemed* more emotional and indecisive, but also warmer and humbler. Men, on the contrary, are considered to be more assertive, resolute, self-confident, analytical, competitive, and risk-taking.[19]

Stereotypes are not only descriptive, they are also prescriptive (how men and women should behave) and even proscriptive (how they should not behave). For example, most people think women should be more interested in the well-being of others and should avoid being dominant, aggressive, or stubborn, while men should be agentic, career-oriented, and independent but should avoid being emotional, uncertain, or weak. By the same token, women are expected to be good at caring for others and hence more able in service jobs, while men are expected to be good at science and engineering jobs.[20] Interestingly, these stereotypes are not necessarily abated by economic development: according mathematical ability to men is actually more frequent in developed countries.[21] Such beliefs probably explain why discrimination against women in the workplace is found to be heterogeneous across sectors, types of position, and the nature of responsibilities.

Stereotypes influence not only perceptions but also hiring and career decisions in real companies. For instance, Elizabeth Gorman studied hiring decision in U.S. medium-size to large law firms in the mid-1990s. For 770 hiring processes, she linked the gender of the person hired to the gender of the decision-maker (the firm's partner in charge of the recruitment). She also identified the stereotypically masculine and feminine attributes listed in the hiring criteria publicized by the firm, such as "independent" and "competitive" versus "cooperative." She found that the number of stereotypically male hiring criteria has a significant negative effect on women's share of new hires: each additional stereotypically male criterion decreased the odds that a woman would be hired to fill a vacancy by about five percentage points. Inversely, stereotypically female hiring criteria had a significant positive effect on women's representation among new hires. The presence of a female hiring partner in the process also had a significant positive effect on women's share of new hires.

To what extent stereotypes are based on some true traits is an empirical question.[22] Surely, some typical feminine versus masculine stereotypes are based on experience with interacting with people of both genders. But stereotypes are also cultural constructs to which people tend to conform (see chapter 2). Their expression may depend on the context and the nature of interactions. Researchers have identified a few personality traits or cognitive characteristics that differ between men and women, but very often differences depend on the context in which men and women make decisions and interact.[23]

Psychologists typically define personality along five basic dimensions: openness (to new ideas, creativity), conscientiousness (attention to details, enjoying structure and schedule), extraversion (enjoying being at the center of attention, meeting new people), agreeableness (caring for other people, empathy), and neuroticism (emotional instability, anxiousness). Explicit personality assessments, whereby people self-assess their traits or those of people around them, consistently show that women are associated with higher levels of warmth (one facet of extraversion), agreeableness, and conscientiousness, but also neuroticism. By contrast, men are associated with higher levels of assertiveness (another facet of extraversion) and openness (to new ideas and experiences). But psychological studies also suggest that differences across genders are small relative to individual variation *within* genders, and that these differences also vary across cultures, with larger gender differences measured in Western societies than in Asia and Africa.[24] Besides, when gender differences are measured by implicit association tests, they turn out to be much smaller than explicit, self-declared ones.[25] Yet women tend to score slightly higher than men on Neuroticism and Agreeableness on those tests.

Similarly, only small differences have been identified in dimensions related to social behaviors, such as temperament, emotions, aggression, and leadership. As shown by Janet Hyde in her comprehensive synthesis, even though stereotypes tend to portray women as the emotional gender, the data available show that differences between genders are very small.[26] Similarly, psychologists have found no significant differences in leadership across genders based on either subjective or objective measures, whereas stereotypes consider leadership as predominantly masculine. Men do tend to behave more aggressively than women, but this depends highly on the context and can stem from the obligation men feel to conform to gender roles.

Hyde also shows that differences in cognitive skills are small, at least for younger generations, in which women outperform men in educational attainment. Actual differences in mathematical performance, including complex problem solving, appear to be negligible. The Program for International Student Assessment (PISA), which evaluates students reading, mathematics, and science competencies at age fifteen, shows that boys outperform girls in mathematics in a majority of countries.[27] Notably, this "outperformance" attribution reflects boys being found in larger proportions among top performers. Similarly, girls significantly outperform boys on reading performance on the PISA, a result driven by the overrepresentation of boys at the lowest level of performance. Girls also slightly outperform boys in science. Overall, however, there seems to be much more difference in actual performance *within* gender than *across* genders. Moreover, there is increasing evidence that gender gaps reflect deeply ingrained social expectations about the roles of men and women much more than they do different abilities between boys and girls. For instance, Gaia Dossi, David Figlio, Paola Giuliano, and Paola Sapienza found that girls' math scores suffer when they grow up in families biased toward sons.[28] To do so, these authors identified families in Florida with a preference for boys by using fertility-stopping rules, that is. families' decision to stop having children after one son is born. They show that girls growing up in a "boy-biased" family score lower on math tests when compared to girls raised in other families. The effect is concentrated among families with high socioeconomic status, probably because better-educated parents invest more in their children's education and hence have a greater influence on their choices. Similar effects are found for girls raised in families where parents show more conservative attitudes concerning gender roles.

How about psychological traits important for economic decision-making, such as risk aversion and taste for competition? By resorting to games performed in a laboratory setting, economists have shown that women are, on average, more risk-averse than men.[29] This finding can have consequences for their choice of occupation insofar as jobs with more unstable remunerations usually are the ones that offer bonuses and other variable components to compensate for a higher level of risk. Similarly, there is evidence from laboratory experiments that, on average, men tend to be more competitive than women. When asked to choose between a piece rate payoff scheme and a tournament-like winner-take-all scheme (where the task is to perform the maximum of additions), women choose the more predictable piece rate payments twice as often as men do.[30] Even top-performing women (with respect to the task) choose to compete less frequently than low-performing men do. In addition, women perform worse when competing with men than when performing the task on their own or in competition with other women only.[31] When offered the choice, men opt to compete at roughly twice the rate of women in a traditional patriarchal society (e.g., the Maasai of Tanzania), but they do not differ from men in matrilineal or matrilocal societies where inheritance and residence are determined by the female lineage (e.g., the Khasi of India).[32] This finding suggests that at least some personality traits are nurtured rather than biologically determined, which in turn calls for policies and interventions quite early in life (see chapter 12).

In Western societies, the fact that women shy away from competition and tend to be more risk-averse, especially as compared to men, has consequences for their educational and career choices. Even at similar levels of academic ability, boys are more likely than girls to choose more prestigious and competitive tracks, and this choice difference can be linked to gender differences in competitiveness.[33] When presented with equivalent job offers with different compensation schemes, women are more likely to choose the compensation package rewarding the individual's performance relative to schemes mentioning that they will compete with coworkers in order to get a bonus, especially when the job can be considered to be a "male" job."[34]

Interestingly, these personality traits explain only a small share of the gender pay gap—about 10 percent, according to Blau and Kahn.[35] In particular, men's earnings benefit from men being antagonistic (the obverse of being agreeable), while this relationship doesn't prevail among women: a one standard deviation increase in antagonism raises the hourly earnings for male workers by 4–6 percent on average. Men also benefit to a lesser extent than women from emotional stability (the obverse of neuroticism).[36] Overall, men and women are associated with both positive and negative traits whose effects may at least partly compensate each other, thereby making their aggregate impact difficult to predict. For instance, Ernesto Reuben, Paola Sapienza, and Lugi Zingales measured the willingness to compete, risk aversion, and the degree of overconfidence among 550 MBA male and female students in 2006 at the University of Chicago Booth School of Business.[37] Men were much more willing to compete than women, and this difference held even after controlling for the fact that they were also less risk-averse and more often overconfident in their performance than women. The authors followed the young graduates for seven years after they completed their MBA program in 2008. Whereas at graduation, taste for competition explained 10 percent of the gender wage gap, it played no role seven years later. This is because over time, the positive effects of taste for competition were mitigated by the negative effects of overconfidence among men. In 2015, competitive MBAs with a low degree of overconfidence earned 26 percent more than those who were highly overconfident.

## Women Are Particularly Hindered in their Career Progression within Firms . . .

Most of the studies on the integration of women into the labor market use observational data: survey data or administrative data. They mostly focus on wages, much less so on access to employment, probably because access is strongly influenced by selection effects that are difficult to control. Women who enter the labor market do not have the same profile as those who stay at home, nor do they have the same motivation or skills, and these differences are not fully measured in national databases.

In this context, the lessons of the experimental approach are particularly valuable. First, correspondence studies reveal no hiring discrimination against women at nonmanagement levels. More precisely, nearly two decades ago, those studies indicated that women faced negative discrimination in male-dominated sectors but positive discrimination in female-dominated ones.[38] This was true in Australia, Europe, and North America.[39] More recently, correspondence studies have failed to document an advantage for men in male-dominated jobs. In particular, a harmonized correspondence study conducted from 2016 to 2018 in six countries (Germany, Netherlands, Norway, Spain, the UK, and the United States) revealed that employers seeking to recruit in nonmanagerial occupations (cook, payroll clerk, receptionist, sales representative, software developer, and store assistant) regarded female applicants as more suitable when these occupations are female-dominated, while there was no evidence that they regarded male applicants as a better fit for any of these occupations.[40]

Second, correspondence studies suggest that hiring discrimination at lower- and middle-management levels against women of childbearing age is losing intensity, whereas this discrimination was once prevalent. In 2002, Pascale Petit carried out a field experiment in France in which she sent the applications of three different types of fictitious male and female job applicants in the banking sector: aged twenty-five years, single, and childless; aged thirty-seven, single, and childless; aged thirty-seven, married, and a mother or father of three children.[41] The results revealed that twenty-five-year-old women were discriminated against compared to their male counterparts if they applied for low- to middle-management positions, whereas they were treated on an equal footing at nonmanagement levels. Indeed, because social norms result in the bulk of domestic and family work being done by women,[42] it is more difficult for women than for men to maintain the same level of involvement in their work after childbirth (which may in turn feed statistical discrimination against women of childbearing age), at least if women hold jobs that are demanding. Discrimination against women, however, disappears altogether by the age of thirty-seven, when the probability of an imminent pregnancy is low. This is the case for profiles both with and without existing children. Stijn Baert and his coauthors found consistent results for women of childbearing age, based on a correspondence study conducted in the mid-2010s in Belgium.[43] They showed that women in their late 20s/early 30s obtained response rates one-third lower than those of men when, after five years of professional experience, they applied for higher-responsibility jobs. That said, a recent correspondence study conducted in France between 2019 and 2021 provides a different picture: the (risk of) maternity of fictitious female job candidates had no bearing on their chance of being invited to a job interview, be it at nonmanagement or at low- or middle-management level.[44] This result stands in sharp contrast to the findings of the correspondence study conducted by Petit nearly twenty years earlier. These divergent conclusions may reflect the effectiveness of policies aimed at alleviating the unpaid work burden for mothers (and thus combat statistical discrimination against them) that several countries, including France, have deployed in the past two decades.

Yet these takeaways do not rule out that women of childbearing age are discriminated against in access to jobs in high-paying firms that search for individuals able to provide excessive working hours rewarded at a disproportionately higher rate than standard ones.[45] Because they anticipate that, relative to men, women are less available for work after childbirth, high-paying firms may engage in hiring discrimination against women "at risk" of pregnancy and against mothers of young children. By the same reasoning, women of childbearing age may also face discrimination in promotion to top management positions *within* their own firm. More generally, the widespread belief that, compared to men, women would be more governed by emotions than by reason (see chapter 1) may help solidify the perception among employers and beyond that *any* women, irrespective of their family obligations, cannot perform as well as men in very demanding and thus prestigious positions, including high-paying and executive-level jobs.

Unfortunately, no correspondence study has been conducted to test whether women are discriminated against in access to those jobs, not least because the experimental approach is hardly suitable in this case. Indeed, hiring in top management positions is typically the outcome of a recruitment process that is based on the promotion of internal candidates rather than on the recruitment of external candidates. However, a promising alternative to correspondence studies exists. It consists in using social security records to link employer and employee data over time to understand the source of the gender wage gap. More precisely, based on a method developed in the mid-2010s by prominent labor economists, these administrative data allow decomposing the gender wage gap into a between-firm component and a within-firm component.[46] The between-firm component captures the role of differences in firm wage-setting practices in the pay gap between similarly skilled women and men (i.e., women and men of the same age and thus with potentially equivalent work experience, and with the same educational attainment) attributable to the sorting of women into low-paying firms. The within-firm component captures differences in pay between similarly skilled women and men in the same firm that are related either to differences in tasks and responsibilities or to differences in pay for work of equal value. A group of researchers recently compiled employer-employee linked data for sixteen OECD countries over the early 2000s to the mid-2010s.[47] The group showed that the large majority (three quarters) of the gender wage gap stemmed from pay differences within firms (only one quarter flowed from between-firm effects). In addition, nearly 90 percent of this within-firm gender pay gap stemmed from women being assigned to different tasks and responsibilities, which may result from unequal opportunities for career progression, either because women refrain from applying for positions too demanding to allow reconciliation of professional and family lives or because employers indulge in promotion discrimination against women. By contrast, only 10 percent of the within-firm gender pay gap stemmed from women being paid a lower wage than men for work of equal value. This finding may reflect outright taste-based or statistical wage discrimination, or it may reflect the fact that employers take advantage of women's weak bargaining power in the context of persistent traditional gender norms.[48] Indeed, the unequal sharing of unpaid work between men and women prevents women from expanding the labor market in which they can search for a job or consider exit options beyond firms located a short commute distance away or firms that provide more family amenities in exchange for lower pecuniary rewards.[49] Moreover, traditional gender norms also negatively operate through their internalization by women, which fuels women's lower assessment of their self-worth in the labor market, as reflected in their tendency to ask for lower salaries than comparable men, the so-called gender ask gap.[50]

A recent paper sheds light on whether the unequal opportunities for career progression that women are facing results at least partly from discrimination in promotion.[51] The answer is a definite yes. Using data on 30,000 management-track employees from a large North American retail chain, the authors found that women receive substantially lower ratings on their career potential by supervisors despite receiving higher job performance ratings. Differences in potential ratings accounted for 30–50 percent of the gender promotion gap. Women's lower potential ratings do not appear to be based on accurate forecasts of future performance: women outperform male colleagues with the same potential ratings. Yet even when women outperform their previously forecasted potential, their subsequent potential ratings remain low.

This situation cannot be accounted for by higher rates of attrition or leave-taking among women: as the authors point out, women in their data set were significantly less likely to leave the firm than men, and, while they were more likely to take leaves of absence, the absolute levels of leave among women were too low to explain the large gap in potential ratings and promotions.

Overall, there is strong evidence that the persistent gender pay gap flows mainly from a glass ceiling effect that prevents women from rising beyond a certain level in a hierarchy, including because of discrimination in promotion. This glass ceiling appears particularly thick and difficult to break. In France, women have a 50 percent lower chance than men to hold one of the highest-paying jobs.[52] Even when women access those jobs, their tenure may be short as a result of work schedules unsuited to family life and a work environment governed by male codes. Based on a large body of data acquired on North American executives over the period 1991–2006, researchers have found that women's chance of survival at top management levels is lower than for men.[53]

### . . . Notably When They Become Mothers

The glass ceiling effect can hurt all women, irrespective of their family obligations. But the subset of women who become mothers may be particularly hard hit. The analysis of employer-employee linked data allows zooming in on women who experience a career break of one or more years at childbearing age, hence presumably following childbirth.[54] This analysis confirms that women face a wage penalty following those breaks. This result is not driven by the fact that mothers of young children move to low-paying firms (in fact, most women return to their previous employer after a career break). Rather, the wage penalty derives from a slower upward mobility within firms owing to a confluence of factors that likely include reduced working hours, reduced work experience, depreciated human capital, and promotion discrimination against women.

However, using observational data to document a motherhood penalty is problematic to the extent that women who decide to have children may not all have the same job prospects or motivations as others: some may be less career-oriented and would have left the job market at some point anyway, at least temporarily. These selection biases make the comparison of labor market trajectories between mothers and childless women difficult to interpret. It is easier to hold constant the qualifications and work experience of women with and without children in experiments using fictitious job applicants. Shelley Correll, Stephen Benard, and In Paik at Cornell University used both a laboratory experiment and a field experiment to investigate why and how mothers are disadvantaged. Laboratory evaluators rated mothers as less competent and less committed to work than nonmothers, and they were offered lower starting salaries, while fathers suffered no such penalty. In addition, employers to whom the same CVs were sent to apply for real jobs mirrored these results, calling back mothers about half as often as childless women, and again not discriminating against fathers in this way.[55]

To further address this identification issue, Petter Lundborg, Erik Plug, and Astrid Würtz Rasmussen used an innovative approach: they combined a national database on in vitro fertilization (IVF) in Denmark with administrative data tracking people over nearly twenty years.[56] Since the success of IVF is essentially a matter of chance that has nothing to do with the employability of prospective mothers, this strategy ensures that women in the data set who become mothers or remain childless are similar except for their maternity status. The authors show that the effects of maternity on career progression are negative, substantial, and lasting. On average, women with one or more children have 30 percent lower labor earnings than childless women. When children are young, the wage gap is due to a reduction in working hours. But when children get older, the penalty is driven by lower hourly wages. These disadvantages emerge from the birth of the first child onward.

Yet women who rely on IVF can hardly be viewed as representative since they are likely more motivated by the prospect of becoming mothers relative to other women. To test the external validity (or generalizability) of the aforementioned results, Henrik Kleven, Camille Landais, and Jakob Egholt Søgaard focused on administrative data comprising all Danish women who become mothers in the course of their lifetime to compare, for different age groups, women who are and women who are not yet mothers.[57] Indeed, among women who want a child and will have one in due course, the date of birth is a matter of chance—meeting the right partner, becoming pregnant, carrying the pregnancy to term—and thus is independent of their employability.[58] The findings show that the birth of a child creates a gender gap in labor earnings of around 20 percent, driven in roughly equal proportions by labor force participation, hours worked, and wage rates. Admittedly, part of the gap in labor market performance may be the result of deliberate choices by mothers to free up time to care for their children. But part may also be attributable to constraints that are beyond their control, such as discrimination on the part of employers.

Henrik Kleven and Camille Landais, along with their coauthor Gabriel Leite-Mariante, take their analysis a step further by demonstrating that the pattern they identify in Denmark is prevalent in most countries worldwide.[59] Using microdata from 134 countries, they construct a global atlas of child penalties in employment. Their findings show that in most of these countries, men and women follow similar employment trajectories before parenthood, but diverge sharply and persistently afterward. While this pattern is widespread, the magnitude of its effects varies significantly across regions. The proportion of gender inequality attributed to child penalties systematically correlates with levels of economic development and structural transformation. At lower levels of development, child penalties account for a small fraction of gender inequality. However, as economies grow—with rising incomes and a transition from subsistence agriculture to salaried work in industry and services—child penalties emerge as the dominant driver of gender inequality. The authors further reveal that women face both marriage and child penalties, but the relative importance of these factors shifts with development. The development process is associated with a gradual substitution of marriage penalties by child penalties, with marriage penalties eventually converging to zero.

* * *

Despite significant progress in the 1970s, 1980s, and early 1990s, women working full-time still made about 88 cents for every man's dollar across OECD countries in 2022, and some two-thirds of this gap remains unexplained. There is strong evidence that this persistent gender pay gap flows mainly from a glass ceiling effect that prevents women, chiefly those of childbearing age, from rising beyond a certain level in their firm's hierarchy, including as a result of discrimination in promotion. This finding suggests that the situation of women in the labor market will change little so long as gender role expectations and men's contribution to domestic and family work remain unchanged.

# 6 The Effects of Race, Ethnicity, and Religion

The horrendous killing of George Floyd in 2020 was a reminder to many Americans that visible minorities, defined as groups perceived as distinct from the majority population, either based on physical characteristics, such as skin color, hair texture, and facial features, or based on cultural attributes, including language, religion, and traditions, are still experiencing discrimination and violence on a daily basis. Distressingly, these minorities' situation does not seem to improve over time. In 2019, more than 150 years after the Thirteenth Amendment abolished slavery in the United States, 63 percent of U.S. adults believed the legacy of slavery affected the position of Black people in American society either a great deal or a fair amount. Moreover, nearly a majority (45 percent) said that the United States had not gone far enough when it comes to giving Black people equal rights with whites.[1] The proportion of people who consider discrimination against Black people to be high is increasing: in 2017, the share of U.S. adults who said racial discrimination was the main reason why many Blacks can't get ahead reached its highest point in Pew Research Center surveys since 1994.[2]

The persistence and even worsening of high levels of perceived discrimination against visible (or racial/ethnic) minorities is not confined to the United States. It also prevails across the EU. The 2012, 2015, 2019, and 2023 editions of the Eurobarometer on the perception of discrimination in the EU reveal that discrimination on grounds of skin color or ethnic origin is seen as the most widespread form of discrimination: 60 percent of respondents rated it as frequent in 2023. These figures are worrying in a context where more than 10 percent of children under age fifteen who were born in the twenty-seven EU countries have parents who were born abroad, mostly in non-European countries.[3]

The perception of discrimination among the public is borne out when one zooms in on visible minorities and their self-reported experience of discrimination. Let's take the example of France. According to Eurobarometer data on the perception of discrimination, France is the EU country with the highest share of respondents in the public who deem discrimination based on skin color and ethnic origin to be widespread. Consistent with this result, immigrants of non-European origin were much more likely than those of European origin to say that they experienced discrimination during the five years preceding the survey, based on the first round of the Trajectories and Origins survey (Trajectoires et Origines, or TeO).[4] This population cites skin color as the main reason for discrimination, far ahead of gender and age, thereby suggesting that discrimination in France is above all "a matter of visible minorities."[5]

This chapter shows that these perceptions of widespread discrimination reflect a reality. Even after the effect of observed productive characteristics has been neutralized, observational data show that visible minorities have lower employment rates and wages. These gaps stem at least in part from the discrimination these minorities face in the labor market as objectively measured by field experiments, with the note that subgroups of racial/ethnic minority background are not equally exposed to unfair treatment: some are more discriminated against than others.

While the concept of visible minorities implicitly touches on the notions of "race" and "ethnicity," it is crucial to emphasize that these notions are not understood in a biological sense, as there are no scientific foundations to interpret them as reflecting genetic distinctions among individuals. Rather, "race" and "ethnicity" are social constructs that highlight physical and cultural differences that society may regard as significant and that, as such, may contribute to determine the positioning of individuals in society.

## Visible Minorities Have Lower Employment Rates and Wages

Labor market surveys provide a preliminary assessment of the situation of racial/ethnic minorities. In the EU, native-born children of immigrants of European background have employment rates similar to those of individuals with no recent immigrant background—that is, native-born children of native-born parents. But this is not the case for native-born children of immigrants of non-European background, that is, those coming mainly from

Africa, the Middle East, and Turkey, and who therefore belong to ethnic minorities. These children of immigrants have employment rates that are 13 percent lower on average than those of individuals whose parents were not immigrants.[6]

The gap narrows when one considers the lower level of education that often characterizes parents of non-European origin. As an illustration, 15 percent of children born in the EU whose parents were born outside the EU have a mother who did not go to school or did not finish primary school, a proportion five times higher than among children without a recent immigrant background. But the employment rate gap is still significant when one neutralizes the effect of differences in parental education level (along with gender and age). A similar unexplained gap emerges if one focuses on the probability of individuals taking up a job calling for qualifications higher than those required by their father's job. Children born in the twenty-seven EU countries of parents who were born outside the EU are much less likely to experience upward social mobility, a deficit that translates into lower wages.

The unexplained differences in employment and wage rates between native-born children of immigrants and native-born children of native-born parents are lower in Canada and the United States, largely because visible minorities are still underrepresented among native-born children of immigrants. In fact, Canada and the United States began receiving significant flows of migrants from regions other than North America and Europe only in the late 1960s.[7] That said, when the analysis is limited to the labor market performance of native-born children of immigrants of racial/ethnic minority background, a penalty emerges.[8] This is also the case for visible minorities who have been settling in the country for much longer, such as African Americans[9] or descendants of Native Americans in the United States and Canada.[10]

Using social security records to link employer and employee data over time sheds additional light on the source of the ethnic wage gap. More precisely, as stressed in chapter 5, employer-employee linked data permit investigating the relative importance of within-workplace differences in wage setting and between-workplace segregation, that is, the sorting of workers from different ethnicities into firms in different parts of the firm-level earnings distribution. Using matched employer-employee data for Britain, Alexander Bryson, John Forth, and Nikos Theodoropoulos find substantial ethnic segregation across workplaces: around three-fifths of workplaces in Britain employ no ethnic minority workers.[11] However, this workplace segregation does not contribute to the aggregate wage gap between ethnic minorities and white employees. Instead, most of the ethnic wage gap exists between observationally equivalent coworkers within the *same* firm: nonwhite male employees earn, on average, around 10 percent less than their white counterparts after accounting for wage differences across workplaces, while the wage penalty for nonwhite female employees is around 6 percent. These findings echo evidence from the United States that also suggests, again based on employer-employee linked data, that the earnings differential between Black workers and white workers "is primarily a within-firm phenomenon."[12]

These findings are consistent with minorities being more often confined to lower-skilled responsibilities than their performance warrants. For instance, studying 9,037 new hires at a U.S. professional services firm, a group of economists documented large racial/ethnic promotion gaps: even after controlling for observable characteristics, Black employees were 18.7 percentage points (26 percent) less likely to be promoted on time than their white counterparts.[13] Similarly, using quasi-experimental data from a U.S. police department, Nayoung Rim and her coauthors found that white supervisors are 28–40 percent less likely to nominate Black officers for awards than they are their white counterparts, even after controlling for work performance.[14] Furthermore, the authors stress that this nomination gap widens as supervisors' prejudice scores increase, as measured by the use of force against Black civilians and citizen complaints.

The findings from employer-employee linked data may also reflect discriminatory practices in wage negotiation. Although research on wage negotiation dynamics related to race and ethnicity is not as well documented as it is for gender, emerging evidence reveals significant influences of racial/ethnic bias on negotiation outcomes. In a 2019 study, a group of researchers conducted a salary negotiation simulation in the United States, which revealed that job evaluators who held biases against Black candidates expected them to negotiate less frequently than their white counterparts, influenced by negative stereotypes about Black employees' job performance and a biased belief that they should not advocate strongly for themselves.[15] Each perceived negotiation attempt by a Black job seeker resulted in a starting salary that was, on average, $300 lower. In contrast, evaluators with less racial bias offered salaries that were more equitable.

### Visible Minorities Are Discriminated Against in the Labor Market

Visible minorities are heavily penalized in terms of employment and wages. In 1970, Roger Jowell and Patricia Prescott-Clarke conducted the first correspondence study in Britain that attempted to determine whether the employment and wages deficit was at least partly a consequence of discriminatory behavior on the part of employers.[16] The authors compared the response rates to UK applicants and to applicants with similar CVs who had immigrated to Britain in their youth and had permanent resident status at the time of application. These applicants come from four different countries or regions: the British West Indies, Australia, Asia (India and Pakistan), and Cyprus. Their geographic origin was indicated by their name (e.g., "Demetriades" for Cypriot applicants) and by the mention of their country of origin in their cover letter. The results showed that applicants from Australia and Cyprus had average interview rates comparable to those of UK applicants with no recent migration ancestry: 74 percent compared to 78 percent for British citizens. But visible minorities, that is, applicants from the West Indies and Asia, were strongly discriminated against, with a job interview rate of only 52 percent, a third lower than that of British citizens.

Since then, hundreds of correspondence studies have been carried out since this first study to verify the existence of discrimination based on race and ethnicity.[17] They almost all confirm Jowell and Prescott-Clarke's conclusion that visible minorities are discriminated against relative to the majority. Notably, a recent meta-analysis reviewed almost one hundred correspondence studies conducted in nine OECD countries in the past two decades.[18] These field experiments consisted in sending out, in response to real job ads, the CVs and letters of applications of fictitious candidates who were identical except for their racial/ethnic identity: they showed similar levels of education, qualifications, and work experience, but their first name and last name conveyed either a racial/ethnic majority or an racial/ethnic minority identity. The results revealed that nonwhite natives, that is, individuals of Asian, Middle East and North African (MENA), or sub-Saharan African background, can be up to two times less likely to be invited to a job interview than white natives with the same CV. For instance, the callback rate for white majority applicants ranged from 24 percent higher in Germany to 78 percent higher in France when compared to candidates of Middle Eastern or North African descent. Similarly, the callback rate gap for Black applicants varied from 5 percent in Belgium (not statistically significant) and 49 percent in Great Britain to 102 percent in France. While there are fewer studies on hiring discrimination against Asian groups, the available data indicate significant disparities. The callback rate gap was estimated at 35 percent in Norway, 42 percent in Canada, 45 percent in France, and 60 percent in Great Britain. Gaps in the Netherlands and the United States were smaller and not statistically significant.

Hiring discrimination also targets Indigenous populations in countries that have been colonized by Europeans since the fifteenth century (Aboriginals in Australia and the Quechuas in Peru), as well as ethnic minorities in countries historically inhabited by different ethnic groups (Mongols, Uighurs. and Tibetans in China).[19]

While most correspondence studies investigating racial/ethnic discrimination in hiring focus on young candidates (under 30), complementary evidence indicates that discrimination against visible minorities does not diminish with age and may even intensify. Economist Nick Drydakis and his coauthors, using a series of correspondence studies in the UK, explored the interplay between race/ethnicity, age, and gender.[20] They found that both white and Black fictitious applicants experienced age discrimination. In their experiments, older applicants (fifty-year-olds) possess thirty-one years of experience in the relevant occupation (applying for low-skilled private sector jobs, such as restaurant employees and sales assistants in England), while younger applicants (twenty-eight-year-olds) only have nine years of experience in this occupation. Despite this gap, the latter were significantly more likely to receive interview invitations. Furthermore, the authors revealed that age-related discrimination was more severe for Black applicants, particularly women. Lastly, the study illustrated that barriers to employment access for visible minorities not only increase with age but also that these groups are more likely to be channeled into lower-paying positions, receiving invitations for vacancies offering lower wages compared to the wages associated with the vacancies for which majority candidates are interviewed.

Importantly, discrimination based on race or ethnicity prevails beyond the labor market. This is for instance the case in amateur sports, even though sports are supposedly an integration tool by enabling social interactions between individuals of different ethnic backgrounds. More precisely, a standardized cross-country correspondence study entailed contacting 23,020 amateur football clubs in twenty-two European countries, using mock email accounts with native-sounding names and foreign-sounding names (the latter being often a signal of ethnic minority background). The fictitious owners of these accounts were asking the club about the possibility of participating in a training session. Although response rates differed across countries, they were, on average, about 10 percent lower for foreign-sounding names.[21]

**Do Sector or Industry, Occupation, and Firm Size Matter?**

Hiring discrimination against racial/ethnic minorities doesn't depend on a specific sector or industry, occupation, or firm size. Meta-analyses of correspondence studies, which assess racial/ethnic discrimination in hiring, control for variables such as the industry and the specific occupation of the fictitious applicant, ensuring that the findings are not skewed by these factors. Yet correspondence studies predominantly examine private sector job listings. It is thus critical to question whether public sector employers exhibit similar discriminatory practices. While only a limited number of studies have explored this angle, the evidence generally indicates that the public sector does not fare better than the private sector in terms of equitable hiring practices.[22] At best, the public sector may demonstrate marginally less discrimination, yet it is by no means free from discriminatory hiring practices.

In addition, although meta-analyses adjust for the occupation of the fictitious candidate, the correspondence studies they examine generally focus on nonleadership positions. To the best of our knowledge, only one correspondence study, conducted in Australia, has compared racial/ethnic discrimination in hiring for both nonleadership and leadership roles.[23] The findings indicate substantial discrimination at both levels, with the most severe discrimination occurring in leadership positions. Specifically, 26.8 percent of job applicants with English names applying for leadership roles received positive responses, compared to just 11.4 percent of those with non-English names, including rates of 14.3 percent for Greek, 11.8 percent for Aboriginal and Torres Strait Islander, 10.3 percent for Chinese, 10.8 percent for Indian, and 9.7 percent for Arabic names. Thus applicants with non-English names experienced a 15.4 percentage point lower positive response rate than those with English names. This result equates to a 57.4 percent lower likelihood of receiving a positive response, with the greatest penalties faced by visible minority groups. Furthermore, when applying to nonleadership roles, applicants with non-English names still faced a significant though slightly lesser disadvantage; their likelihood of being invited to a job interview was 45.3 percent lower than that for applicants with English names.

Last, an examination of the influence of firm size on hiring discrimination reveals a consistent pattern of bias, irrespective of whether a company is classified as large, medium, or small based on revenue, operating income, workforce size, and stock market listing.[24] This consistency suggests that discriminatory hiring practices are pervasive across different types of firms.

### Is Hiring Discrimination Measured by Field Experiments Driven by the Names Used to Convey a Racial/Ethnic Minority Background?

Estimates of hiring discrimination against racial and ethnic minorities may be exaggerated because the names used for these groups in various experiments might also suggest a lower socioeconomic status.[25] However, a recent correspondence study has ruled out this possibility, clarifying that the discrimination is not based solely on socioeconomic cues. Meanwhile this research also has the merit to demonstrate that race triggers discriminatory behavior independently of or in combination with ethnicity.

Specifically, previous studies conveyed race and ethnicity through the applicants' first and last names, which combine ancestry and phenotypical triggers of discrimination into a single treatment. Under these circumstances, it is challenging to discern whether phenotype (race) plays a separate role when ancestry (ethnicity) is held constant. To investigate this question, a group of researchers utilized a large-scale correspondence study on hiring discrimination based on racial appearance across Germany, the Netherlands, and Spain.[26] Nearly 13,000 fictitious résumés were submitted to actual job vacancies, with applicants' ethnic ancestry and phenotype varied randomly. Phenotype was conveyed through applicants' photographs. Specifically, the authors created eight photographs representing four phenotypic groups: Black, Asian/Indigenous, dark-skinned Caucasian, and white. Ancestry was signaled by ethnic-sounding names *carefully selected to avoid strong religious or class connotation*, mother tongue, and parental country of birth. Regarding the latter, the study included forty-four different ancestries, grouped into five main regions: Asia, Europe (together with the United States), Latin America and the Caribbean, MENA countries, and sub-Saharan Africa. Sub-Saharan Africa was uniquely associated with Black applicants, while the other regions included applicants across all four phenotypic groups. The results revealed strong evidence that both race and ethnicity trigger discriminatory behavior in all three countries. In Germany and the Netherlands, race influenced discriminatory behavior independently of ethnicity, whereas in Spain, it affected hiring outcomes through a more complex interaction with ethnicity. In other words, the findings confirm that immigrant descendants in Europe face hiring discrimination based on both atypical (nonwhite) phenotypes and distinct cultural heritage (ethnicity), *regardless of the socioeconomic status associated with their names*.

### Is Hiring Discrimination against Visible Minorities Taste-Based or Statistical?

Many correspondence studies have attempted to determine whether discrimination against visible minorities is taste-based or statistical. Evidence for taste-based discrimination is typically measured through three main approaches. The first focuses on employer bias. This approach involves assessing how discrimination correlates with employers' prejudiced views of racial and ethnic minorities. The second strategy concentrates on customer contact. It consists in comparing the level of discrimination in jobs with high customer interaction versus those with low customer interaction, with more discrimination in high-customer-contact jobs indicating taste-based discrimination. The third method centers on coworker contact. This method examines the extent of discrimination in jobs requiring significant interaction with coworkers compared to those with minimal interaction. Higher discrimination in high-coworker-contact jobs serves as evidence for taste-based discrimination.

Concerning evidence of statistical discrimination, it is typically measured by introducing an experimental condition that provides additional information about candidates' language skills, academic achievements, job qualifications, and other productivity indicators. Researchers then evaluate whether this additional information moderates the relationship between race or ethnicity and discriminatory behavior. If discrimination remains equally high or increases despite the additional information, it suggests that statistical discrimination is not the primary driver. Conversely, if discrimination decreases, it indicates that statistical discrimination is at play.

A review of the literature reveals that both statistical and taste-based discrimination are at play in hiring practices.[27] Providing employers with more information about candidates' productivity typically reduces their reluctance to invite racial and ethnic minority candidates to job interviews. However, strong evidence also points to taste-based discrimination, showing that the degree of discrimination correlates with employers' biases and the level of customer and coworker contact required by the job. Moreover, if ethnic discrimination were solely statistical, one would expect significantly lower hiring discrimination for second-generation immigrants of non-European origin compared to first-generation immigrants. This is because recruiters' concerns about the quality of a foreign education or language proficiency should be less relevant for applicants born in the host country.[28] However, empirical evidence does not support this assumption: hiring discrimination against individuals of immigrant and ethnic minority backgrounds is only slightly lower for those born in the host country compared to newly arrived immigrants.[29] This finding may explain why second-generation immigrants often perceive higher levels of discrimination than first-generation immigrants do.[30] This perception may be driven by heightened expectations of fair and equal treatment, as well as a deeper understanding of discrimination processes.

That discrimination based on ethnicity or race is a matter of both beliefs (or stereotypes) and distaste (or prejudice) is not surprising, in light of the close interweaving of the two: both are shaped by cognitive bias (see chapter 1). Further evidence confirms that experimental employers in an online experiment stubbornly engage in inaccurate statistical discrimination despite being given the opportunity to correctly revise their beliefs about different social groups: they seek additional information about the individual performance of candidates (e.g., grades in high school English classes or college GPA) when a piece of information contradicts their initial beliefs and stop seeking additional information once their information set is consistent with those beliefs. In addition, they underweight (overweight) information that contradicts (supports) their stereotypes.[31] This dynamic explains, for instance, that declines in Black hiring following managers' negative experience with a Black hire is larger and more persistent than declines in white hiring following a negative experience with a white hire.[32] What is more, taste-based and statistical discrimination can fuel each other. As discussed in chapter 2, taste-based discrimination against a specific group can lead to a loss of self-confidence and self-esteem among its members that has the potential to permanently erode their productivity and thus expose them to statistical discrimination. Conversely, the perceived productivity deficit of a particular group may arouse hostility toward its members.

This mutual reinforcement may account for another important finding from the literature on hiring discrimination against racial/ethnic minorities, namely, it does not seem to be decreasing. For example, based on the analysis of all the correspondence studies carried out in the United States between 1989 and 2015 involving fictitious white and African American applicants, a group of sociologists has shown that the intensity of hiring discrimination experienced by African Americans has remained unchanged over the period.[33] Similarly, a review of correspondence studies from the late 1960s to the late 2010s across six European and North American countries (Canada, France, Germany, Great Britain, the Netherlands, and the United States) found that racial/ethnic discrimination has remained largely stable or slightly increased for most countries and visible minority groups.[34] Focusing on the results of correspondence studies published between 2005 and 2020, Louis Lippens and his coauthors find no evidence of recent change in discrimination against racial/ethnic minorities.[35]

That said, cyclical variations in the intensity of ethnic discrimination are possible. Although few correspondence studies have been devoted to this topic, the results suggest that discrimination against minority groups is weaker when fictitious candidates apply for jobs in occupations where there is a shortage of labor.[36] In other words, discrimination might be stronger in times of economic crisis but weaker in periods of recovery, a surmise that has been confirmed in the US,[37] and, more recently, in France.[38] Drawing on five waves of correspondence studies conducted between 2015 and the period following the first lockdown in France, Laetitia Challe, Yannick L'Horty, Pascale Petit, and François-Charles Wolff demonstrate that racial and ethnic hiring discrimination has generally decreased in France since the mid-2010s, in the context of an improving labor market. However, this trend reversed sharply during the COVID-19 health crisis, as economic conditions deteriorated, suggesting that discrimination tends to follow a counter-cyclical pattern. Notably, the temporal trends in discrimination, as measured by callback rates, closely track fluctuations in the unemployment rate.

### Visible Minorities Perceived as Muslim Are Doubly Penalized in Christian-Heritage Societies

Visible minorities are discriminated against in the labor market. However, in the absence of data, for a long time little was known as to whether some groups are more discriminated against than others. Among the many correspondence studies conducted in Europe, North America, and Australia to assess discrimination against individuals of non-European origin, few have considered several geographic origins at the same time.

During this period of uncertainty, economists Anthony Edo, Nicolas Jacquemet, and Constantine Yannelis hypothesized that racial/ethnic minorities, irrespective of their extra-European origin, are equally discriminated against with respect to hiring in European countries (and countries whose populations are mostly European in origin), which would reflect a tendency by recruiters to favor candidates who look like them—and therefore white, as opposed to any candidate of color. To test this hypothesis, these researchers carried out two correspondence studies, one in the United States and one in France.[39] Their approach involved comparing the interview rates for an applicant from the racial/ethnic majority (e.g., "Kristen Smith" in the United States and "Pascal Leclerc" in France) and two applicants who were citizens of the country under consideration but with a non-European origin. The first of these was an applicant whose surname suggested that he belonged to one of the country's main visible minorities: an African American individual in the United States (e.g., "Ebony Williams") and an individual of North African origin in France (e.g., "Rachid Benbalit"). The second was an applicant whose surname suggested a non-European origin, without a specific region of origin being attributable to it (e.g., "Aferdita Dzaghig" in the United States and "Jatrix Aldegi" in France, which are fictitious foreign names). The results were clear: both applicants of non-European origin experienced discrimination of similar intensity relative to the applicant of ethnic majority background. The researchers conclude, "The question of discrimination is much more a matter of opposition between the majority group and all individuals with a non-European background, than of antagonism with specific non-European groups."[40] However, a compilation of findings in the literature (or meta-analysis) conducted in 2016 by sociologists Eva Zschirnt and Didier Ruedin casts doubt on this interpretation.[41] Based on an analysis of all correspondence studies carried out in OECD countries from 1990 to 2015, these authors show that individuals of non-European origin who are most discriminated against come from the MENA region. However, to the extent that the religious tradition of these individuals, Islam, is much easier to infer than that of individuals from sub-Saharan Africa or Asia, where religious diversity is greater, it is legitimate to ask whether Zschirnt and Ruedin's findings reveal a double penalty for racial/ethnic minorities identified by recruiters as Muslim.

Indeed, the results of Edo, Jacquemet, and Yannelis's correspondence study in the United States does not exclude the possibility that an applicant of MENA country origin would have been penalized more than the African American fictitious applicant they relied on. The only correspondence study conducted in the United States that included all of these origins showed that applicants with Arab-sounding first and last names are the most discriminated against.[42] Similarly, the results of the correspondence study that the aforementioned researchers conducted in France are compatible with applicants of Asian or sub-Saharan African background being treated better than applicants of North African origin. This is precisely the conclusion of the CV testing conducted internally by the Casino Group in 2008, one of the very few in France that included several non-European origins. Specifically, this self-administered testing showed that French people of sub-Saharan African, Asian, and North African origin are all treated less well than French people perceived as members of the majority group. However, among these penalized applicants, French people of North African origin are discriminated against the most.[43]

But how can we know whether racial/ethnic minorities perceived as Muslim are treated unfairly because of their presumed geographic origin or because of their religious beliefs? To answer this question, it is first necessary to isolate the religious component of discrimination from its racial and ethnic component in a context where, with the exception of Albania, Muslim-majority countries are located outside Europe and its former colonies. Consider, for example, the correspondence study carried out in France in 2006 by the economists Emmanuel Duguet, Noam Leandri, Yannick L'Horty, and Pascale Petit.[44] The study revealed that the French male applicant of North African origin ("Yassine Mokraoui") was four times less likely than the French male applicant of French origin ("Clément Meunier") to be contacted by the recruiter for a job interview.[45] But the experimental setup did not allow explaining why this discrepancy occurred: the difference in the response rate to Clément and to Yassine could as easily be attributed to their different ethnic origins (European for Clément, North African for Yassine) as to their presumably different religious traditions (Christianity for Clément, Islam for Yassine). To be able to attribute the different response rates for Clément and Yassine to their distinct religious cultures, it would have been necessary to assign them the same ethnic origin.

Identifying religious discrimination presents a further challenge since Islam is often associated with more intense religious practice than Christianity. For example, using data from the World Values Survey, the American political analyst Steven Fish has shown that people who declare themselves to be Muslims attach more importance to religion than those who claim to be Christians.[46] A similar finding for France emerged from the Trajectoires et Origines survey.[47]

In other words, measuring the religious discrimination experienced by applicants perceived as Muslim, and that alone, involves eliminating two confounding factors that are associated with Islam rather than Christianity: belonging to an ethnic minority and strong religious commitment. To this end, one of the authors of this book (Marie-Anne Valfort) carried out an extensive correspondence study in France involving fictitious Christian and Muslim applicants from the same country of origin, one known for its religious pluralism, namely, Lebanon.[48] The identical national origin of applicants made it possible to eliminate a first confounding factor, namely, whether they belonged to a racial/ethnic minority. Specifically, the fictitious applicants were born Lebanese in Lebanon. They also had the same surname, "Haddad," which means "blacksmith" in Arabic. This surname is as widespread in Lebanon as is the surname Durand in France and can apply indifferently to those of Christian or Muslim faith. The applicants arrived in France at the beginning of upper secondary school, obtained their baccalaureate and BTS (vocational training certificate), and acquired French nationality. They also presented strictly equivalent educational and professional paths. The applicants differed, however, in terms of their religious confession, which was indicated on their CV in two ways: first, through their given name—Michel and Nathalie for Christian, and Mohammed and

Samira for Muslim[49]—and second, through the denominational lower secondary school in Beirut where they obtained their passing out certificate. For Michel and Nathalie, this was the "Notre Dame de Nazareth bilingual French-Arabic Catholic private junior high school" and for Mohammed and Samira it was the "Amilieh bilingual French-Arabic Muslim private junior high school."

But these precautions were not enough to remove the second confounding factor, namely, the strong correlation between an individual's affiliation with Islam rather than Christianity and that person's actual religiosity. The experimental setup thus included this variable through reference to the scouting association where the applicant supervised young people (under the heading "Areas of Interest" on the CV). Practicing applicants stated that they were active in a religious scouting association: the Catholic association "Scouts and Guides of France" for applicants of the Christian religious tradition and the association "Muslim Scouts of France" for those of the Muslim religious tradition. Nonpracticing candidates stated that they were involved in the nonreligious scouting association called "Éclaireuses et Éclaireurs de France."[50] It might be thought that recruiters do not pay attention to these signals, but a follow-up survey of two hundred recruiters shows that this is not the case. Not only do they consider it relevant to mention scouting activities on a CV because of the valued soft skills the scouting experience reveals, they also view applicants involved in the "Muslim Scouts of France" and the "Scouts and Guides of France" as more religious than members of the "Éclaireuses et Éclaireurs de France."

Analysis of the response rates to these different profiles revealed that candidates of the Muslim religious tradition were more discriminated against in hiring than their Catholic counterparts: the rate of invitation to interviews of the former (11.7 percent) was lower by almost seen percentage points than the invitation rate of the latter (18.4 percent). However, this overall result masks substantial variation according to the applicants' degree of religious practice. Employers do not discriminate against applicants of the Muslim tradition compared to their counterparts of the Christian tradition if these applicants are not religious. But the gap widens when candidates of the Muslim religious tradition practice their religion. In fact, whereas religious practice penalizes Muslims, it benefits Christians. These results are largely driven by male candidates: the penalty of religious practice is particularly strong for Muslim men, while its benefit is very pronounced for Christian men. The religious practitioner Michel needs to send only five applications to get a job interview, whereas the religious practitioner Mohammed needs to send twenty.

As with discrimination against racial/ethnic minorities, discrimination against Muslim practitioners seems both statistical and taste-based. Muslim tradition applicants are penalized if they practice their religion unless they show outstanding profiles that reassure recruiters about their performance. These results suggest that employers associate practicing Muslims with a risk of problematic behavior in the workplace.[51] But practicing Muslims are also victims of taste-based discrimination. One way to test whether this type of discrimination exists is to look at employers' behavior toward these candidates once they have decided not to recruit them. At this point, their beliefs about the applicants' productivity when hired should no longer apply. The data reveal that recruiters are indeed more hostile toward practicing Muslims than toward their Christian counterparts, even after rejecting their application.[52] They are less likely to inform them of their decision not to interview them and, when they do inform them of this decision, they are less cordial in the email they send.

It is important to underline that hiring discrimination against practicing Muslim applicants in France appears to be very specific to Muslims and does not concern other religious minorities, such as practicing Jews.[53] Moreover, such discrimination does not seem to be limited to France. Survey data reveal that practicing Muslims of the same ethnic origin are also penalized in the labor market in other European countries and in the United States.[54] More recently, a standardized cross-national field experiment examined discrimination against Muslim job applicants in five European countries (Germany, the Netherlands, Norway, Spain, and the UK). By focusing on candidates originating from several Muslim-majority countries of whom some signaled closeness to Islam in their job application while others did not, the experiment design allows disentangling anti-Muslim discrimination more strictly speaking (a "disclosed Muslim" effect) from the possible stigma of originating from countries where Islam is prevalent (a "Muslim by default" effect). The results uncovered alarming levels of discrimination against applicants from Muslim majority countries, especially when they are male. Both the "disclosed Muslim" and the "Muslim by default" independently contribute to the severe disadvantage faced by the ethnoreligious minorities analyzed in this correspondence study, with the authors noting that this disadvantage is especially severe in the Norwegian labor market.[55] Further findings reveal that, although Muslim women face less discrimination than their male counterparts, this is no longer the case when they wear the headscarf, at least in countries such as Germany and the Netherlands, where Muslim minorities are descendants of immigrants who settled more than five decades ago and thus form a significant part of the population.[56] By contrast, the level of discrimination against veiled Muslim women is much smaller in Spain, where the size of the Muslim population was negligible until the 2000s and is still low. The penalty observed in Germany and the Netherlands emerges when veiled Muslim women apply for jobs that require a high level of customer contact.

## A Threat to Social Cohesion

Muslim tradition applicants are widely perceived by recruiters as practicing their traditional religion.[57] People with a North African–sounding surname are therefore very likely to suffer a twofold penalty in the labor market, linked to their extra-European origins and their supposed practice of Islam, which may in turn lead them to accentuate, either deliberately or unintentionally, the cultural differences separating them from those who exclude them, thereby further aggravating the discrimination they face. This mechanism was clearly identified in the American context by the economists Eric Gould and Esteban Klor.[58] Muslims living in states where Islamophobic acts increased the most after the attacks of September 11, 2001, were seemingly practicing a more uncompromising form of their religion ten years later, suggesting that exclusion might push people to hold more extreme versions of the beliefs that others exclude them for holding. The shift is notably reflected in an increase in intracommunity marriages and a lower participation of women in the labor market. Apparent withdrawal of this kind is likely to heighten the sidelining of Muslims. Consistent with these findings, complementary research suggests that the difficulties of Muslim immigrants and their descendants in integrating into rich, secularized, and homogeneous societies may have led them to radicalize and become ISIS foreign fighters.[59] For instance, using data from fourteen EU countries, Philip Verwimp found that the number of a country's ISIS foreign fighters is positively correlated with the gap in employment between natives with native parentage and natives with foreign parentage.[60]

Survey data collected by Claire Adida, David Laitin, and Marie-Anne Valfort further illustrate these phenomena.[61] For example, a survey of five hundred people of Senegalese origin living in France revealed that, while feelings of exclusion and detachment from the host society and its values are exacerbated from one generation of immigrants to the next among Muslims, the reverse happens among Christians.[62] The authors drew similar conclusions when using data from other European countries and the United States.

Of course, the discrimination that some racial/ethnic groups face does not always discourage them from making costly investments in assimilation despite these investments' lower economic returns compared to a situation in which discrimination is absent. This positive scenario is even more plausible since the minority's demonstrated efforts to integrate likely lower the majority's incentives to indulge in discrimination. The political scientist Vasiliki Fouka confirmed that this assimilation dynamic can emerge when the ethnic minority is culturally closer to the ethnic majority and thus when the cost of assimilation is low.[63] More precisely, she shows that, in the face of anti-Germanism in the United States during World War I, Germans increased their assimilation investments by Americanizing their own and their children's names and filing more petitions for U.S. citizenship, noting that these assimilation responses to increased native hostility were stronger in states that registered higher levels of anti-Germanism. Yet even for ethnic minorities that are culturally close to the ethnic majority, the cost of assimilating can become prohibitive when discrimination against the minority group is so high that it boils down to denying the minority's identity. As an illustration, in another research effort Fouka investigated the effect of German-language bans that several U.S. states adopted after World War I on Germans' integration and identification with the host country.[64] She shows that these forced and radical assimilation policies instigated a backlash that heightened the sense of cultural identity among the minority instead of facilitating the assimilation of immigrant children: the second-generation German Americans who were exposed to German-language bans at school were more likely to marry other ethnic Germans, choose German-sounding names for their children, and refrain from volunteering for the U.S. Army in World War II.

Unfortunately, the expected increase in the proportion of individuals of non-European background in European countries (or in countries whose populations are mostly European in origin),[65] and the opportunities for contact that ensue, do not seem to be able to break the cycle resulting from some discriminated minorities reacting by radicalizing. On the contrary, this demographic trend may exacerbate some ongoing negative dynamics.

According to the intergroup contact theory developed by the psychologist Gordon Allport, greater ethnic diversity can potentially improve relationships between people of different ethnic backgrounds, but not unconditionally.[66] In particular, the interactions induced by ethnic diversity must take place in a context in which it is clearly in the interest of the different groups to cooperate. While certain situations satisfy this prerequisite (e.g., when students of different ethnic backgrounds share the same classroom or dormitory), others are more conducive to confirming the predictions of group threat theory developed by sociologist Hubert Blalock.[67] This theory suggests that an increase in the proportion of racial/ethnic minorities will exacerbate discrimination against them because of the majority's perception that its cultural identity is under threat.

The laboratory experiments carried out by Claire Adida, David Laitin, and Marie-Anne Valfort support this intuition.[68] The authors show that French people without a recent migration history are less cooperative with respect to Senegalese Muslim immigrants when the latter's proportion increases. On the other hand, an increase in the proportion of Senegalese Christian immigrants does not affect the way in which this French cohort behaves toward them. The authors call this decline in cooperation the "Hortefeux effect," referring to the comment made on September 5, 2009, by Brice Hortefeux, then French minister of the interior: "When there's one [Muslim], that's OK; it's when there's a lot of them that there are problems."[69] The experiments show that, in a dictator game setting, moving from a ten-player environment with one Senegalese Muslim to a ten-player environment with two Senegalese Muslims is sufficient for the attitude of the French players toward them to deteriorate.[70] The results of the large-scale correspondence study conducted by Valfort to identify anti-Muslim discrimination (discussed above) are consistent with these findings:[71] hiring discrimination against Muslims intensifies as the proportion of Muslims at the local level grows. These conclusions do not seem specific to France or to Muslims. Drawing on random assignment to projects and coworkers for more than 9,000 newly hired employees in an elite U.S. professional services firm, a group of economists found that a 20 percent increase in the percentage of white coworkers increased turnover for Black (female) employees by sixteen percentage points. Moreover, Black women assigned to teams with more white coworkers tended to receive more negative performance evaluations: evaluators were more likely to identify them as "at risk of low performance" and were less willing to "want the [given employee] on their team."[72]

* * *

Discrimination on the ground of race and ethnicity is viewed as the most widespread form of discrimination. Indeed, a plethora of studies have shown that visible minorities, for example individuals of non-European background in countries whose population is mostly of European origin, are systematically disadvantaged in the labor market and beyond. These gaps at least partly stem from the discrimination these minorities face, as objectively measured by field experiments. For instance, across nine OECD countries, nonwhite natives, that is, individuals of Asian, MENA, or sub-Saharan African background, can be up to twice less likely to be invited to a job interview than white natives with the same CV. This discrimination is particularly strong when directed at individuals from Muslim-majority countries unless they emphasize that they do not practice Islam. Racial/ethnic discrimination is a threat to social cohesion because it induces groups who are culturally more distant from the majority to react to discrimination by radicalizing and undertaking explicit oppositional actions to reaffirm their identity.

# 7 The Burdens of Age

Daniel Blake is a fifty-nine-year-old joiner from Newcastle, UK, who recently suffered a heart attack. Although he would like to return to work, his doctor advises against performing the same type of work because of his health. Daniel faces a bureaucratic nightmare as he has to find a different type of job in order to receive financial support. Age discrimination becomes a prominent theme in Ken Loach's film, *I, Daniel Blake*, especially as Daniel tries to navigate a world that feels increasingly alien to him. While his skills as a carpenter may be in demand in certain contexts, he finds it difficult to translate those skills to modern job applications, which often require digital literacy.

This reflects a wider societal problem: older workers are often left behind or marginalized because their skills don't mesh perfectly with the rapidly changing digital age. They are often asked by potential employers if they can adapt and if they are really motivated by the job, only to be rejected. The film poignantly depicts the struggles and frustrations many older people face when reentering the labor market, especially after decades of stable employment. Although discrimination on the ground of age may affect only a minority of the population—those who are approaching retirement age—it also has the potential to start hurting individuals at an earlier stage of their life cycle. This pervasive risk could explain why age discrimination is a major source of worry among employees.

Consistent with the existence of significant age discrimination in the labor market, the incidence of long-term unemployment among over-fifties is high, as is the incidence of low employment within this age group. But discrimination may not be the only culprit. Other factors may account for the poor performance of seniors in the labor market, such as obsolescent skills, few incentives to invest in reskilling and upskilling as retirement nears, or the choice to ramp down as one ages. The objective of researchers is to disentangle these different factors. Yet identifying age discrimination in the labor market is not a given since older workers may also be more experienced and thus potentially more productive.

## Higher Wages but Declining Access to Employment with Age

Let us start with a quick review of the situation of older people in the labor market. Data are readily available since age and date of birth, like gender, are always included in employment surveys (which is not the case for race/ethnicity, religion, sexual orientation, or gender identity).

The first observation is that wages clearly increase with age. In the United States, full-time employees aged between fifty-five and sixty-four years earn about 10 percent more than the median employee, and 19 percent more than those aged twenty-five to thirty-four years (figure 7.1). This difference is striking since younger cohorts typically have higher education levels than older ones. The beneficial effects of work experience in the labor market are felt up to about age fifty-five, beyond which labor earnings tend

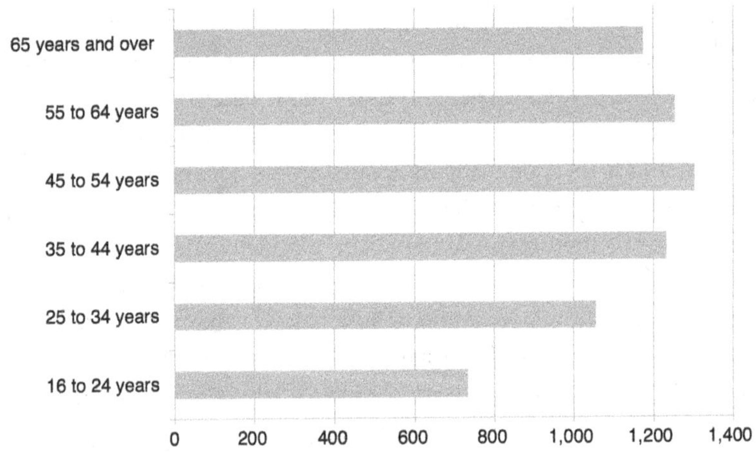


**Figure 7.1**
Median Usual Weekly Earnings of Full-Time Employees in the United States in 2024 (in U.S. Dollars). *Note:* Data represent earnings before taxes and other deductions and include any overtime pay, commissions, or tips usually received (at the main job in the case of multiple jobholders). *Source*: Bureau of Labor Statistics, U.S. Department of Labor (https://workingnation.com/wp-content/uploads/2020/05/BLS-Average-Income-Q1-2020.pdf).

to level off. Various factors may contribute to this slowdown, including the stagnation of productivity and fewer career moves.[1]

By contrast, differences in employment rates between older and younger people follow an opposite pattern (figure 7.2). On average in OECD countries, the employment rate of twenty-five- to fifty-four-year-olds is sixteen percentage points higher than that of individuals aged fifty-five to sixty-four years.[2] In the United States, the difference is equal to the OECD average, while it reaches twenty points in Canada, and even twenty-five points or more in several European countries. The normal retirement age—that is, the age of eligibility for pensions schemes without penalty based on a full career—obviously affects these differences. But it is not the only factor at play. As shown in figure 7.2, the employment rate of seniors varies by country, including among those with similar retirement ages.

When they are not in employment, seniors are usually not in the labor force. The incidence of long-term unemployment (one year or more) is higher among people aged fifty-five to sixty-four years because once they become unemployed, they have great difficulty finding another job.

Finally, few older people enroll in educational or training programs with a view to improving their skills, thus penalizing their employability. The rates of participation in formal and informal training in a given year differ greatly from one age group to the next: 24 percent among fifty-five-year-olds and older but 46 percent among twenty-five- to fifty-four-year-olds, on average in the OECD.[3] The gap is similar in the UK and Canada, and slightly lower but still significant in the United States (40 percent for older workers compared with 53 percent for the middle-aged). The situation is even worse among older people who do not have tertiary education.

## Stereotypes Regarding Older Workers

Age is the discrimination criterion that typically worries employees the most, for it also concerns the relatively more privileged groups in the labor market, such as white, native-born, Christian males. In the United States, three out of five workers aged forty-five years or older have seen or experienced discrimination, with the proportion higher among women than men (64 percent versus 59 percent, respectively).[4] The same holds true in many European countries. For instance, about half of all French employees believe they might eventually be discriminated against because of their age.[5]

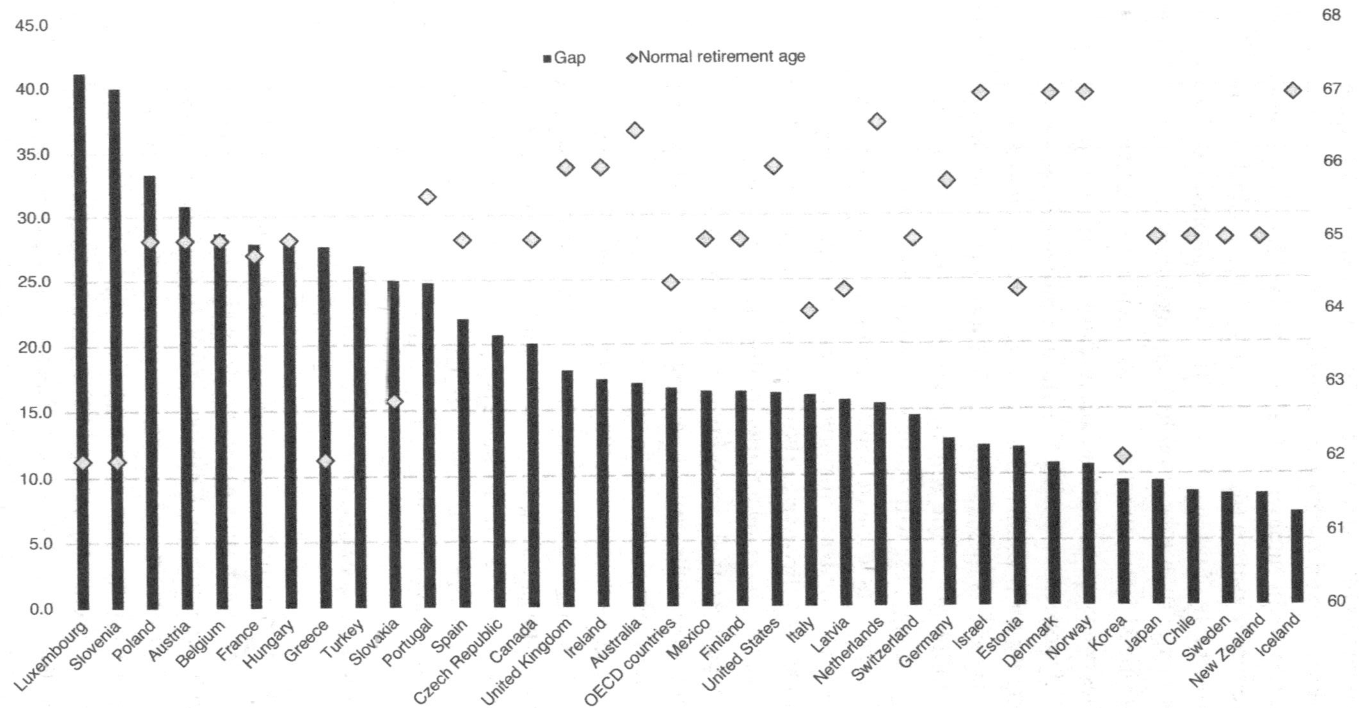


**Figure 7.2**

Employment Rate Gap between 25–54 and 55–64 Age Groups in 2022 (as a percent) and the Normal Retirement Age in OECD Countries. *Note:* The employment rate gap is represented by the vertical bars (left scale) as of 2022. The normal retirement age, which is the age of eligibility for all pensions schemes combined without penalty based on a full career, is represented by dots (right scale) as of 2022. When the retirement age differs with gender, the average retirement age for men and women is used. *Sources*: OECD, OECD Employment and Labor Market Statistics database (https://www.oecd-ilibrary.org/employment/data/oecd-employment-and-labour-market-statistics_lfs-data-en) and OECD indicators on pensions (https://www.oecd.org/en/topics/sub-issues/public-pensions.html#:~:text=Retirement%20ages,64.4%20years%20old%20for%20men).

Yet these perceptions are no proof that age discrimination is a reality. The impact of age on employability results from a mixture of factors that are difficult to disentangle and that, for many of them, have nothing to do with discrimination. For example, the experience accumulated by older people during their career is an asset in many occupations. Yet it is also possible that hourly productivity levels off or falls with age, a factor that hampers employability if wages are not adjusted accordingly. In addition, certain skills acquired through education and training and subsequently during the person's professional life may eventually become obsolete. The lack of professional training after the age of forty-five puts older people at risk of unemployment. Last, when people approach retirement age they tend to value more free time, which may worry employers looking for a committed workforce. Such factors do not, strictly speaking, come under the heading of discrimination, but their negative consequences in terms of employment may be perceived as discrimination by those who experience them.

These considerations do not, however, mean that the possibility of discriminatory behavior against seniors should be brushed aside. Panel data, which track a given cohort over a period of several years, show that people reporting age discrimination have a greater risk of losing their job in the period that follows. They are also more likely to become unemployed at some point, while their pay increases at a slower rate.[6]

In addition, employers do indeed entertain certain stereotypes regarding seniors. Admittedly, the experience, know-how and professionalism of people aged fifty and older are viewed as a strength by a large majority of employers when questioned in the context of specific surveys.[7] But the over-fifties are also seen as less productive and motivated than their younger counterparts. They are also considered to be less mobile, more resistant to organizational and technological change, and less willing to participate in training and to master new skills. Employers often consider them more likely to experience health problems or more likely to retire earlier than planned, or to quit faster, meaning that they are associated by employers with shorter job tenure. In a word, they are viewed as less dynamic and less committed to their job.[8] These stereotypes are fading in OECD countries where the population is aging at a quick rate, but they are still widespread.

Survey evidence is confirmed by experimental data. For example, a group of economists asked HR managers in Germany and Norway to evaluate three CVs that were similar apart from the applicant's age (which randomly varied from twenty-seven to fifty-three).[9] The results revealed that older people's CVs are consistently ranked lower than those of younger applicants. This is particularly the case in Germany, where older people are perceived as less flexible and less able to learn. Similar results have been obtained in Australia.[10]

Such stereotypes are most often at odds with actual employee behaviors in the workplace. Indeed, based on 380 empirical studies, Thomas Ng and Daniel Feldman have shown that stereotypes about seniors are generally not consistent with the cumulated research evidence, in the United States and other countries.[11] For instance, there are greater differences in terms of job performance within age groups than between age groups. There is also no empirical evidence to support that older workers would be more resistant to change. The only stereotype that seems to be validated empirically is that older workers are less willing to participate in training.

These stereotypes, whether or not they are well-founded, likely feed statistical discrimination against older job applicants. An aversion to the physical appearance of older individuals may also contribute to taste-based discrimination against them. Yet testing the existence of age discrimination through labor market field experiments is a challenge.

## Lower Interview Rates for Older Workers

The gap in employment rates between older and younger people have led researchers to turn to field experiments for analyzing hiring behaviors toward these groups. Such experiments help to determine whether some of the observed discrepancies result from discrimination rather than from other factors such as differences in skills, salary requirements, or even motivation.

Virtually all correspondence studies aimed at testing the existence of age discrimination reveal that older job applicants are invited to interviews less frequently than younger applicants with similar experience in the occupation tested. This is the case in most sectors studied. Moreover, the proportion of seniors in the working population in the countries considered makes no difference: discrimination against older applicants is not limited to certain countries, but is common to all of them.

Yet these correspondence studies may overestimate age discrimination since they typically solve the "Difference in Post-Educational Years

Problem"[12]—that is, the fact that an older person inevitably has, in comparison with a younger person with the same educational background, a higher number of posteducational years at the moment of application—by simply introducing gaps in relevant work experience in the fictitious applications of older job candidates. Indeed, if a researcher trying to measure the incidence of age discrimination "fills" these additional years in the résumé of the fictitious older candidates with supplementary in-field employment, then one may underestimate discrimination against them by giving them an advantage in terms of human capital valued by employers. If, by contrast, one "fills" these additional years with out-of-field employment or inactivity (or let employers fill them in themselves by limiting the mentioned professional experience to the most recent career years), then one may overestimate age discrimination by introducing in older job candidates' fictitious applications gaps in relevant career. One of the first studies, carried out by Marc Bendick, Charles Jackson, and Horacio Romero during the 1990s in the United States, involved sending unsolicited job applications that were identical in every respect except for the applicant's age—either thirty-two or fifty-seven.[13] Nearly eight hundred companies, representing a wide range of business sectors, were tested. The results revealed that older job seekers received a less favorable employer response almost 30 percent of the time. But the study went further than this. The researchers varied the content of the CVs to counter certain negative stereotypes that recruiters might hold toward older applicants. Some CVs thus placed less emphasis on age (focusing on skills rather than on the applicant's career history), some emphasized the positive aspects of age (accumulated experience, maturity), and some sought to reassure the recruiters by emphasizing in the cover letter the applicant's "energetic" personality, capacity to "adapt to the latest technologies," and "career commitment." These changes reduced discrimination against the older applicants by half, suggesting that it was partly statistical in nature: when employers were given more information on older workers' productivity, they discriminated less. But discrimination nonetheless remained significant, highlighting a substantial taste-based component.

Marc Bendick and two other colleagues then set out to identify at what stage of the recruitment process discrimination occurs.[14] Accordingly, between 1995 and 1996, they targeted a hundred sales and management jobs in stores in Washington, D.C. As before, for each of these positions, they sent out two CVs identical in all respects except for the applicant's age. But they also sent actors to the job interviews, thereby complementing the correspondence study with an audit study (see chapter 4). The findings showed that three quarters of the total discrimination against older applicants occurred during the CV selection stage. Only a quarter of the discrimination took place during the job interview, perhaps because the interview allows candidates to elaborate on their career and demonstrate their skills.

These results date back to the 1990s, but things have not changed much since then. Notably, finding oneself in an unemployment situation seems particularly harmful for older workers. Between 2012 and 2014, Henry Farber, Dan Silverman, and Till von Wachter sent out nearly 10,000 applications from unemployed individuals in response to three thousand job advertisements for administrative positions in the United States.[15] They varied the applicants' age, but also the duration of their periods of unemployment. Although, unlike in other studies, this latter variable had no significant average effect on employers' callback, the authors found that unemployed people aged fifty-five and older had callback rates on average 20 percent lower than those of unemployed persons in the thirty-five -to thirty-seven-year-old age group or forty- to forty-two-year-old age group.[16]

The United States is no exception regarding discrimination against older job candidates. Very similar results have been obtained in Europe. For example, Peter Riach conducted correspondence studies for men aged twenty-seven or forty-seven years and with the same professional experience as waiters in Germany, the UK, Spain, and France.[17] He found that young men were between 1.5 times and twice as likely as older men to be invited to a job interview in Germany and the UK. The advantage of being young is even larger in France and Spain, where young men were 3.5 times as likely as their older counterparts to be called back by recruiters. These results suggest that age discrimination may affect applicants well before the age of fifty, at least in occupations involving customer contact. These conclusions were confirmed by Ali Ahmed, Lina Andersson, and Mats Hammarstedt, who in 2011 tested the behavior of nearly five hundred recruiters for waiting staff and sales assistant jobs in Sweden.[18] Despite Sweden's reputation as a very inclusive country, thirty-one-year-olds were three times more likely on average to be invited to a job interview in this sector than forty-six-year-old applicants with equal skills.

While age discrimination may affect people starting in their mid-forties, it tends to increase with age. David Neumark of the University of California,

Irvine, and his colleagues sent out no fewer than 40,000 CVs in response to job advertisements across the United States for several low- to middle-skill positions, distinguishing between applicants aged forty-nine to fifty-one years and seniors aged sixty-four to sixty-six years.[19] The authors found that discrimination against applicants who are approaching retirement age is twice as high as that against middle-aged applicants: rates of invitation to job interviews for sixty-four- to sixty-six-year-olds and forty-nine- to fifty-one-year-olds were 35 percent and 18 percent lower respectively than those for younger applicants. This is an important finding since greater discrimination at the approach of retirement may in the short or medium term hinder the implementation of public policies encouraging older people to work longer.

Age discrimination tends to be more pronounced in large cities, where the imperative of being an energetic person may be more salient. In France, Peter Riach and his colleague Judith Rich have shown that age discrimination is higher in Paris than in the rest of France.[20] The same two researchers came up with similar findings for the UK. They sent out CVs of men aged twenty-seven or forty-seven years for jobs as waiters.[21] While young waiters were one-third more likely than their older counterparts to be called back by recruiters outside London, their probability of being invited to a job interview was four times as high in the capital city!

It is possible that women are even more exposed than men to age discrimination. Aging affects physical appearance, and, as we will see in chapter 8, women are particularly subject to discrimination based on looks. Joanna Lahey of Texas A&M University has focused specifically on women.[22] She varied the ages of applicants from thirty-five to sixty-two years in CVs she sent out between 2002 and 2003 to nearly four thousand companies in various economic sectors in Boston, Massachusetts, and St. Petersburg, Florida. Her results revealed that younger female applicants (aged thirty-five or forty-five years) were 40 percent more likely to be interviewed than older women (aged fifty, fifty-five, or sixty-two years). The difference was substantial and appeared to prevail regardless of the recruiter's gender or the proportion of older employees in the company. Another particularly depressing finding was that emphasizing the applicant's adaptability, computer skills, or already in possession of health insurance—which can be very expensive for employers in the United States—had no effect on the response rate to older women. Discrimination against older women appears to be even greater when the job involves a lot of contact with customers, as was demonstrated in a correspondence study carried out in the UK with women aged twenty-four or fifty.[23] For bar staff jobs in pubs, young women are between two and three times more likely to be contacted than older women, whereas for personal assistant jobs the difference is not statistically significant. Similarly, in the United States, the large-scale correspondence study conducted by David Neumark and his colleagues has shown that discrimination rates against older workers are almost twice as high for women than for men for sales assistant jobs. This heightened discrimination against women occurs from the age of fifty upward.[24]

The above-mentioned correspondence studies are not devoid of methodological flaws, however. In most of them, applicants' CVs show a similar number of years of experience in the occupation being tested for both older and younger applicants. The goal is to avoid underestimating discrimination against older workers, since longer in-field work experience would signal better know-how and expertise among older job applicants that young people would not have had time to acquire. In most cases, the CVs of older applicants are thus "filled" with years of experience in other occupations, or sometimes even periods of unemployment.

This approach runs the risk of overestimating age discrimination since employers may well question the employability of older workers who have changed occupations several times or have had periods of inactivity. This negative signal may lead them to reject older workers' applications more often, quite independently of any discriminatory intent. When, on the contrary, older workers are given in-field work experience on their CVs that is commensurate with their age, discrimination against them tends to diminish, as has been shown by Stijn Baert and his colleagues at Ghent University.[25] Between December 2014 and May 2015, they sent out 1,200 fictitious applications in response to 600 job offers in Flanders, in northern Belgium. The youngest candidates were aged thirty-eight, while the older ones were aged either forty-four or fifty. The age difference—six or twelve years—was filled in by the researchers either by adducing professional experience in another sector, or by inactivity, or by more extensive experience in the sector being tested. Six different professions were considered, ranging from low-skilled (manual worker, administrative assistant, waiter) to middle-skilled (laboratory assistant, assistant manager, salesperson). The experiment showed that younger applicants had an average callback rate

1.6 times higher than that of older applicants. But this difference was fully accounted for by older applicants whose CVs had been filled with professional experience in sectors other than the one tested or by a period of inactivity. There was no difference, however, in the case of older candidates who had more experience in the job they were applying for, a finding that contrasts with those of Nick Drydakis and his coauthors in the UK. In their experiments, despite older applicants (fifty-year-olds) possessing thirty-one years of experience in relevant low-skilled private sector occupations—such as restaurant and café staff, or sales assistants—compared to younger applicants (twenty-eight-year-olds) with only nine years of experience, the younger applicants were significantly more likely to receive interview invitations.[26] Interestingly, irrespective of how the "difference in post-educational years problem" was solved, discrimination measured by Stijn Baert and his colleagues was again stronger for jobs where interaction with customers was more frequent, that is, for waiting staff and sales assistants. These findings suggest that the hiring rate of seniors depends not only on employers' stereotypes about candidates' commitment, flexibility, or familiarity with the latest IT tools but also on employers' expectations about customer preferences.

On top of the "difference in post-educational years problem," another methodological obstacle challenges the possibility of measuring age-based hiring discrimination with precision. Older workers are given ample opportunity to differentiate from each other over the course of their careers. Some will have accumulated a significantly greater array of skills over the years, while others will have gradually lost their competencies. Employers are aware of this, and it is possible that they perceive older people as a more heterogeneous group on average than younger ones. Consequently, they may consider that, compared to young people, applications from older people will include both more very strong profiles and more very weak ones.

As discussed in chapter 4, this factor can lead to differences in response rates to young and older applicants that have nothing to do with discrimination. For example, if the employers' requirements are exacting—if the bar is set high compared to the CVs sent—then they will be inclined to interview older applicants more often because the chances of coming across a candidate able to meet their requirements are higher among this more heterogeneous group. In this setting, outcomes may be biased in favor of older people, thus masking any discrimination they may face.

As further noted in chapter 4, David Neumark in 2012 came up with a method to offset this bias, based on the observation that employers weigh differently the characteristics mentioned on a CV when the applicant comes from a group that they perceive as more heterogeneous and therefore riskier.[27] Consequently, the way in which various applicant characteristics affect the hiring decision for different groups shows whether the employer views these groups as more or less heterogeneous. Neumark and his colleagues applied this method in the context of the large-scale correspondence study already mentioned in which they distinguished between applicants aged forty-nine to fifty-one years and seniors aged sixty-four to sixty-six years.[28] They concluded that although the neutralization of the bias flowing from different beliefs on the variance of applicants' unobserved characteristics has no effect on the intensity of discrimination against older women, it does alter the extent of discrimination against older men, sometimes reinforcing it, sometimes diminishing it, depending on the occupations considered.

It is worthwhile noting that age discrimination does not disappear when one relies on age-blind application procedures. Indeed, even though the written application may not reveal any information on age (because information on years of graduation and on the exact length of work experiences is removed), age cannot be concealed at the stage of the job interview. This is David Neumark's finding, based on nonexperimental data stemming from a lawsuit over age-based hiring discrimination for a restaurant chain that opened locations throughout the United States.[29] When applications are completed in stores and handed in in person, age is revealed at the same time as all other information about the applicant. Applicants aged forty and over then obtain job offers at a rate 68 percent lower than younger applicants. When selection for interviews is made on-line, in an age-blind manner, older applicants are selected at the same rate as younger applicants. But in the end, after the interviews have taken place, they still receive job offers at rate 46 percent lower than that of younger applicants.

* * *

More research is necessary to understand better at what times in people's professional life, in which occupations, and for which profiles age discrimination is most pronounced. The work currently available to us nonetheless provides a clear-cut conclusion: discrimination on the ground of age is a powerful obstacle to older workers maintaining their jobs or returning to employment, especially in occupations involving contact with customers, in which case older women are at a particular disadvantage. This discrimination is not only statistical but also taste-based. Age discrimination not only hampers the labor market trajectories of individuals who approach retirement age, it also hurts individuals well before they reach the age of fifty.

# 8 The Advantages Conferred by Beauty

Perhaps the most widespread and certainly the most spontaneous form of discrimination—to the point that few people notice it in day-to-day life—is based on physical appearance. If the saying "First impressions are always right" is widely shared, then such physical attributes as facial features, body size, or height may well have a significant impact on hiring and pay decisions.

This is what Henri, at the age of only twenty, found out to his own cost: "I had an interview at a real estate agency. The boss told me he'd call me back. Several days went by and still no news. I went back to the agency to renew my application. A sales representative told me that the boss refused to hire me. Why? Because he thought I was too ugly."[1] The explanation could hardly have been more explicit. Most often, recruiters remain discrete about their real motives, but the outcome is not less ambiguous. Joseph, thirty-seven years old, got an offer as a cook at a fast-food chain during a job fair. He was invited, with other newly hired workers, to report to the restaurant. Candidates were asked their clothing size for uniforms. For months, Joseph, whose waist size was fifty-four inches, waited to be contacted but never heard back, except that his uniform pants were not ready yet. He even went in person to the restaurant but never got a chance to talk to the manager. He noticed on that occasion that all the other candidates recruited on the same day were actually working there. None was wearing uniform pants.[2]

Some employers thus follow their inclinations and surround themselves with good-looking employees. Rightly or wrongly, they think that the most beautiful people are also more sociable, more balanced, more ambitious, less aggressive, and even more intelligent.[3] But in the great majority of cases, the reason for the refusal is never made explicit to the unfortunate candidates whose applications are declined. In the case of Henri, the employer perhaps thought that an attractive physical appearance would directly benefit his business. After all, real estate agents must be able to appeal to people, both to acquire property and to sell it. Being good-looking, slim, and tall may be viewed as advantageous in occupations that involve frequent contact with customers, not only in real estate agencies but also in sales and reception positions and even in highly qualified occupations such as medicine or the law. These associations may feed statistical discrimination by employers in the labor market, while simultaneously reflecting customer distaste. Taste-based discrimination by employers against unattractive, obese, or short individuals may also be at work.

## Beauty Stereotypes

Consciously or not, most people have positive a prioris with respect to the psychological traits and skills of attractive individuals and negative a prioris regarding unattractive people. Psychologists have uncovered such stereotypes among adults as well as children. In two experiments where they presented pictures of individuals to participants and asked them to judge these individuals' personality traits, Angela M. Griffin and Judith H. Langlois found that, among adults, unattractiveness is associated with negative ratings when participants are required to assess whether the person in the picture is helpful and smart. Besides, unattractive subjects are viewed as less sociable, while the reverse occurs for attractive subjects.[4] These stereotypes develop early in life: children aged seven to nine years deem people with unattractive faces to be significantly less altruistic, intelligent, and sociable than people with more attractive faces.

Meta-analyses based on a plethora of studies confirm these results. Attractive adults are judged more positively than unattractive ones with respect to both interpersonal and occupational skills. Consequently, attractive individuals are treated substantially better on average: they get more help and support, and face unfriendly behaviors less frequently.[5] This process is at work from the first years of life on: attractive children get more attention from their caregivers and teachers and benefit from more positive interactions in general.

## Is Beauty in the Eye of the Beholder?

While this saying certainly contains a kernel of truth, it is also true that beholders generally perceive the appearance of the people they look at in much the same way. If not—if there were no agreement on what constitutes beauty—investigating the effects of physical appearance on people's labor market paths would be pointless.

Contrary to what is often claimed, beauty is not purely subjective; in fact, most people share the same standards and react in the same way to specific physical traits.[6] Although the criteria for beauty may vary over time and across cultures, there seems to be a consensus, among both men and women, that facial symmetry, features corresponding to those most frequently observed in the population (rather than atypical traits), and marked female and male characteristics are associated with greater beauty.[7]

This consistency of standards prevails not only over time for the same individual but also from one individual to another. For example, in a study conducted in Canada among a representative sample of about 3,500 people, the same individuals were surveyed up to three times by different interviewers—in 1977, 1979, and 1981.[8] On each occasion, the interviewers were asked to "categorize the respondent's physical appearance" on the following scale: 5—strikingly handsome, 4—above average (good-looking), 3—average, 2—below average (plain), and 1—homely. More than half of both men and women were given the same score for all three survey rounds, and fewer than 3 percent experienced a difference of more than one in their scores on any two successive rounds. In another study on the professional prospects of law students in the United States, a panel of four independent observers was asked to rate the photographs of approximately two thousand graduates from the school's official gallery on an assessment scale from 5 to 1. Total agreement by all four panelists was unusual (14 percent), but near unanimity (three out of four panelists giving the same score) occurred in two-thirds of cases for women and three quarters of cases for men.[9] Total disagreement (none of the four panelists giving the same score) occurred in only 0.1 percent of cases.

Observers tend to give women more extreme scores and to be more prejudiced against aging in women. In two representative surveys of the American population in the 1970s, participants were asked to rate the physical appearance of thousands of respondents aged eighteen to sixty-four on a scale of 5 to 1.[10] Compared to men, women were more often considered to be above or below average. Young people were also perceived as more beautiful than older ones. The combination of these two effects yielded the following outcomes: for young people aged eighteen to twenty-nine years, 45 percent of women were rated above average, compared to 36 percent of men, but among women aged fifty to sixty-four years, only 18 percent of women were rated above average, compared to 21 percent of men. The effect of age on the assessment of physical appearance is thus more negative for women than for men.[11]

## Beauty Pays, Not Least Because Employers Indulge in Statistical and Potentially Taste-Based Discrimination

There are at least three reasons why recruiters might be willing to recruit and reward attractive individuals at a higher rate. The first is simply that they prefer to be around good-looking colleagues rather than unattractive ones. This is sheer taste-based discrimination. The second is that they believe, wrongly or rightly, that attractive workers have skills that make them more productive, for example they are more convincing, have more charisma, and so forth. The third is the fact that, for some jobs, employers anticipate customers to value the beauty of employees in contact with them. Obvious examples are sales jobs in the fashion and cosmetics sectors. In department store or clothing retailing, there are very few salespeople selling face cream, make-up, or perfume that could be described as ugly. For instance, Abercrombie & Fitch was very explicit in the past about its preference for hiring "young, attractive, mainstream athletic" and "good-looking" people for store sales positions.[12] In the case of the second and third reasons, employers' beliefs relate to the supposedly higher productivity of attractive workers and thus provide a basis for statistical discrimination. Prejudice (preferences) and stereotypes (beliefs) are not easy to discern, but, regardless of their respective influence on employers' decisions, they all lead to attractive job candidates and employees being favored in the recruitment process and paid higher wages once hired.

In their 1994 seminal study, Daniel Hamermesh and Jeff Biddle were the first to reveal the existence of a "beauty premium" on pay.[13] The authors used U.S. and Canadian survey data to combine assessments of respondents' physical appearance with information about their living conditions, income, and employment. They found that plain-looking people earned less than average-looking people, who in turn earned less than people deemed to be very good-looking, even after offsetting the effect of other characteristics such as age, education, ethnicity, and self- reported health. Those whose appearance was below the average suffered a penalty that ranged from 7 percent to 10 percent, while the premium accruing to the most good-looking people was 5 percent. The wage gap between the bottom and the top of the beauty scale was therefore equal to nearly 15 percent, or $240,000 over an entire professional career.[14] The effects of beauty on pay for men are on average at least as great as those for women, but being above average is more advantageous for women (+8 percent compared to +4 percent). The wage premium for very good-looking women is almost equivalent to the benefit brought by an additional year of studies, while it is equivalent to the returns of about five years of additional mid-career work experience for very good-looking men.[15] Furthermore, beauty also has a positive impact on women's participation rates in the labor market. These findings are confirmed by more recent evidence. For example, a representative health survey of 15,000 American high school students in the mid-1990s tracked them for six years (National Longitudinal Study of Adolescent to Adult Health, or Add Health). The survey had the merit of providing extensive information on the students' background and skills, as well as an assessment by the interviewer of their physical appearance. Jason Fletcher of Yale University focused on the professional trajectories of those who joined the job market just after graduation from high school. He estimated an income advantage of 5 percent to 10 percent for young people considered to be better-looking than average, and a penalty of 5 percent for those considered to be less attractive than average.[16] Similar earning premia conferred on beauty have been identified in other countries and across a wide range of occupations, and these premia tend to persist over a lifetime.[17] John Karl Scholz and Kamil Sicinski followed a cohort of more than 10,000 male individuals who graduated from Wisconsin high schools in 1957 and were subsequently surveyed five times until 2004.[18] Attractiveness was measured by twelve independent "judges" who rated the photographs of surveyed individuals based on photos in senior year high school yearbooks. Even after controlling for a sizable set of characteristics that can influence wage and could possibly be correlated with attractiveness, such as self-confidence, family background, IQ, and high school activities, they found that beauty induces a wage premium in the mid-thirties that persists until respondents reach their fifties.[19]

Overall, the impact of people's appearance seems largely independent of their occupation, a fact that Hamermesh and Biddle (and several scholars after them) interpreted as evidence of taste-based discrimination on the part of employers. For if beauty is read by employers as a signal of productivity, it should matter especially in occupations where the impact of beauty on productivity is strong, such as those requiring contact with customers.[20]

This interpretation is debatable, however, for at least two reasons. First, beauty may be the cause or the consequence of unobserved characteristics that matter for economic success, irrespective of an individual's occupation. Surveys confirm that attractive people experience better physical and mental health, have higher self-esteem, and possess better social skills than unattractive people.[21] These features are key ingredients for individuals to thrive in the labor market, including during wage negotiations, regardless of the sector or occupation considered. In a laboratory experiment conducted in 2002 and 2003, Markus Mobius of Harvard University and his colleague Tanya Rosenblat of the University of Michigan tested whether a "beauty premium" operated during the salary negotiation process by randomly assigning students to two distinct roles, that of the recruiter and that of the job candidate.[22] The physical appearance of candidates was assessed based on facial photographs rated from 1 to 5 by fifty evaluators. Whereas beauty had no effect on the wage offered by recruiters who could only access the job candidates' CVs without a photograph, it led recruiters who could see the job candidates' photographs or the candidates in person to offer significantly higher wages to those deemed to be attractive. While 40 percent of the beauty premium stemmed from the visual interaction between recruiters and job candidates (during which discriminatory intents may have emerged among recruiters), 60 percent flowed from other factors: 20 percent was driven by the fact that beautiful candidates manifested greater self-confidence and 40 percent by the fact that they exhibited better oral skills, including when interactions with recruiters were blind.

The second reason why Hamermesh and Biddle's interpretation of employers' taste-based discrimination is questionable flows from novel and richer data that allowed Ralph Stinebrickner, Todd Stinebrickner, and Paul

Sullivan to reexamine the labor market mechanisms generating the beauty wage premium.[23] More precisely, these authors followed about five hundred individuals who entered a U.S. college in 2000 and were surveyed at several points in time through 2014, to learn what precise tasks they were performing on the job and thus to develop job-level measures of the amount of time spent performing interpersonal tasks versus data-related tasks. The authors found a large wage premium associated with attractiveness but only in jobs requiring substantial amounts of interpersonal interactions, both in high-skill positions (e.g., management[24]) and lower-skill ones (e.g., sales positions). The researchers did not find that attractiveness predicted wages for jobs requiring primarily working with data. These results suggest that the beauty premium is not primarily driven by employer taste-based discrimination—which would imply a premium in all sorts of jobs—but rather stems from productivity-based factors or customer taste-based discrimination, which in turn can trigger statistical discrimination on the part of employers.

That said, it is unlikely that individuals viewed as homely are able to avoid taste-based discrimination, including during interactions with employers. Indeed, such discrimination occurs in public places and even in front of millions of people without anyone finding anything untoward, as Michèle Belot and her colleagues Venkataraman Bhaskar and Jeroen van de Ven strikingly demonstrated in 2012.[25] They looked at the results of a TV game show that was a variant of *Going for Gold* (originally broadcasted in 1987 in the UK) and aired in the Netherlands in 2002. In this game, contestants accumulated cash prizes by correctly answering questions. Players' winnings depended on the accuracy of their answers, how quickly they pressed the buzzer, and their investment decisions. The contestants' performance was easily observable and depended on their skills and their success as investors. But, unlike in *Going for Gold,* the contestant with the highest winnings had to decide which contestant to eliminate at the end of each round, before starting the next one. It is at this stage that Belot and her coauthors found that less attractive contestants were more often eliminated, regardless of their performance. Only 27 percent of the less good-looking contestants reached the final round compared to 49 percent of the better-looking contestants, irrespective of their answers or their investment decisions. Even worse, the less attractive contestants were eliminated even when they performed better and were more cooperative than others—two attributes that, given the structure of the game, made their elimination particularly costly for the contestant with the highest potential winnings. The study thus shows that beauty-based discrimination is not only statistical but also stems from a sheer taste for better-looking individuals or distaste for less attractive individuals.

Correspondence studies confirm that employers discriminate against unattractive job candidates. For instance, Florencia López Bóo, Martín Rossi, and Sergio Urzúa sent fictitious résumés for sales, secretarial, receptionist, or unskilled positions in Buenos Aires.[26] They used digitally manipulated images constructed to match or deviate substantially from two golden ratios of facial proportions that condition attractiveness. They found that the faces that corresponded to the golden ratio generated 36 percent more callbacks than those that deviated from it. Similarly, Eleonora Patacchini, Giuseppe Ragusa, and Yves Zenou found a beauty premium in Rome and Milan for women, but not for men, for positions as administrative clerk, bookkeeper, call center operator, receptionist, secretary, and shop assistant.[27] By contrast, after sending similar CVs with attractive versus plain-appearing photographs or no photograph at all to 2,656 job ads in Israel, Bradley Ruffle and Ze'ev Shtudiner observed a beauty premium for men but not for women for various positions in sales, banking, finance, accounting, programming, and engineering.[28] They even found a negative effect on the callback rate for the applications of attractive women compared with similar applications submitted without a photograph. A survey of a randomly chosen subset of firms participating in the experiment revealed that jealousy likely accounted for this result, in a context where 90 percent of the application screeners were women.

The impact of physical appearance on hiring outcomes may be exacerbated by the expansion of social media that allows employers to easily access job candidates' photographs, in addition to a trove of information on their professional and personal lives. Stijn Baert confirms that publicly available information on Facebook about job applicants affects employers' hiring decisions.[29] After sending mock applications differing only in the photograph that could be seen on the fictitious job candidate's Facebook account to more than one thousand real job openings in Belgium, Baert found that fictitious applicants with the most attractive picture obtained nearly 40 percent more job interview invitations than fictitious applicants with the least attractive picture. This beauty premium was higher for highly educated applicants, that is, college rather than high school graduates.[30]

### Being Overweight Affects Job and Earnings Prospects

Obese individuals also experience discrimination based on physical appearance, regardless of how attractive they may be. Dan-Olof Rooth tested this surmise by relying on a correspondence study.[31] In Sweden, applicants often include a photograph of themselves with their CV. Rooth made use of this practice by digitally manipulating photographs of people of average appearance to make them look obese (or not). He then randomly allocated photographs of the obese and nonobese applicants to a set of CVs, which he then sent out in response to job advertisements. The results showed that obesity reduces the response rate by six (for men) to eight (for women) percentage points on average—for response rates that are usually between 30 percent and 50 percent, depending on the sector—for all the occupations tested except nursing. The study also included assessments of the attractiveness of each fictitious candidate. Obese men and women are systematically perceived as less attractive. When the attractiveness rating (based on the nonmanipulated photographs) was included in the analysis of response rates, the results for women seemed to be driven primarily by obesity, while the results for men seemed to be driven by being less attractive. Another interesting finding was that the penalty for obesity was higher in sectors requiring customer contact (e.g., sales), which may reflect taste-based discrimination on the part of customers.

Although hiring discrimination against obese job candidates is a reality, overweight individuals who successfully pass the recruitment process do not seem to suffer from discrimination afterward. To be sure, obesity is also associated with a wage penalty. For example, John Cawley of Cornell University found that a weight difference of about 30 kilograms is associated with a wage disparity of 9 percent, equivalent to the effect on labor earnings of 1.5 years of education or three years of additional professional experience.[32] Similar results flow from European data: obese women earn on average 10 percent less than nonobese women.[33] But this does not mean that obesity per se is the cause of such wage penalties.

Indeed, further research suggests that no share of the wage gap between obese and nonobese individuals is unexplained. In other words, this gap can be entirely accounted for by differences in individuals' productive characteristics. More precisely, in 2014, Petter Lundborg and his Swedish colleagues focused on 450,000 male Swedes whose weight, cognitive and noncognitive skills, and physical fitness were measured between 1984 and 1997 on entering military service (which at that time was compulsory for eighteen-year-old Swedish men).[34] These authors were also able to track these young men for several years, together with a subsample of 150,000 of their male siblings to neutralize the effect of family determinants. The authors found that obesity is associated with significantly lower cognitive and noncognitive abilities, thereby accounting for approximately a fifth of the obesity-related wage penalty. The mechanisms that could account for this association are many. For instance, overweight children may be bullied at school because of their stature, which might alter their self-esteem and hamper their school performance. The authors also found that obese individuals are more likely to stem from poor families, who generally face barriers to a healthy diet, in addition to other barriers to skill development faced by people from less privileged backgrounds. But an even larger share of the obesity-related wage penalty is the result of obese people's lower physical fitness. Overall, skills and fitness account for most of the effect of obesity on labor earnings. Similar results have been obtained in the United States. Based on the U.S. National Longitudinal Survey of Youth, Euna Han, Edward Norton, and Lisa Powell found that late-teen obesity lowers hourly wages of both men and women by 3.5 percent later in life, noting that this effect entirely transits through fewer years of schooling.[35]

### Height Matters . . . Especially for Men

The positive correlation between and among height, social status, and income is well known to social scientists and has been frequently demonstrated in various countries in Europe and North America. For example, in 2004, Nicola Persico, Andrew Postlewaite, and Dan Silverman showed, based on British and American survey data, that an extra inch in height increased income by 2 percent on average.[36] Given the height distribution of the male population, this means that the tallest quarter of the population has a median salary more than 13 percent higher than the lowest quarter, all other things being equal. The advantage conferred by height is thus comparable to that associated with gender or ethnicity.

The advantage of height seems to be most marked for men. In France, for example, Nicolas Herpin found that greater height is associated with men's greater access to managerial positions.[37] Similar results have been found for the UK and the United States.[38]

Disentangling the effect of height from that of the other factors associated with being tall is not easy. For instance, taller individuals tend to benefit from greater cognitive skills. Anne Case and Christina Paxson show that taller children at the age of three obtain better results on cognitive tests in the UK and the United States, and that they retain this advantage throughout their lives: as adults, they are taller than average and are more likely to select into higher-paying occupations that require more advanced verbal and numerical skills and greater intelligence, for which they thus earn handsome returns.[39] Taller individuals also develop better noncognitive skills. Nicola Persico and his coauthors show that those who were relatively short when young are less likely to participate in school-sponsored social activities (e.g., athletics and clubs), which explains half of their observed wage differential with taller people as adults.[40] Participation in these activities is expected to foster essential noncognitive skills that are highly valued in the labor market, such as interpersonal competencies. More generally, the societal preference for height might give taller individuals more confidence in many situations, translating into taking more opportunities to develop and demonstrate their skills.

No correspondence study was conducted to test for the existence of hiring discrimination against short job candidates, but a decomposition of the wage gap between short and tall individuals shows that part of this gap is unexplained and thus could flow from employers' discriminatory practices. For example, it is possible that employers associate height with greater ability to exert authority over teams, which in turn helps tall employees, especially male ones, to move up the hierarchy faster even when they show poor management skills. More precisely, unlike for obesity, Petter Lundborg and his colleagues found a residual wage premium associated with height, even after accounting for the better cognitive and noncognitive skills and the better health observed among taller individuals.[41]

* * *

A rich body of evidence shows that employers indulge in discrimination against homely, obese, or short job candidates or employees. Whether the advantage conferred on beautiful, slim, or tall individuals stems from a pure preference for physical appearance unanimously judged as attractive or from the hope that these individuals will attract new customers or will be exceptionally productive, this phenomenon is worrying. The expansion of social media and the search for bodily perfection it dictates, combined with the ongoing obesity pandemic, suggests that discrimination based on physical appearance and its negative economic consequences will only worsen in the future.

# 9 Sexual Orientation and Gender Identity: Just Private Matters?

Mario is a promising young footballer in a local Swiss club. One autumn day, a young German player, Leon, joins the team. These two lads, who are earmarked for the first division and are under the wing of coaches and the federation, share the same apartment. Mario falls in love for the first time in his life—with Leon, it's love at first sight. Leon fully accepts the relationship, but it's more difficult for Mario, who fears for his career. The other players on the team start spreading rumors, and there's even talk of blackmailing the two young men. The club officials ask for an explanation, while Leon's and Mario's agents recommend they maintain the utmost discretion. They know that if their relationship becomes public knowledge, both players' chances of being selected for the first division will be ruined. Mario stands his ground and denies everything, but Leon is suffering from the constant harassment, is playing less well, and can no longer carry on with the deception. The most promising player in the team, he ends up throwing in the towel and quits professional sport altogether. Mario, on the other hand, manages to do well in the first division, but at the cost of lasting psychological distress.

Marcel Gisler's film *Mario*, released in 2018, offers a powerful illustration of the waste and suffering caused by prejudice against lesbians, gay men, bisexuals, transgender, intersex, and queer (LGBTIQ+) people. Hatred of LGBTIQ+ individuals (also referred to as LGBTIQ+ phobia) is in evidence among a wide range of stakeholders, including employers (in the film *Mario*, the club and the federation), work colleagues (the other players), and customers (the team's supporters), leading talents such as Leon's to be forgone in sectors and occupations where attitudes toward LGBTIQ+ individuals are the most hostile. All too often the chances of being hired, promoted, or receiving equal pay for work of equal value are reduced when their sexual orientation or gender identity is detected on their application, during the job interview, or over the course of their career. Staying closeted is not without consequence either, for the career prospects of those who cannot bring their whole self to work are damaged by the stress and psychological sufferings involved, and by the risk of being viewed as withdrawn by colleagues and managers, while extraversion and sociability are key to moving up the ladder in the workplace.

### Who Are LGBTIQ+ Individuals?

LGBTIQ+ people are defined with respect to three distinct features: sexual orientation, gender identity, and sex characteristics. Oftentimes, a plus sign (+) is added to leave the demographic category open-ended and to acknowledge additional sexual orientations and gender identities that are not explicitly present in the initialism.

Sexual orientation allows for differentiating among heterosexuals, homosexuals, and bisexuals. It is indicative of a person's capacity for emotional or sexual attraction to different-sex, same-sex, or both different- and same-sex individuals. In this context, the "plus" refers to additional sexual orientations, such as "asexual" (lacking emotional and/or sexual attraction to anyone) or "pansexual" (considering gender as irrelevant in determining whether one will be emotionally or sexually attracted to someone), among others.

Gender identity refers to a person's internal sense of being masculine, feminine, androgynous, or neither, regardless of sexual orientation. For individuals for whom gender identity corresponds to their biological sex, the Latin prefix *cis* ("on this side of") is used to characterize them as "cisgender." For those where this is not the case, the Latin prefix *trans* ("on the other side of") is used to characterize them as "transgender." A transgender person can be (1) a transgender man (a person who was assigned the female gender at birth but whose gender identity is male); or (2) a transgender woman (a person who was assigned the male gender at birth but whose gender identity is female). In this context, the "plus" refers to additional gender identities, such as "nonbinary" (a person who was assigned either the female or male gender but who identifies with neither, both, or a combination of male and female genders), gender fluid (identifying oneself as not having a fixed gender), among others.

Sex characteristics refer to chromosomal patterns, hormonal structures, reproductive organs, and sexual anatomy that determine an individual's biological sex. Sex characteristics are sometimes ambiguous in comparison to medical standards rooted in binary concepts of male and female. An individual whose sex characteristics are neither wholly female nor wholly male is called intersex. Because of this nonbinary pattern, and although being intersex is distinct from a person's sexual orientation or gender identity, intersex individuals are overrepresented among the LGBTQ+ population[1]—this explains why the letter "I" is typically added to the LGBTQ+ acronym to include intersex people. Importantly, being intersex is not a pathological condition and rarely is life-threatening.[2]

LGBTIQ+ individuals are also referred to by the umbrella term "queer people". Consistent with its original meaning of describing something strange, odd, or eccentric, the word "queer" began to be adopted in the early 1990s to represent an identity that challenges normative concepts of sexuality and gender. Prior to this, "queer" had been used colloquially, often pejoratively, to refer to men who were sexually attracted to other men. From the early 2000s, its usage expanded, increasingly serving as an umbrella term that encompasses the wide spectrum of sexual orientations and gender identities represented by the LGBTIQ+ acronym. Although historically derogatory, "queer" has since been reclaimed by nonheterosexual and noncisgender individuals as a positive and empowering identifier. Today, it is widely understood as an affirming and inclusive term for all individuals within the LGBTIQ+ community.[3]

## LGBTIQ+ Inclusion Is about the Well-Being of Hundreds of Millions of People Worldwide

Thus far, only two OECD countries have included a question on sexual orientation or gender identity in their census: Canada in 2021 regarding gender identity, the UK, also in 2021, regarding sexual orientation (Great Britain and Northern Ireland) and gender identity (Great Britain only). A few other OECD countries have deployed self-identification questions on sexual orientation (and more rarely on gender identity) through representative surveys conducted by national public institutions.[4] However, the share of nonresponses or of individuals who indicate "prefer not to say" in response to questions measuring sexual orientation or gender identity remains high, which suggests that a significant percentage of LGBTIQ+ individuals do not yet live openly as such, or do not yet feel comfortable with disclosing this personal information in a survey conducted by public authorities.

In a context where respondents may feel more secure in disclosing sensitive information to nongovernmental polling companies, these companies' efforts to measure the share of LGBTIQ+ individuals deserve attention, although caution is warranted: in this field, polling companies typically rely on opt-in panels rather than probability sampling, which can lead to potential biases and, notably, to an overstatement of the size of the LGBTIQ+ population if individuals more inclined to participate in such surveys may be those who identify more strongly with LGBTIQ+ issues.

The LGBT+ Pride Global Survey that IPSOS conducted in 2021 is the first attempt to quantify the size of the LGBTIQ+ population across twenty-seven countries, including nineteen OECD countries.[5] Of respondents in OECD countries, 9.1 percent declared themselves to be nonheterosexual, with bisexuals making up the largest share (3.8 percent of respondents), followed by individuals who self-identified as "lesbian, gay or homosexual" (2.7 percent), followed by individuals who self-identified as "other," such as pansexual (2.6 percent)—the category "other" does not include respondents who indicated "don't know" or "prefer not to say." In addition, an estimated 1.6 percent of respondents self-identified as noncisgender, which included individuals who self-identified as "transgender," "nonbinary/nonconforming/gender fluid," or as belonging to another unspecified group of noncisgender individuals. In other words, the share of LGBTIQ+ individuals in OECD countries varies between 9.1 percent (if one assumes that *all* noncisgender individuals are also nonheterosexual) and 10.7 percent (if one assumes that *no* noncisgender individual is nonheterosexual). Applying these rates to the total population worldwide, estimated to be equal to 8.2 billion people in 2024,[6] LGBTIQ+ inclusion is about the well-being of between 746 and 878 million individuals.

Although these figures may be subject to upward bias, they could still underestimate the actual share of LGBTIQ+ individuals. Indeed, regarding sexual orientation, these figures rely on questions that ask respondents to self-identify as heterosexual, homosexual, or bisexual—not on questions that ask respondents to report their sexual behavior (the sex of individuals with whom one has sexual intercourse) or their sexual attraction (the sex of individuals one feels sexually attracted to). Yet sexual attraction is a more inclusive concept than sexual behavior, which is itself more inclusive than sexual self-identification: not all people who feel sexually attracted to people of the same sex engage in same-sex sexual behavior, and not all people who engage in same-sex sexual behavior view themselves as homosexual or bisexual. Consistent with this idea, the size of the LGB population is 70 percent larger when it is calculated based on individuals' sexual behavior (instead of individuals' sexual identification), and more than twice as large when sexual attraction is taken as a criterion.[7]

The underestimating effect of relying on sexual self-identification to measure the size of the LGBTIQ+ population is compounded by the fact that LGB people are more likely to refrain from disclosing who they are if they are asked to self-identify as homosexual or bisexual rather than to specify the sex of the persons with whom they have sex or to whom they feel sexually attracted. In arriving at this conclusion, Katherine Coffman, Lucas Coffman, and Keith Marzilli Ericson compared the likelihood of individuals reporting LGB status, depending on whether the sexual orientation question is asked through a self-administered online survey or through an item count technique (ICT) also conducted online.[8] Coffman, Coffman, and Ericson showed that the proportion of LGB respondents is significantly higher when the ICT is used, especially if the question on sexual orientation is based on sexual self-identification. In this case, the proportion of LGB individuals increases by 65 percent with the ICT (compared to the self-administered online survey), while the impact of the ICT is smaller when sexual orientation is measured based on sexual behavior and almost nonexistent when it is based on sexual attraction. These findings suggest that experiencing sexual attraction to a person of the same sex is viewed as socially more acceptable than defining oneself as lesbian, gay, or bisexual.

It is worthwhile stressing that the share of individuals who self-identify as LGBTIQ+ is on the rise. This trend is consistent with improving social acceptance of LGBTIQ+ individuals, which in turn encourages them to come out of the closet. This evolution is strikingly illustrated by data from the Gallup Daily Tracking Survey in the United States: the share of adults who self-identify as LGBT rose from 3.5 percent in 2012 to 7.1 percent in 2021, and the increase was driven by younger cohorts—a pattern common to all countries where data are available.[9] In 2021, 10.5 percent of U.S. adults born between 1981 and 1996 self-identified as LGBT, compared to 5.8 percent in 2012. By contrast, the share of self-identified LGBT individuals stagnates or even declines over time among older cohorts: 1.8 percent of U.S. adults born before 1946 viewed themselves as LGBT in 2012, but only 0.8 percent did so in 2021. One wonders whether this pattern reflects a true shift in sexual orientation and gender identity among younger generations or whether it merely reflects a greater willingness of younger people to identify as LGBT, in a context where social acceptance of LGBT people is increasing but perhaps not sufficiently for elderly LGBT people, who have been exposed to greater marginalization in their life course, to disclose who they are. Regardless of the underlying mechanism, the share of LGBTIQ+ individuals as measured on surveys should continue to grow in the future.

## Attitudes toward LGBTIQ+ Individuals

### The Source of LGBTIQ+ Phobia

LGBTIQ+ phobia is a well-documented phenomenon that flows from emotional disgust (or distaste) toward individuals viewed as "unnatural" because they violate traditional gender norms.[10] Based on a survey conducted in twenty-three countries representing both Western and non-Western societies, Maria Laura Bettinsoli and her coauthors showed that endorsement of traditional gender norms by respondents is significantly associated with negative attitudes toward gay men and lesbians in most countries surveyed (attitudes toward transgender and intersex individuals were not explored).[11]

Indeed, traditional gender norms are based on three assumptions that are antinomic to the recognition of the diversity of sexual orientations, gender identities, and sex characteristics. The first assumption underlying traditional gender norms is that individuals are born as one of two distinct biological sexes, male and female. This exclusively binary view of sex at birth denies the possibility that intersex people can live as who they are and explains why intersex babies continue to be subjected to surgery to normalize (or "disambiguate") their reproductive organs and sexual anatomy for the child to be clearly assigned as female or male, even in cases where the life of the intersex newborn or child is not at risk.[12] These interventions on healthy bodies, which are purely cosmetic, are still presented by many doctors as "medically necessary" as they are considered beneficial for the psychosocial development of the child in a society that would otherwise stigmatize them for not conforming to the female-male binary system.

The second assumption underlying traditional gender norms is that individuals' gender identity conforms to their sex at birth and is thus determined by it: people born male feel male, while people born female feel female. This conservative view leaves no space for noncisgender individuals, who are thus viewed as pathological. Although "gender incongruence," the terminology used to refer to being transgender, is removed from the list of mental health disorders in the eleventh revision of the *International Classification of Diseases* (ICD-11), which was adopted in 2019 by the member states of the World Health Organization, many countries still pathologize transgender individuals.[13] To the extent that being transgender is not a mental disorder, a person whose gender identity is at odds with their sex at birth should not have to receive psychiatric therapy for the purpose of realigning their self-perceived gender with their body. Along this line, transgender individuals should be entitled to change their gender marker in the civil registry, that is, their sex and first name revealing their gender. Yet many countries still do not grant this right, and others are backsliding. In Hungary, for instance, a bill was passed in 2020 that defines gender based only on sex assigned at birth, meaning that transgender individuals can no longer change their gender marker on their identity documents. Moreover, among countries that legally recognize the gender identity of transgender individuals, several still condition legal gender recognition on eugenic obligations such as sterilization or sex-reassignment surgery or treatments that typically lead to infertility. Most countries also request a psychiatric diagnosis confirming the medical condition of the transgender person.[14]

The third assumption underlying traditional gender norms is that men and women are "complements" to one another who are assigned rigid roles obstructive to women's empowerment and gender equality, with men expected to behave in "manly" fashion and women expected to be more passive and caring.[15] This view makes heterosexual coupling the only possible normality (the condition of "heteronormativity"). By contrast, homosexual coupling is viewed as an against-nature perversion.

This belief, which hampers any move toward LGBTIQ+ inclusion, is still pervasive, although the World Health Organization decided to declassify homosexuality as a mental disorder as early as May 17, 1990. As of 2024, same-sex conduct remains criminalized in sixty-two UN member states, in seven of which the death penalty is the legally prescribed punishment for consensual same-sex sexual acts: Brunei, Iran, Mauritania, Nigeria (the twelve Northern states), Saudi Arabia, Uganda, and Yemen.[16] Uganda exemplifies an alarmingly regressive trend in LGBTIQ+ rights observed in some countries. Laws criminalizing consensual same-sex sexual acts were originally imposed under British colonial rule and were retained, and later expanded, after the country gained independence. Notably, however, the death penalty was not applied to such acts until the passage of the Anti-Homosexuality Act in 2023. This legislation prescribes the death penalty for "aggravated homosexuality," which is defined as repeated instances of same-sex sexual relations, as well as sexual relations involving individuals living with HIV, minors, or other vulnerable groups, such as people with disabilities.[17]

In addition, as of 2024, the prohibition of discrimination based on sexual orientation (not to mention gender identity or sex characteristics) is absent from cross-continental international agreements, which are binding on all signatory and ratifying states. For example, the United Nations has adopted various agreements aimed at eliminating all forms of racial discrimination (1965), discrimination against women (1979), and discrimination against persons with disabilities (2006)[18]—but nothing about sexual orientation. The same is true of Convention 111 of the International Labour Organization (1958), which mentions race, color, sex, religion, political opinion, national extraction, and social origin as prohibited grounds for discrimination, but not sexual orientation.

This lack of consensus among countries on the need to prohibit discriminations against homosexuals and bisexuals was well illustrated by the dispute that followed the declaration on sexual orientation and gender identity that France and the Netherlands proposed in 2008 at a meeting of the UN General Assembly. The declaration affirmed "the principle of non-discrimination which requires that human rights apply equally to every human being regardless of sexual orientation or gender identity." The declaration was approved by fifty-seven nations but prompted a counterdeclaration by fifty-seven others, backed by the Organization of Islamic Cooperation, that led the initial declaration to not be adopted by the General Assembly. Stressing that the concepts of "sexual orientation" and "gender identity" have no legal basis, the counterdeclaration also claimed that the declaration filed was conducive to "social normalization and possibly the legitimization of many deplorable acts, including pedophilia." The Holy See's Permanent Observer to the United Nations echoed these claims and asserted that "the categories 'sexual orientation' and 'gender identity', used in the text, find no recognition or clear and agreed definition in international law."[19]

That said, legal inclusion of LGBTIQ+ individuals is strongly improving, at least in countries that are the most economically and socially advanced. As an illustration, discrimination in employment explicitly based on sexual orientation was prohibited in thirty-two out of then thirty-six OECD countries in 2019, up from eleven OECD countries in 1999.[20] EU members states are overrepresented among those countries, which reflects the strong normative framework in favor of LGBTIQ+ equality required by EU institutions. Notably, as of 2019, all EU member states have transposed the 2000 Employment Equality Directive that prohibits discrimination on the grounds of, among other things, sexual orientation.[21] But considerable strides have also been made in non-EU OECD countries, with three quarters of them protecting LGB employees against discrimination in 2019. Ever since, progress has been continuing in those countries, as demonstrated, for instance, by the U.S. Supreme Court groundbreaking ruling of June 2020 according to which LGBTIQ+ people can no longer be discriminated against in the workplace.

### Social Acceptance of LGBTIQ+ Individuals Is Globally on the Rise, but Remains Limited

Consistent with significant improvement in legal LGBTIQ+ inclusion in several countries, the social acceptance of this population is on the rise globally. Regular, representative cross-continent data on attitudes toward homosexuals have been collected since as early as 1981, beginning with the World Values Survey (WVS). Similar inquiries have since been conducted by the European Values Survey, AmericasBarometer, LatinoBarometer, AsiaBarometer, AfroBarometer, and Gallup. The LGBT Global Acceptance Index (LGBT-GAI), established by Andrew Flores, shows that acceptance of LGBTIQ+ people (and notably of LGB individuals since most of the seventy-one factors used to compute the index focus on acceptance of homosexuality) improved between 1981 and 2017 across the globe, with only limited polarization: while 131 of 174 countries experienced increases in acceptance, only sixteen are characterized by a decline (twenty-seven experienced no change). In the United States, for instance, nearly three quarters of Americans (71 percent) in 2022 said they supported same-sex marriage, as opposed to barely a quarter (27 percent) in 1996.[22]

The Special Eurobarometer on Discrimination provides a valuable complement to these cross-continental data by also measuring attitudes toward transgender and intersex individuals. in addition to attitudes toward a "gay, lesbian or bisexual person." As such, it permits a more comprehensive analysis of levels and trends in social acceptance of LGBTIQ+ individuals, although data are limited to EU member states and cover a shorter time frame—a maximum of four rounds, conducted in 2012, 2015, 2019, and 2023. The results reveal that, as of 2023, only a small majority (59 percent) of respondents in the EU declared they would feel comfortable if one of their children were to enter into a love relationship with a person of the same sex as their child, while a minority (48 percent) would feel comfortable with a transgender or intersex son- or daughter-in-law, indicating that the acceptance of noncisgender individuals is lower than the acceptance of nonheterosexual individuals. Using a nationally representative online sample in the United States, Billur Aksoy, Christopher S. Carpenter and Dario Sansone confirmed that attitudes toward transgender people are less positive than attitudes toward lesbians, gay men, and bisexuals, even after correcting for social desirability bias, which turns out being higher when individuals report their views about noncisgender than when they report their views about nonheterosexual individuals.[23] On average, women report substantially greater acceptance of LGBTIQ+ individuals than men.

## Employers Discriminate Based on Sexual Orientation and Gender Identity

Many employers justify that LGBTIQ+ individuals are not part of the priority groups targeted by their inclusion policies by insisting that sexual orientation and gender identity are private matters that should have no bearing in the labor market.[24] Although this explanation sounds reasonable at first glance, a closer examination reveals its high degree of prejudice against LGBTIQ+ individuals. Sexual orientation is in fact ubiquitous in the workplace: no one is offended—everyone finds it even normal and nice—that heterosexual persons express themselves about their family life at work, for instance by recounting their holidays with their husband or wife and children at the coffee machine, displaying photos of their family in their office, participating with their family in social events organized by their employers, talking to colleagues about preparations for their marriage or the arrival of a new child, and so on. Gender identity is equally present in the workplace, with many cisgender employees adopting dress codes that demonstrate their efforts to fit in with the gender expectations of their peers, for example outfits that are ostensibly feminine for women and masculine for men. The marginalization of LGBTIQ+ inclusion in the workplace thus cannot be attributed to deemphasizing talk about private life at work but to disgust at hearing LGBTIQ+ people talk about *their* private life.

This propensity to express distaste LGBTIQ+ people in the workplace was confirmed in a laboratory experiment in which participants were asked to evaluate job applications. With the same CV, gay or lesbian applicants were rated significantly lower on competence, social skills, and employability than heterosexual applicants, a gap that increased with how strongly "employers" endorsed traditional gender norms.[25] But anti-LGBTIQ+ discrimination is not confined to the laboratory. This finding consistently emerges from analyzing three types of evidence: data on perception of discrimination, the comparison of labor market outcomes between LGBTIQ+ and non-LGBTIQ+ individuals with representative observational data, and field experiments.

### Perception of Discrimination by LGBTIQ+ People

In 2012, 2019, and 2023, the EU's Agency for Fundamental Rights (FRA) conducted three cross-country surveys among nonheterosexual and non-cisgender individuals (93,000 LGBT respondents in 2012, 140,000 LGBTI respondents in 2019, and 100,577 LGBTIQ respondents in 2023). In all rounds of the FRA-LGBT(IQ) survey, respondents were asked whether they felt personally discriminated against over the previous twelve months in a variety of situations, such as "when looking for a job" or "at work." In 2019, 42 percent of LGBTI respondents reported having felt personally discriminated against in the past year in at least one of the eight areas of life listed, with no improvement since 2012, even though the question measuring perception of discrimination then covered more areas of life, eleven versus eight, a methodological inconsistency that runs toward finding an amelioration in levels of perceived discrimination. Nonetheless, a slight improvement can be observed in more recent years: the proportion of those who felt personally discriminated against in at least one of the eight key areas of life in the twelve months preceding the survey decreased from 42 percent in 2019 to 36 percent in 2023. A closer look at the eight scenarios used in 2019 and 2023 highlights that the perception of discrimination among LGBTIQ respondents is particularly high in health care, education, and the labor market. The acute feeling of being discriminated against expressed by LGBTIQ+ people in the EU echoes findings from the Survey of LGBT Americans" that was conducted in 2013 by the Pew Research Centre: less than a quarter of LGBT respondents then considered that social acceptance of the LGBTIQ+ population in the United States was high.

### Comparing Labor Market Outcomes Based on Representative Observational Data

A plethora of studies that rely on representative observational data collected in Australia, Europe, or North America consistently reveal that LGBTIQ+ individuals suffer, on average, from a substantial disadvantage relative to non-LGBTIQ+ individuals with respect to various labor market outcomes, including employment rates and (hourly) labor earnings. This finding holds even when the effect of potential differences in observable characteristics across these two groups is neutralized, such as differences in age, education, occupation, type of work contract (full-time, part-time), or sector.[26]

This penalty prevails for most LGBTIQ+ subgroups. For instance, reviewing studies published between 2012 and 2020, Nick Drydakis found that gay men, bisexual men, and bisexual women experience labor earnings penalties of 7 percent, 9 percent, and 5 percent, respectively, relative to their heterosexual counterparts.[27] Moreover, transgender individuals are also at a significant disadvantage relative to their cisgender counterparts. In the United States, they are 9 percent less likely to be employed than cisgender people, an average figure that hides great disparities.[28] Transgender men, that is, individuals born female but who feel themselves to be male, have an employment rate similar to that of cisgender men. But the employment rate of transgender women is 24 percent lower than that of cisgender women. The vulnerability of transgender women has been confirmed by the Dutch economists Lydia Geijtenbeek and Erik Plug.[29] The researchers used administrative data from the Netherlands to track transgender individuals before and after their gender transition, that is, their recourse to surgery and hormonal treatment to change sex and alter their secondary sexual characteristics. The authors found that, before transitioning, transgender women faced earnings penalties of 4 percent compared with cisgender men, and that transgender men experienced earning penalties of 53 percent in comparison with cisgender men. This result suggests that, before transitioning to another gender, transgender men face a double penalty: as transgender persons (which also harms pretransition transgender women) and as registered women. In addition, the study revealed that posttransition transgender women experienced a 20 percent fall in labor earnings, whereas transgender men faced an 8 percent rise.

Lesbians are an exception. Relative to heterosexual women, they experience both higher employment rates and higher hourly labor earnings. This situation presumably flows from the fact that their unpaid work burden is lower than that of heterosexual women. Indeed, women in different-sex couples devote considerably more time to childcare than their partner, while family responsibilities are fewer for lesbians: lesbians not only are less likely to live with a partner or have children, they are also more likely to share paid and unpaid work equally with their partner when in a couple—an observation that also applies to gay men.[30] Failure to identify a disadvantage for lesbians in the labor market due to the "household specialization bias" (i.e., the asymmetry across different-sex and same-sex couples in the way paid and unpaid work is shared between partners) does not mean that lesbians are not discriminated against by employers. On the contrary, a wide range of evidence suggests that the premium for lesbians would become a penalty should representative observational data allow solving the household specialization bias. For instance, comparing *single* lesbian women with their heterosexual counterparts is conducive to the emergence of a penalty for lesbians.[31] Furthermore, several studies have shown that lesbians are as likely as gay men to report less satisfaction with their pay, promotion prospects, and respect received from their manager, relative to their heterosexual counterparts.[32] Recently, a laboratory experiment revealed that, when they interact with individuals who could "punish" them for not being heterosexual, lesbians are less likely than gay men to disclose their sexual orientation.[33]

Regarding the mechanisms behind the penalty that LGBTIQ+ individuals endure in the labor market, a paper by Marc Folch provides interesting insights.[34] Based on data from a representative sample of bachelor's degree recipients in the United States, the author first shows that LGBTIQ+ individuals experience 22 percent lower earnings ten years after graduation than their non-LGBTIQ+ counterparts. Folch then estimates that half of this gap is the result of sorting: LGBTIQ+ individuals avoid professions that are more masculine and thus higher paid, in a context where men tend to show more hostile attitudes toward LGBTIQ+ individuals than women do.[35] The other half of the pay gap (i.e., the remaining 10 percent gap) could flow from labor market discrimination since nearly half of LGBTIQ+ respondents report having experienced workplace discrimination for being LGBTIQ+ during the first ten years after graduation. This discrimination could reflect differences in pay for work of equal value or discrimination in promotion to top management positions. Representative data collected in the UK are consistent with the existence of a glass ceiling that prevents LGBTIQ+ from rising beyond a certain level in a hierarchy: LGBTIQ+ employees are on average 11 percent less likely to hold a high managerial position.[36]

It is worthwhile stressing that the penalties presented in this section likely constitute lower bounds of the disadvantage faced by LGBTIQ+ individuals in the labor market. Evidence suggests that LGBTIQ+ people who disclose their sexual orientation in surveys are not representative of the LGBTIQ+ population as a whole: only the better off reveal who they are, perhaps because they mostly interact with wealthy individuals who, on average, are less LGBTIQ+-phobic than poorer individuals.[37] For instance, among men who report having sex with men in the United States, those of advantaged background are more likely to self-identify as homosexual or bisexual.[38] Similarly, analysis of nationally representative surveys that include a question on sexual self-identification shows that the share of individuals who answer "other," "don't know," or who refuse to answer the question is disproportionately high among underprivileged individuals. This disclosure bias could explain a puzzling feature of the literature on the socioeconomic status of homosexuals and bisexuals.[39] Long-term analyses that involve interviewing adolescents several times up until they enter adulthood produce consistent findings: students who experience same-sex physical attraction during their teenage years on average do less well in school, partly because of homophobic and biphobic harassment that they are, or fear being, subject to.[40] Yet nationally representative surveys among adults with a question on sexual self-identification all point to higher educational achievements for lesbians, gay men, and bisexuals relative to heterosexuals.[41] This discrepancy is not observed among transgender individuals, who are both more exposed to violence at school and more likely to report low educational attainment in adulthood relative to cisgender individuals.[42] Either the disclosure bias does not exist among transgender respondents or it is too weak to offset the negative consequences in adulthood of transphobic bullying at school.

## The Unequivocal Verdict of Field Experiments

### Hiring and Wage Discrimination against Homosexual Applicants

Until the early 2010s, thirteen correspondence studies with results published in academic journals had been conducted to measure hiring discrimination against homosexual applicants in OECD countries, covering ten of them (Austria, Belgium, Canada, France, Germany, Greece, Italy, Sweden, the UK, and the United States).[43] These studies used three different approaches to signaling sexual orientation in job application materials. The first approach, used in nine of the thirteen studies, consisted in emphasizing on the CV the volunteer engagement or work experience of the homosexual applicant in a gay or lesbian organization, such as a local chapter of the Gay People's Alliance or a gay and lesbian campus association, in a context where volunteering in an association is highly valued by employers—a volunteer engagement or work experience in an organization aimed at the common good is typically mentioned on the CV of the heterosexual applicant that does not give any evidence of being gay or lesbian, such as the Swedish Red Cross or an environmental organization.[44] The second approach, implemented in two of the thirteen studies, both of which focused on fictitious female job applicants, entailed revealing on the CV the sex of the candidate's partner.[45] This strategy is adopted in countries where it is common to specify the partner's first and last name on a CV (e.g., the Flanders region in Belgium or Germany). The third approach, used in three of the thirteen studies, relied on a weaker set of signals, such as mentioning the candidate's volunteering activities or the sex of the candidate's partner only in the letter of application, manipulating candidates' sexual orientation on their Facebook profile, or signaling on the CV the candidate's participation in LGBTIQ+ events not restricted to LGBTIQ+ participants, such as the Gay Games.[46]

Homosexual female and male applicants are 1.5 times less likely to be invited to a job interview when sexual orientation is conveyed on their CV through their volunteer engagement or work experience in a gay or lesbian organization. By contrast, insisting on the family prospects of fictitious female candidates by signaling homosexuality through the sex of the candidate's partner on her CV leads to the virtual disappearance of hiring discrimination against lesbians. This pattern could reflect that employers attach a lower risk of maternity to lesbians relative to heterosexual women and are therefore less inclined to discriminate against them. Not surprisingly, hiring discrimination against gay men and lesbians is nearly nonexistent in correspondence studies that rely on a weak signal for sexual orientation.

When aggregating the results from three types of correspondence studies and incorporating additional, more recent research, the findings reveal that homosexual applicants, on average, are 36 percent less likely to receive a callback from employers compared to heterosexual candidates. This conclusion comes from a meta-analysis of eighteen studies from OECD countries, involving more than 50,000 job applications, conducted by Alexandre Flage.[47]

Among correspondence studies that measure hiring discrimination against homosexual job candidates, some have also tried to detect wage discrimination. The credit for this innovation goes to Nick Drydakis. In the two audit studies he conducted in Athens, Greece, he trained research assistants to play the role of fictitious homosexual and heterosexual candidates, using a strictly identical script and voice intonation for both.[48] The results confirm a wage penalty, especially for female homosexual applicants: the monthly wage offer was lower by 1.6 percent for gay men (not statistically significant) and by 6.1 percent for lesbians.[49]

Let's conclude with three important additional results from field experiments in the labor market. First, fictitious female homosexual applicants are somewhat less discriminated against than their male counterparts. The nine correspondence studies that relied on a strong signal of sexual orientation and involved both male and female job candidates showed that, while heterosexual women are 40 percent more likely to be invited to a job interview than their homosexual counterparts, this advantage is equal to 60 percent for heterosexual men when they are compared to gay men. Similarly, in his meta-analysis, Alexandre Flage finds that gay men are 39 percent less likely to receive a response than their heterosexual peers, while lesbian women are 32 percent less likely.[50] This finding is consistent with a well-known result according to which gay men are disliked more than lesbians,[51] a pattern driven by male respondents: men's acceptance of lesbians is like women's acceptance of both lesbians and gay men, but men show more negative attitudes toward gay men.[52]

Second, anti-LGBTIQ+ discrimination seems to originate both in the preferences of employers, colleagues, or customers (taste-based discrimination) and in employers' beliefs (statistical discrimination). Consistent with the existence of taste-based discrimination, the difference in callback rate between fictitious heterosexual and homosexual applicants is positively correlated with prejudice against homosexuality among the public. In the United States, employers strongly discriminate against sexual minorities in the southern and midwestern states (Texas, Florida, Ohio), whereas they tend to treat heterosexual and homosexual candidates on an equal footing in the West and Northeast (California, New York, Pennsylvania), regions known to be less hostile toward LGBTIQ+ people.[53] A correspondence study performed in two German cities characterized by opposite value orientations, Munich and Berlin, yielded similar findings. While the population in Munich displays conservative attitudes, that of Berlin is known to support liberal views. The results reflect this divide: homosexual applicants are discriminated against in Munich but not in Berlin.[54] These relationships also persist when attitudes toward homosexuality are measured at the recruiter level. In the correspondence study he conducted in Greece in 2006–2007, Nick Drydakis found that employers who invited both heterosexual and gay male applicants for job interviews showed significantly less prejudice against gay men than employers who called back only heterosexual male applicants.[55] Local levels of acceptance of homosexuality not only affect employers' hiring decision, they also seem to have an impact on the wage employers offer to homosexual employees: relying on U.S.-based representative survey data, Ian Burn found a significant positive relationship between the share of individuals in a state who are prejudiced against homosexuals and the labor earnings penalty for gay men.[56]

As for statistical discrimination, hiring discrimination against gay men and lesbians depends on the gender composition in the occupation in which they seek work, in a way that suggests that employers stereotypically view gay men as lacking "masculine" productive characteristics and lesbians as lacking "feminine" productive characteristics. In Sweden, for instance, gay men are discriminated against when they apply to male-dominated occupations (e.g., construction or mechanic worker), while these occupations are not particularly hostile to lesbians. Similarly, lesbians are discriminated against when they apply to female-dominated occupations (e.g., preschool teacher or nurse), but this is not the case for gay men.[57] In the UK, gay men receive fewer callbacks for vacancies for which personality traits perceived as masculine are stressed in the job ad; that is, the ideal job applicant is described as "ambitious," "assertive," or "having demonstrated leadership qualities." Conversely, lesbians receive fewer invitations to job interviews for vacancies for which personality traits perceived as feminine are emphasized; that is, the ideal job applicant is described as "affectionate," "cheerful," or "sensitive to the needs of others."[58]

Beyond personality traits that do not meet social expectations, another source of statistical discrimination against LGBTIQ+ individuals could potentially be at play: the fact that LGBTIQ+ people exhibit less robust physical and mental health. In part owing to their disproportionate practice of anal sex, gay and bisexual men experience the greatest burden of HIV compared to any other group.[59] According to the U.S. Centers for Disease Control and Prevention (CDC), gay and bisexual men accounted for 70 percent of new HIV infections in the United States in 2019. But there is more. LGBTIQ+ individuals are also characterized by worse mental health outcomes. For instance, LGBTIQ+ respondents are more than twice as likely to have ever been diagnosed with a depressive disorder (Germany), nearly three times as likely to have experienced a major depressive episode in the year preceding the survey (United States), and nearly ten times as likely to have attempted suicide in the past year (Sweden).[60] As stressed in chapter 2, psychological distress among LGBTIQ+ individuals at least partly flows from the discrimination they face, and diminished mental health in turn has the potential to further impair homosexual and bisexual people's physical health by providing a fertile ground for other pathologies to emerge, such as cardiovascular diseases. In Germany, LGBTIQ+ individuals are 2.5 times more likely to have been diagnosed with a heart disease, such as heart failure or cardiac insufficiency, than non-LGBTIQ+ individuals (10 percent versus 4 percent).[61] Despite the significant health gap between LGB and non-LGB individuals, there is no evidence thus far that it feeds hiring discrimination. Drydakis has shown that underlining the applicant's good physical and mental health by emphasizing his or her excellent academic and professional performance (through submitting transcripts of records and letters of recommendation from previous employers) does nothing to reduce the gap between heterosexual and homosexual applicants.[62] Eleonora Patacchini,

Giuseppe Ragusa, and Yves Zenou came up with similar findings from a correspondence study carried out in Italy.[63]

A third important result that emerges from correspondences studies is that global improvement in attitudes toward LGBTIQ+ individuals does not coincide with lower discrimination rates against them everywhere and anytime. In the mid- to late 2010s, Drydakis again innovated by being the first to rerun in the same country (Greece) the experimental setup of the correspondence study he had conducted a few years before (2006–2007).[64] He found that discrimination against gay men worsens over time, with gay men, in comparison to heterosexual men, being nearly 15 percent less likely to receive invitations for interviews in 2013–2019 than in 2006–2007. This result is consistent over the course of the 2010s in Greece, which was experiencing the influence of a far-right rhetoric that exalted virility and rising economic difficulties (prejudice against minorities is known to follow a countercyclical trend and to rise during periods of higher unemployment for majorities).[65] In the same vein, Alexandre Flage's meta-analysis shows that the disparity in callback rates between homosexual and heterosexual applicants has remained fairly stable over time.[66]

### Hiring Discrimination against Transgender Applicants

To the best of our knowledge, two correspondence studies with results published in academic journals were conducted to measure hiring discrimination against transgender applicants. These field experiments concerned two OECD countries, Germany and Sweden. The results suggest that transgender applicants are discriminated against in gendered occupations. More precisely, in Sweden, a group of economists sent more than two thousand fictitious applications to employers with job vacancies in twelve low-skill sectors.[67] The authors exploited the common practice in Sweden of an applicant prefacing a CV with a short cover letter. In this letter, the fictitious applicants introduced themselves by name (e.g., "Hello, my name is A Eriksson)." In the second paragraph, they then mentioned: "For future contact I would like to clarify that I have changed my name (from B Eriksson), so a few of my old documents are in my previous name." For transgender applicants, the names A and B were drawn from a pool of common differently gendered names and for cisgender applicants the names were drawn from same-gendered names. The results indicate that transgender women are discriminated against relative to cisgender men in applying for work in male-dominated occupations (this is not the case for female cisgender applicants), while transgender men are discriminated against relative to cisgender women in female-dominated occupations (this is also the case for male cisgender applicants). By contrast, transgender applicants are not discriminated against in mixed-gender occupations.

In Germany, a group of sociologists found consistent results. They showed that candidates assigned male at birth (cis men and trans women) are invited to a job interview at the same rate when they apply for dramaturgical internships in German-speaking theaters, which are known to have a mixed-gender workforce (and to be open to minorities).[68] That said, more evidence is needed to get fully conclusive results since a correspondence study conducted in Texas that targeted mixed-gender occupations found that cisgender applicants had a 50 percent higher chance of being invited to a job interview than their transgender counterparts.[69] This result echoes the findings of a small-scale audit study that was conducted in 2008 in Manhattan's retail sector, which is also characterized by gender balance.[70] Out of twenty-four employers tested, transgender applicants (men, women, and gender-nonconforming) were six times less likely than their cisgender counterparts to be hired: the job offer rate for the cisgender applicants was 50 percent, as opposed to 8.3 percent for the transgender applicants.

Transgender individuals are exposed to greater psychological distress than are LGB individuals. In Germany, for instance, 39 percent of transgender respondents report having ever been diagnosed with an anxiety disorder, compared to 9 percent of cisgender LGB persons.[71] On top of the deleterious effect of stigma on their mental health, which also affects homosexuals and bisexuals, transgender applicants are likely to experience gender dysphoria, a state of distress arising from the experience of conflict between an individual's gender identity and the sex they were assigned at birth.[72] In addition, like LGB people, transgender individuals also face a high risk of HIV, including because they are overrepresented among individuals participating in survival sex.[73] Nevertheless, this health penalty, which is compounded by the fact that noncisgender individuals face discrimination in access to health care,[74] does not seem to feed statistical discrimination against them, or else discrimination against transgender applicants would be observed in all types of occupation.[75] One reason why this is not the case could be that, as demonstrated by Baert and coauthors, employers hold both positive and negative beliefs about transgender job applicants that, at the aggregate level, may cancel each other.[76]

* * *

Although social acceptance of LGBTIQ+ individuals is improving worldwide, anti-LGBTIQ+ discrimination in the labor market is a reality, as consistently revealed by three different types of evidence: the perception of discrimination by LGBTIQ+ people, the comparison of labor market outcomes between LGBTIQ+ and non-LGBTIQ+ individuals with representative observational data, and field experiments. One could object that the empirical results reported here apply only to a subset of LGBTIQ+ individuals, those who are out of the closet in the labor market. But these results are also valid for individuals who, while not disclosing their sexual orientation or gender identity, are perceived by their work environment as nonheterosexual or noncisgender. These cases may not be exceptions. For instance, individuals who self-identify as homosexual are significantly more likely to be viewed as homosexual by external observers not informed of their sexual orientation.[77] As for those who refuse to disclose who they are because of fear of retaliation (and who manage to pass as heterosexual cisgender persons), staying closeted is not without consequence either. The career prospects of people who remain closeted are damaged by the stress and psychological suffering involved and by the risk of being viewed as withdrawn by colleagues and managers, whereas extraversion and sociability are key to moving up the hierarchy in the workplace.

# III Combating Discrimination

# 10 The Limits of Antidiscrimination Legislation

On the historic day of July 2, 1964, when signing the Civil Rights Act, which forbids discrimination on the basis of sex and race in hiring, promoting, and firing, President Lyndon B. Johnson remarked:

> We believe that all men are created equal. Yet many are denied equal treatment. We believe that all men have certain unalienable rights. Yet many Americans do not enjoy those rights. We believe that all men are entitled to the blessings of liberty. Yet millions are being deprived of those blessings—not because of their own failures, but because of the color of their skin. . . .
>
> This Civil Rights Act is a challenge to all of us to go to work in our communities and our States, in our homes and in our hearts, to eliminate the last vestiges of injustice in our beloved country. . . . It does say that those who are equal before God shall now also be equal in the polling booths, in the classrooms, in the factories, and in other places that provide service to the public.[1]

Even with such momentous legislation, sixty years later the challenges of discrimination persist. The age-old narrative continues to resound, with individuals declaring, "I did everything right. I went to school, applied for jobs, but received no responses." To address these systemic disparities, it's vital not only to recognize them but also to rigorously enforce antidiscrimination laws.

A comprehensive strategy is in place in the United States and other developed economies that prohibits discriminatory practices and creates mechanisms to identify and penalize them. The intent is to instill a genuine fear of legal consequences for offenders.[2] Because in principle it is the most direct way to prevent discrimination, this approach appeals to many governments. However, even if legal prohibition is essential, the possibility of pinpointing discrimination on the ground, especially in employment, remains limited. This relative powerlessness may at least partly explain why, for instance, fewer than a third of Europeans and American surveyed considered that efforts to combat discrimination in their country were effective.[3]

**Legal Protection against Discrimination in Employment Is Widespread . . .**

The "right to work" is one of those rights that, according to the Universal Declaration of Human Rights of 1948, should be guaranteed to everyone, "without distinction of any kind, such as race, color, sex, language, religion, political or other opinion, national or social origin, property, birth or other status."[4] An examination of the extent of antidiscrimination legislation in all 193 UN countries reveals that many seek to align with the human rights obligation of not discriminating in employment: nearly all (89 percent) guarantee some protection from discrimination in the workplace based on gender, while almost three quarters legislate some protection on the ground of disability (79 percent), religion (77 percent), or race/ethnicity (76 percent). Of course, there is still room for improvement. For instance, some grounds of discrimination are left behind by a significant share of countries: less than a third of UN countries provide at least some protection from discrimination at work based on sexual orientation, and far fewer (10 percent) do so based on gender identity. Moreover, although most countries provide at least some protection from discrimination in employment based on gender, disability, religion, or race/ethnicity, only a minority provide a comprehensive protection by explicitly prohibiting discrimination in all five key work areas of hiring, pay, promotions/demotions, terminations, and harassment.[5]

Despite these downsides, the trend is globally positive, even for grounds of discrimination that are still lacking consensus. As an illustration, the number of OECD countries where discrimination in employment based on sexual orientation is legally prohibited nearly tripled in only two decades (between 1999 and 2019), rising from eleven to thirty-two.[6]

There are reasons to celebrate these levels and trends in legal protections against discrimination. It is indeed essential to provide sanctions against employers who discriminate. After all, how can one claim to combat discrimination if, to begin with, the law finds nothing wrong with it? Legal sanctions have another advantage in that they help to change the social norm. Academic work suggests that individuals perceive changes to the law as changes in social norms, which they then are anxious to conform to. This wish to conform was demonstrated in a laboratory experiment conducted shortly before the Supreme Court legalized same-sex marriage in the United States. The participants were randomly divided into two groups. Those in one group were invited to read an article presenting the legalization of same-sex marriage by the Supreme Court as likely, and those in the other group were invited to read an article arguing that this legalization was unlikely. The authors show that participants in the first group were significantly more supportive of gay marriage and more comfortable with homosexuality than those in the second.[7] This finding has been confirmed outside the laboratory. The acceptance of homosexuality has improved much more in European countries that have legalized same-sex marriage than in those that have not, whereas this trend was not in evidence until these states legally recognized marriage for all.[8] Similarly, same-sex marriage legalization across U.S. states led to an increase in employment of people in same-sex couples, a change driven by improvements in attitudes toward homosexuality and, hence, lower discrimination against LGB individuals.[9] Furthermore, Samuel Mann demonstrates that sexual orientation–based antidiscrimination laws across the United States lowered the number of poor mental health days among men in same-sex households by around 11 percent (no significant impact was observed in women in same-sex households) because these laws reduced prejudice primarily against non-heterosexual men.[10]

### . . . and Significant Efforts Have Been Made to Enforce Laws That Prohibit Discrimination in Employment

In all jurisdictions, it typically falls on the claimants who engage in legal actions to establish the facts they allege. Yet this standard rule concerning the burden of proof constitutes a threat to the effectiveness of antidiscrimination legislation since discrimination usually leaves no material traces. Against this backdrop, many countries have moved toward lightening the burden of proof weighing on claimants in discrimination cases, at least in civil legal proceedings. For instance, the sharing of the burden of proof between the complainant and the respondent has been part of EU antidiscrimination law since the late 1980s. Initially articulated by the Court of

Justice of the European Union in the seminal cases of *Danfoss* and *Enderby*, it is now enshrined in the various EU antidiscrimination directives.[11]

This burden-shifting framework does not mean that complainants in discrimination cases are exempt from providing evidence of their claims. Rather, it eases their task by requiring that they "simply" establish facts from which it may be presumed that there has been discrimination. To make a prima facie claim of discrimination, the plaintiff has to prove several elements, which turn out not to vary much across jurisdictions. For instance, U.S. employees and job candidates who wish to demonstrate discrimination under Title VII of the Civil Rights Act of 1964 must show that (1) they are a member of a protected group; (2) the discriminator knew of this membership; (3) acts of harm occurred (their job application was declined, they were denied a promotion or a bonus, they were fired, etc.); and (4) others who were similarly situated were either treated more favorably or not subjected to the same or similar adverse treatment, where "similarly situated others" is defined as individuals who are of a different, race, color, gender, religion, and so forth than the complainant but whose employment situation is nearly identical (e.g., they occupy the same position or job title, in the same supervisory chain).[12] This fourth element is the most challenging to prove. That said, the complainants do not have to demonstrate a clear causal link between their membership in the protected class and the harm. They are only required to provide evidence that this causation is likely.

If the court finds that the complainant can establish a prima facie case of discrimination, then the burden of the proof shifts to the respondent, who is then responsible for rebutting this presumption. There are two ways in which the respondent can demonstrate that no discrimination occurred. First, they can seek to invalidate the elements established prima facie by the complainant, by proving that the latter did not in fact receive unfavorable treatment. Second, the respondent can seek to provide a legitimate, non-discriminatory reason for its actions, that is, that the unfavorable treatment was not based on the complainant's membership in a protected group.

If the court ascertains that the elements provided by the respondent allow a reversal of the presumption, then the complainant is usually given another chance to demonstrate that the respondent's stated reason is merely a pretext for discrimination. If, however, the court is not convinced by the respondent's attempt to rebut the prima facie elements provided by the complainant, then the court will arrive at a finding of discrimination.

## But Proving Discrimination Remains a Challenge

The sharing of the burden of proof between the complainant and the respondent has given rise to an extensive case law, often under the impetus of equality bodies[13] which, at least in countries where they have litigation powers, engage in proceedings that allow bringing clarifications on the law or setting a legal precedent.

Cases that are particularly easy to plead are those that involve discriminatory language used in job ads or stated by employers or employees themselves, even when no victim of discrimination is identified.[14] Such public statements are generally viewed as sufficient to establish a prima facie case for discrimination, including in criminal proceedings where the burden of proof weighs entirely on the complainant.[15]

In the United States, for instance, the Equal Employment Opportunity Commission (EEOC) oversees cases of employment discrimination. The Civil Rights Act of 1964, particularly Title VII, prohibits employers from discriminating against employees based on race, color, religion, sex (which includes sexual orientation and gender identity), or national origin. Flagrant cases of discrimination are unfortunately not absent, as seen in several cases. For instance, in 2009 the EEOC sued the restaurant chain Applebee's. The company allegedly allowed racial slurs and derogatory remarks about AfricanAmerican, Hispanic, and Asian customers and failed to address an African American employee's complaints about the matter. In 2022 the same chain agreed to pay $100,000 to settle a sexual orientation and race discrimination lawsuit filed by the EEOC. According to the lawsuit, two members of the restaurant's staff verbally harassed a Black employee by subjecting him to racial and homophobic epithets on a consistent basis. The employee complained to various levels of management at the restaurant, but no actions were taken by the employer. In a high-profile case, the EEOC brought a suit against Abercrombie & Fitch, a popular clothing retailer, on behalf of a Muslim woman who wore a headscarf as part of her religious practice. Samantha Elauf applied for a sales job at Abercrombie & Fitch and wore her headscarf during her interview. Despite being deemed qualified for the position, she was denied employment because, as explained by the company, her headscarf conflicted with the retailer's "Look Policy." Ms. Elauf was awarded $20,000 by a jury. The case eventually made its way to the U.S. Supreme Court. In an 8–1 decision, the court ruled in favor of Ms. Elauf, stating that to refuse to hire someone based on a religious practice, even if the employer has a mere suspicion that the practice exists (and the potential employee hasn't explicitly stated it), constitutes religious discrimination.[16]

These cases, among others, highlights overt discriminatory practices where the evidence is clear-cut. In a less overt case from 2016, a national department store, Dillard's Inc., was ordered to pay $900,000 to settle an EEOC lawsuit. The suit claimed the company had imposed broad English-only rules on its staff and had publicly reprimanded of those found speaking other languages, even during their breaks.

While such instances are relatively obvious, many cases in the United States and elsewhere pose challenges in proving discrimination.[17] Unlike overt discriminatory remarks, these subtle cases require thorough investigation and often hinge on patterns of behavior and statistical analyses. More precisely, the case law allows for three main approaches to establish a prima facie case for discrimination when no discriminatory public statements have been made. First, the complainant can in theory rely on audio or video recordings. But in practice, recordings made without the respondent's knowledge or consent have been deemed inadmissible as proof by several courts, including in some U.S. states, depending on the circumstances under which they were obtained.[18]

Second, to prove hiring discrimination, the complainant can rely on "situation testing" whereby complainants compare their treatment with that of other similarly situated individuals. This approach resembles the correspondence and audit studies described in chapter 4, except that the role of one of the applicants is played by the complainant herself. Situation testing emerged in the United States in the 1960s, where they were first applied to the housing market: when a complainant claimed she had been unfairly denied access to an apartment or a house because of a protected ground (say, her skin color), so-called fair housing agencies sent a fictitious white applicant to inquire about the same unit.[19] If the latter was offered the possibility to buy or rent the unit that had been refused to the complainant, then the agency had powerful evidence of discrimination that she could then bring to court. In the labor market, situation testing aimed at detecting unequal treatment of job applicants differing only with respect to a protected characteristic expanded in the 1990s. However, the set of conditions that such testing must meet to be deemed reliable and conclusive

**Books From California**
51 W. Easy St
Simi Valley, CA 93065
UNITED STATES
customerservice@booksfromca.com

**Books From California**
51 W. Easy St
Simi Valley, CA 93065
UNITED STATES

**To:** Alibris APEX DC 76901964-54 - APEX
800 Avondale Ave.

Grandview Heights, OH 43212-3473
UNITED STATES

If this order is shipping from the US to an international buyer, remember to attach proper documentation. Complete and attach USPS Form CN-22 for all Priority Mail International Envelopes or First-Class Mail International shipments (available at your post office).

---

| | |
|---|---|
| **Order Number:** | 33958570 |
| **Ship Method:** | Standard |
| **Customer Name:** | Alibris APEX DC 76901964-54 - APEX |
| **Order Date:** | 9/10/2026 |
| **Alibris Order #:** | 76901964-54 |
| **Email:** | |

---

**Items:**

| Qty | Item | Locator | Item ID | Condition |
|---|---|---|---|---|

by courts is very strict. In this context, situation testing results are rarely sufficient to convince judges. They must generally be supported by other sources of evidence to lead to a finding of discrimination.

A third way to establish a prima facie case for discrimination in employment consists in relying on statistics. For instance, to document that she was discriminated against at the hiring stage based on her ethnic origin, the complainant can gather statistical data showing that the employer never hires people sharing the same ethnic background, or that the employer hires them but only on an interim or fixed-term contract, or only in positions involving little or no contact with customers, and so forth.[20] Similarly, with regard to discrimination in the course of an employee's professional career, the plaintiff may compare her professional trajectory with that of similarly situated others.[21] However, gathering such statistical evidence is not a given since the information is generally in the hands of the discriminator, in a context where case law does not provide complainants in discrimination proceedings the right to require the disclosure of this information. In two cases (*Kelly* and *Meister*), national domestic courts asked the Court of Justice of the European Union (CJEU) to provide clarification on these issues.[22] Although the CJEU acknowledged that a respondent's refusal to disclose information could be one of the factors helping to establish a prima facie case for discrimination, the court insisted that this refusal could not in and of itself trigger a presumption of discrimination.

Unfortunately, and contrary to conventional wisdom, collective legal actions are not necessarily a more efficient way to prove discrimination in employment compared to the individual legal actions described above. Modern class action lawsuits originated in the United States, following a revision of Rule 23 of the Federal Rules of Civil Procedure in 1966.[23] This revision, which emerged under the impetus of the civil rights movement, provides that all the claims of all class members can be resolved in a single proceeding through the efforts of the representative plaintiff(s) and appointed class counsel, instead of each damaged person bringing their own lawsuit. At first sight, this class action device was considered a revolutionary vehicle for achieving mass justice.[24] Certainly a group of persons claiming to be victims of the same type of discrimination by an employer is a stronger indicator of discriminatory behavior than a lone person in an individual lawsuit. Moreover, aggregating many individualized claims into one representational lawsuit lowers the cost of litigation for all class members. However, class action lawsuits also face sharp criticism. Starting in the mid-1990s, courts began expressing concern about the pressure on defendants to settle after a decision certifying a class.[25] As a result, there is a tendency among courts to strengthen their requirements to grant class certification, including the obligation for the class to bring more evidentiary proof ahead of courts' certification decision.[26] These case law trends may explain why employment discrimination class action lawsuits are still predominantly a U.S. phenomenon that did not widely spread beyond U.S. borders. As an illustration, while the European Parliament adopted legislation in November 2020 giving European consumers the right to U.S.-style class action lawsuits, it did not provide the possibility to use this class action device to address cases of discrimination.

## Antidiscrimination Legislation Should Be Complemented by Further Policies

It is of course critical to pursue efforts to properly enforce antidiscrimination legislation by informing the public, including people who believe they have been discriminated against as well as their advisers, such as staff representatives, trade unions, or lawyers, of the illegality of discrimination in the labor market and of the means of proving such discrimination. In this regard, national human rights institutions have an important role to play in terms of implementing awareness-raising campaigns, organizing online training, and maintaining well-designed interactive websites that allow users to easily engage with their content. For instance, following the best practice example from the Equality Commission in Northern Ireland, human rights institutions' websites should deliver clear information on the grounds and fields that are protected by antidiscrimination laws. They should also provide users with concrete guidance on how to compile the discrimination case, based on real examples pf previous successful discrimination complaints, that is, complaints that allowed the complainant to obtain reparation.

But these actions won't be sufficient to counter discrimination in the labor market. Indeed, the difficulty complainants face in providing evidence compelling enough to establish a presumption of discrimination discourages many to report the discriminatory behavior. Nonreporting is the default response of victims of discrimination, even when they are aware of their rights. As an illustration, the EU Survey on Immigrants and Descendants of Immigrants that was conducted in 2022 by the European Union Fundamental Rights Agency revealed that 47 percent of respondents of African descent felt racially discriminated against in the five years before the survey.[27] However, few of them (9 percent) reported or made a complaint about the most recent incident, even though most respondents (75 percent) are aware of antidiscrimination legislation in their countries of residence.

In this setting, it is critical to complement antidiscrimination legislation with policies aimed at combating discrimination (see chapter 11). These complementary policies would also have the advantage of countering a potential unintended effect of antidiscrimination laws, namely, that they may reduce the employment rate of the groups they are supposed to protect. Indeed, it is objectively more difficult to prove discrimination in hiring than discrimination in career development (including discrimination in labor contract termination) simply because collecting information on similar others and comparing oneself to them is easier when these others are colleagues rather than competing unknown job candidates. In other words, antidiscrimination laws raise the costs of terminating protected workers because they create an incentive for them to claim the dismissal was unfair (even if it was not) to receive compensation. The fact that this rise occurs without a parallel increase in the risk of retaliation against employers who discriminate at the recruitment stage opens the possibility that antidiscrimination laws in employment unintentionally reduce the hiring of protected groups. Evidence suggests that these perverse effects could be at work under certain conditions, although this conclusion comes from studying the impact of age discrimination protection, which, in principle, should be less conducive to unintended consequences of antidiscrimination laws: as recalled by the economist David Neumark, "even if age discrimination laws increase termination costs, such costs may not weigh heavily in employers' decisions because many older workers might not plan on remaining in a particular job for very long."[28] Research on the impact of age discrimination protection suggests that economic downturns are conducive to stronger discrimination protections deterring the hiring of protected workers through the termination cost channel. More precisely, the literature indicates that, in normal times, antidiscrimination legislation helps the hiring of protected workers.[29] However, during an experience such as the Great

Recession, stronger discrimination protections become less productive or even counterproductive for protected workers.[30] An explanation could be that economic crises elevate product and labor demand uncertainty to a level where employers, in contemplating hiring a protected worker, perceive a stronger possibility of wanting to terminate that worker before the worker voluntarily chooses to leave.[31]

* * *

Legally prohibiting discrimination in the labor market based on criteria such as gender, age, sexual orientation, or racial/ethnic identity is paramount. For doing so ensures that recruiters will not openly discriminate on such grounds and, more fundamentally, introduces a zero-tolerance culture around labor market discrimination. Regulation is also likely to gradually modify social norms. But we must remain realistic about the effectiveness of antidiscrimination legislation: despite the best intentions, discrimination is very difficult to prove when it is not blatant. Under these circumstances, it is important to recognize that antidiscrimination legislation alone is insufficient and that additional policies aimed at combating discrimination need to be implemented.

# 11 Beyond Antidiscrimination Legislation

While antidiscrimination legislation is crucial, it alone isn't sufficient to combat labor market discrimination. Employers often implement additional antidiscrimination policies, but the effectiveness of these measures can be dubious. Consider Starbucks' reaction to the highly publicized arrest in April 2018 of two Black men at one of its eight thousand U.S. locations. Despite the men explaining they were having a business meeting, the store's staff called the police on them, alleging trespassing. In response to the backlash, a month later, Starbucks closed all its shops one afternoon to conduct diversity training for its 175,000 employees, aiming to address and mitigate racial bias.

This may seem like a surprising choice. Decades of evidence suggest that diversity training on its own is unlikely to produce significant and lasting improvements in attitudes (not to mention behaviors), especially among those most prejudiced against outgroups.[1] While employers often present diversity training as just an initial step, many in fact do not move beyond it. This stagnation frequently arises from a combination of insufficient incentives and inadequate knowledge about effective strategies to reduce exclusionary attitudes and behaviors.

It is urgent to address this lack of progress as it likely has contributed to the concerning absence of a decline in racial discrimination during recruitment processes. Recent findings from field experimental studies spanning several decades have shown no significant change in such discrimination in the United States, the UK, Canada, France, Germany, and the Netherlands.[2]

This chapter is geared toward making a tangible difference in the realm of antidiscrimination.[3] It unfolds in four comprehensive steps. First, it offers an in-depth analysis of the efficacy of two commonly acclaimed antidiscrimination strategies in the workplace: affirmative action and blind job application procedures. Following this, the chapter delves into strategies to motivate employers to proactively combat discrimination and discusses a set of proven remedies. Subsequently the scope widens to reflect on educating society at large about nurturing positive intergroup dynamics. In conclusion, the chapter illuminates policies that drive change by focusing on the victims' perspective, ensuring those discriminated against are equipped to challenge and defy the stereotypes ascribed to them.

## Affirmative Action to Address Hiring Discrimination Does Not Deliver on its Promise

Many see affirmative action as a pivotal antidiscrimination strategy in the labor market.[4] This approach encompasses policies specifically designed to promote the hiring and retention of individuals from historically discriminated-against groups. While these policies may seem to deviate from the standard principle of equal employment access outlined in antidiscrimination laws, they have been upheld as essential, given the long-standing injustices experienced by these groups.

### Quotas, Targets, Hiring Subsidies, and Employment Subsidies: What Are We Talking About?

In the labor market, affirmative action can take two different forms. First, it can be based on sanctions through employment quotas or targets. Employment quotas oblige employers to allocate to a certain group a minimum percentage of jobs, which is fixed across employers subject to this policy. For instance, in the aftermath of World War I, employment of people with disabilities became a national duty to the war-disabled and their families in many countries that participated in the conflict.[5] Today, employment quota systems for disabled people targeting both private and public employers are implemented in a majority of EU countries (the exceptions are Denmark, Estonia, Finland, Latvia, the Netherlands, Sweden, and the UK). These quotas range from 2 percent (Spain) to 7 percent (Italy) of the workforce and apply above an employee threshold that varies between fifteen (Italy) and fifty (Greece, Lithuania, Spain) employees. In case employers fail to meet their obligations, they typically have to pay a fee (which can reach up to 4 percent of the payroll, as is the case in France, Italy, and Poland) to a special fund whose resources are used to support disabled people and help complying employers offer adequate facilities to their disabled employees.[6]

But quotas are not restricted to the case of disability and can apply to a range of other characteristics. In India, the 1950 constitution abolished the practice of untouchability and introduced measures of affirmative action in both educational institutions and public services in favor of groups that had been exposed to centuries of caste-based discrimination. These policies originally applied to Scheduled Castes (SC) and Scheduled Tribes (ST) but were extended in 1987 to Other Backward Classes (OBC).[7] More recently, several European countries have introduced gender quotas on corporate boards following Norway's lead in 2001 as well as a proposal for a directive on gender balance among nonexecutive directors of companies listed on stock exchanges submitted in 2012 by the European Commission and approved by the European Parliament and the Council of the European Union in June 2022.[8] In France, for instance, private and public listed companies have been subject to an obligation of 40 percent women on corporate boards since 2011. Public companies were required to reach this quota by 2017 and private companies by 2020. Failure to comply with these schedules results in nullity of appointments made in violation of the gender quotas and suspension of payment of attendance fees to board members. In a historic vote in 2021, France's Parliament went a step further by extending gender quotas on corporate boards to executive leadership.

Employment targets are more flexible than employment quotas and thus can vary based on local labor market characteristics. In the United States, for instance, this type of affirmative action applies to firms that have sizable contracts or subcontracts with the federal government; these firms employ about a quarter of the U.S. workforce. Regulated employers are mandated to make a "good faith" effort to employ minorities at rates (at least) proportional to their share in the local and qualified workforce. Failure to comply with this requirement implies financial sanctions, with the ultimate punishment for a contractor consisting of being debarred from doing business with the federal government, sometimes permanently. Similarly, in South Africa, compliance with the Broad-Based Black Economic Empowerment (BBBEE) Act of 2003 entails that the representation of Black individuals in management positions be commensurate with the local supply of Black managers. Otherwise employers may not be able to compete for contracts for government work or to access services (e.g., bank loans) from suppliers committed to serving only clients whose BBBEE scores are sufficiently high.[9]

But affirmative action relates not only to sanctions through employment quotas or targets. It can also be grounded in incentives through wage subsidies, that is, financial compensation to encourage employers to hire (hiring subsidy) or retain (employment subsidy) candidates or employees from eligible groups. Whereas an employment quota or target system means firms can *avoid* sanctions if they recruit and retain more individuals from a minority group, they are *rewarded* for hiring (or retaining) more of these individuals under a hiring subsidy (or employment subsidy) system. In France, for instance, the "Emplois francs" ("free jobs") scheme has been implemented since 2018. It consists in granting monetary assistance for the hiring of a job seeker living in a deprived area, designated Quartiers de la Politique de la Ville (QPV, city policy districts) where the share of individuals of (non-European) immigrant background known to be subject to substantial labor market discrimination is disproportionately higher than in the general population. Not surprisingly, the unemployment rate in QPVs (approximately 25 percent) is more than 2.5 times the national unemployment rate.[10] The sum paid for each inhabitant of a QPV recruited is €5,000 per year over a maximum of three years for any open-ended contract. When the group eligible for a subsidy is not only subject to discrimination but also potentially characterized by lower labor productivity—for example, as individuals suffering from a work-limiting disability such as blindness—it may be necessary to replace hiring subsidies with employment subsidies. In this case, the wage subsidy is virtually paid as long as the individual is employed. In Flanders, for instance, the Dutch-speaking part of Belgium, the Flemish Supporting Subsidy (FSS) aims to improve the integration of disabled people into the labor market. It is automatically paid over a five-year period to employers who recruit a worker eligible for the FSS. Moreover, the employer can apply for an extension of another five years if it can demonstrate that the disability of the employee still results in a productivity loss. In practice, provided the employee remains employed with the employer, the employer can continue to extend the premium.[11]

### What Is the Impact of Affirmative Action Policies on Minority Group Employment?

While subsidies can be effective in boosting employment among groups most at risk of unemployment, there is a lack of evidence to date on their effectiveness when they focus specifically on individuals belonging to groups targeted by affirmative action policies, unlike employment quotas or targets.[12] For instance, a group of French economists recently evaluated the impact of the Emplois francs scheme mentioned above.[13] To that end, the group ran a correspondence study to compare the callback rate for fictitious applicants of French and North African background, depending on whether the applicant lived within or outside the deprived area granting eligibility to the wage subsidy. They did so at two different points in time: a few months before the launch of the Emplois francs scheme (period 1) and one year later (period 2). To avoid getting a null result driven by employers ignoring the existence of the scheme, the authors made sure that eligibility for the wage subsidy of fictitious candidates living in a QPV was explicitly stated in period 2. Instead of having it appear only in the cover letter, they also mention this eligibility in the email they sent to recruiters. Moreover, they attached to this email the flyer prepared by the French Public Employment Service to present the scheme to employers. Despite this strong signal, the authors found no effect of the Emplois francs scheme: the gap between the callback rate for applicants living in a QPV and for applicants living in a non-QPV neighborhood did not narrow between period 1 and period 2.[14] It is worth stressing that the odds of minority candidates of getting hired are not better when one focuses on employment rather than hiring subsidies. Based on a correspondence study, Stijn Baert shows that the likelihood of a disabled candidate receiving a positive response to a job application is not improved by revealing entitlement to the FSS.[15]

By contrast, employment quotas or targets are effective at improving the hiring and retention of groups they target. For instance, Rafael Lalive, Jean-Philippe Wuellrich, and Josef Zweimüller estimate the impact of the Disabled Persons Employment Act in Austria, which provides that firms must hire at least one disabled individual per twenty-five nondisabled employees, thereby leading to quota thresholds at firm size twenty-five, fifty, and so on. Firms that fail to comply to this quota are subject to a tax. The authors' empirical strategy to gauge the employment effect of this regulation basically consisted in comparing the number of disabled workers in firms just below and just above the quota threshold. The results indicate that firms with twenty-five nondisabled workers employ about 12 percent more disabled workers with than without the tax.[16] Evidence also reveals that targets in the United States benefited the employment of women and African Americans during the 1960s and 1970s.[17]

Two possible explanations may account for the lower effectiveness of hiring and employment subsidies relative to employment quotas or targets.

First, wage subsidies are more stigmatizing for minorities because they entail paying employers for hiring and retaining minority candidates, rather than sanctioning them for not doing so. As such, they entail a greater risk of instilling or reinforcing the belief among employers that minority candidates suffer from a productivity deficit for which employers need to be compensated. In other words, it is possible that the incentive effect of wage subsidies is partly or fully offset by a concomitant perverse effect, the worsening of negative representations about the productivity potential of minority candidates and therefore the strengthening of statistical discrimination against them. This mechanism was recently confirmed by Axana Dalle, Elsy Verhofstadt, and Stijn Baert, who examined the effectiveness of hiring subsidies targeted at unemployed individuals aged fifty-eight and over.[18] Through an experiment involving 292 real recruiters evaluating fictitious candidates on their employability and perceived productivity, the study revealed that subsidized candidates had even lower interview and hiring prospects than their nonsubsidized counterparts, despite the latter having similar profiles (notably, all were unemployed and only a few months away from turning fifty-eight). Furthermore, the study demonstrated that this unfavorable treatment arises from the negative signals recruiters associate with the hiring subsidy, casting doubt on the employability of the candidates. This finding sheds light on why, despite significant public investment in subsidies aimed at encouraging the employment of older workers, their effectiveness remains limited in many OECD countries, as evidenced by peer-reviewed research.[19]

The second reason that may explain the lower effectiveness of hiring and employment subsidies compared to employment quotas or targets is that these subsidies often place more administrative burdens (red tape) on employers than quotas or targets. While it is usually enough in the framework of the latter policy to measure the share of minority groups in the workforce and compare it to the quota or target under consideration, entitlement to a wage subsidy is often characterized by a strong bureaucratic burden. For instance, although the 2018 version of the Emplois francs scheme in France aimed to reduce the excessive paperwork attached to the initial version implemented between 2013 and 2015, the range of rules to conform to remains large in the latest version.[20]

### Are Quotas and Targets Effective at Combating Taste-Based and Statistical Discrimination?

Should we conclude, based on this evidence, that quotas and targets constitute a magic bullet to combat taste-based and statistical discrimination? Research does find that quotas and targets reduce statistical discrimination: firms required to hire more minority candidates do so by investing in recruitment methods that better reveal the productivity of job applicants, such as recruitment by simulation or the use of employment intermediaries such as recruitment firms.[21] As an illustration, affirmative action policies in the United States improved the employment of women and African Americans without leading companies to recruit underperforming employees. Notably, Harry Holzer and David Neumark have shown that the educational and experience levels of the minority candidates thus hired were often inferior to those of their white colleagues but their productivity was comparable, presumably as a result of the more careful screening they went through.[22] Interestingly, the change in recruitment strategies induced by employment quotas or targets seems to outlast implementation of these policies. Conrad Miller has shown that the share of African Americans in companies required to comply with affirmative action policies does not drop fully back to its initial level once these policies cease to apply.[23] In other words, even when these companies no longer have sizable contracts or subcontracts with the federal government, once they have invested in recruitment procedures that better reflect candidates' productivity, they continue to apply these procedures, although such is no longer required to meet quotas or targets.

Unfortunately, the impact of quotas and targets on taste-based discrimination against minority groups is less promising. On the one hand, according to intergroup contact theory (see chapter 6), affirmative action policies should help decrease prejudice against minority candidates and employees, at least among the staff of firms to which quotas or targets apply. On the other hand, affirmative action policies may generate a reverse effect by fueling resentment among the majority. This resentment flows from the fact that the value of a quota or even a target is necessarily wrong since it varies by firm, not simply by country (as assumed by quotas) or by the local labor market (as assumed by targets). Indeed, this share hinges not only on the local supply of skills by majority and minority job seekers but also on the demand for skills, which is firm-specific (it depends on the firm's sector, activity, and growth stage, among others). Yet the extent of discrimination against minorities *in each firm* and consequently the share of jobs that minorities would hold in the absence of discrimination is *unknown.* In this setting, quotas and targets can easily be suspected by the majority group of being too high, and thus of offering undue advantages to minority candidates and employees by increasing the probability that a person from the minority group is recruited even when, following an objective assessment, that person is less suited to the job offered. Research in social psychology yields results consistent with the surmise that affirmative action policies induce resentment. One of these studies, based on a lab experiment, entailed providing managers with objective descriptions of the work done by different employees and asking them to evaluate these employees' performance.[24] The findings revealed stigmatization of those described as eligible for affirmative action policies: for objectively equal work, their performance was deemed to be poorer than that of employees whose recruitment was presented as unrelated to affirmative action of any kind. Complementary lab experiments confirm that, unless compelling evidence is provided to individuals in the majority group that, *within their work environment,* minority candidates would be discriminated against in the absence of a quota or target (a proof it is hardly feasible to provide in real life), they strongly oppose these policies and even retaliate against members of the minority, which in turns results in productivity losses.[25]

The increased prejudice of the majority against the minority induced by affirmative action policies is observed not only in lab experiments. It also emerges in the field, although evidence in this case is available for quotas in politics, not in the labor market. One of the papers contributing to this evidence evaluated the impact of mandated exposure to female leaders across village councils in India ten years after the policy was established.[26] Since 1998, in every village council election, one-third of councilor positions in each council and one-third of chief councilor (*pradhan*) positions across councils in a district have been randomly "reserved" for women. The authors found that this policy reduced the probability that male voters indulged in statistical discrimination against female candidates contesting councilor and *pradhan* positions on village councils: men who had never been exposed to a female *pradhan* judged men as more effective leaders than women, while this evaluation gap disappeared in villages where at least one woman had been elected as *pradhan* in the previous ten years. However, these results did not hold when the authors assessed the effect of the policy on the propensity of male voters to engage in taste-based discrimination against female candidates: men expressed stronger distaste for female leaders in villages where the *pradhan* position was reserved to a woman than elsewhere. Subsequent studies have confirmed that this significant male backlash against female leaders is driven by men considering women who become village heads as engaging in socially inappropriate behavior rather than by men judging women leaders to be ineffective.[27] Distressingly, the increased distaste of the majority for the minority following the implementation of affirmative action policies can lead to extreme violence. As an illustration, the economist Victoire Girard demonstrates that the enactment of caste quotas in India in 1993, that is, the reservation of a fixed share of seats in local elections for members of the lower castes, led to an increase in the number of murders targeting individuals belonging to these castes. Moreover, based on Indian households' answers to a nationally representative survey, she shows an increase in intercaste tensions and discrimination following the implementation of caste quotas.[28]

Overall, while quotas and targets generally allow more members of the minority to be hired and retained in firms that are subject to these policies, their effects on the underlying causes of discrimination are mixed: on the one hand, implementation of quotas and targets tends to dampen negative stereotypes about the productivity potential of minority candidates, but on the other hand it exacerbates prejudice against the minority. As such, contrary to proponents' claims, affirmative action policies are unlikely to help society reach a nondiscriminatory equilibrium and thus be transitory. The unintended negative consequences of affirmative action policies on taste-based discrimination may explain why, despite implementation of these policies in the aftermath of the civil rights movement, the intensity of hiring discrimination against African Americans as measured by correspondence studies has remained virtually unchanged over time.[29] These unintended effects may also explain why the expected positive spillover effects of implementing quotas or targets have difficulty materializing. These difficulties have been well documented by Marianne Bertrand and her coauthors in the framework of the law that Norway passed in 2003 to mandate 40 percent representation of each gender on the board of directors of public limited liability companies.[30] The authors show that seven years after it fully came into effect, this board quota policy had had very little discernible impact on women in business beyond its direct effect on the women who made it into boardrooms. More precisely, the proportion of women on boards did reach the 40 percent target following the quota mandate, and the women appointed to boards of directors were more qualified than those who preceded them. However, the authors did not find that an increase in the female share of board members translated into the recruitment or promotion of more women within the firms (including among those who were as highly qualified as women on the board of directors), which may reflect that the board quota policy failed to reduce prejudice against women in leadership position.

## Blind Job Application Procedures Are No Magic Bullet to Counter Hiring Discrimination Either

Beyond affirmative action, blind job application procedures have been viewed by many as a magic bullet to combat discrimination, at least at the hiring stage, following the success of blind auditions that were progressively adopted by U.S. symphony orchestras during the second half of the twentieth century. This approach, which was first introduced in 1952 by the Boston Symphony Orchestra, consists in recruiting musicians based on how they perform behind a screen, hidden from the evaluators. Claudia Goldin and Cecilia Rouse have found that blind auditions substantially reduced hiring discrimination against women.[31] They estimate that blind auditions accounted for a quarter of the increase in the proportion of women in American symphony orchestras during the 1970s and 1980s.

Yet, on top of the fact that developing job tests for recruiting job candidates exclusively based on their skills is not an easy task outside orchestras (i.e., among more standard private or public employers), the outcome of such tests is rarely the only criterion used by employers to make their hiring decision. Blind application procedures are typically followed by job interviews or at least the final assessment of an HR staff or a manager, who are encouraged to factor the test into their assessment but are not required to hire strictly according to test recommendations. In other words, if HR staff or managers involved in the recruitment process are biased, there is a risk that at least part of the hiring discrimination that would have occurred at the CV screening stage will be postponed to a later stage.

Empirical evidence has confirmed the existence of this risk. Relying on personnel data from U.S. firms that introduced job testing, a group of economists has explored how managers use job test information that allows categorizing applicants as "green" (high-potential candidate), "yellow" (moderate-potential candidate), or "red" (lowest rating), based on candidates' performance on job testing.[32] The researchers found that not all HR managers align their hiring decisions with the job test information, meaning, for example, that they end up hiring an applicant with a yellow test score when one with a green score had also applied but is not hired (or similarly, when an applicant with a red score is hired while one with a yellow or green score is not). When HR managers deviate from the test recommendations, evidence shows that it is not because they have additional information about job applicants, resulting in better hires for the firm. Rather, deviations happen when HR managers are biased and indulge in hiring discrimination, thereby leading to worse hires: HR managers more likely to deviate bring in workers who leave their jobs more quickly.[33]

Similarly disappointing findings have been documented regarding the impact of anonymous CVs, that is, CVs that do not contain (or do not allow inferring) the applicant's surname, first name, postal address, gender, age, nationality, and racial/ethnic identity. The reason is simple: even though the CV may not reveal any information on the job applicant's non-productivity-related characteristics, these characteristics cannot be concealed during the job interview. David Neumark has confirmed this suspicion in the field of age discrimination, as briefly mentioned in chapter 7. Relying on personnel data from a restaurant chain in the United States, David Neumark first shows that applicants aged forty and older obtain job offers at a rate 68 percent lower than younger applicants with similar CVs when applications are completed in stores and handed in in person (in which case age is revealed at the same time as all other information about the applicant).[34] He then uncovers that part of this hiring discrimination persists even when date of birth and information on years of graduation and on the exact length of work experiences are removed from job applicants' CV. More precisely, when selection for interviews is made online in an age-blind manner, older applicants are selected at the same rate as younger applicants. But in the end, after the interviews have taken place, older applicants still receive job offers at rate 46 percent lower than that of younger applicants, holding their productive characteristics constant.

Anonymous CVs are not only inefficient at fully addressing hiring discrimination, they may also put marginalized groups at a disadvantage compared to standard CVs, at least among employers keen on making their workforce more diverse. According to an experiment carried out in France among employers committed to diversity, anonymous CVs penalize applicants of racial/ethnic minority background relative to standard CVs because anonymity prevents employers from favoring minority job candidates, either by systematically choosing them when credentials are equal or by "forgiving" defects on their CV, such as misspellings or career breaks, that are more likely to appear on the CV of minority applicants (who disproportionately stem from underprivileged backgrounds and face labor market discrimination). As a result, minority candidates have a one in twenty-two chance of obtaining an interview with anonymous CVs (against one in six for other candidates), whereas they have a one in ten chance with CVs that give their name (against one in eight for other candidates).[35]

### Monitoring Employers' Hiring *and* Career Management Behavior through Rigorous Data Collection

In their recent book, *Getting to Diversity: What Works and What Doesn't*, sociologists Franck Dobbin and Alexandra Kalev insist that discrimination in the labor market is unlikely to wane in the absence of data to monitor employers' hiring and career management behavior with respect to minority groups.[36] Without regular numerical assessments, employers' commitment to promoting diversity is doomed to go not much beyond window dressing.

As an illustration, Sonia K. Kang and her colleagues found that job candidates of racial/ethnic minority background who "whitened" their CVs (i.e., concealed or downplayed racial cues) were twice as likely to be invited to a job interview by ostensibly pro-diversity employers, compared to their peers with unwhitened CVs.[37] Indeed, although those firms presented themselves as valuing diversity, thus attracting fewer whitened CVs from minority applicants, they were not less likely to discriminate against unwhitened résumés, thereby leading to the paradox that minority candidates were at a strong disadvantage when applying to pro-diversity employers.

Even worse, when not accompanied by mechanisms aimed at holding employers accountable, diversity policies have been shown to generate worrisome unintended effects.[38] Using laboratory experiments, a group of researchers in social psychology has demonstrated that the presence of diversity structures in an organization causes high-status group members (i.e., white men) to automatically assume that members of underrepresented groups are treated more fairly. This "illusion of fairness" in turn results in high-status-group members legitimizing the status quo by becoming less sensitive to discrimination and reacting more harshly toward underrepresented group members who assert discrimination.[39] Evidence suggests that the illusion of fairness also extends to judges and minority groups. For instance, an examination of over one thousand federal employment discrimination opinions between 1965 and 1999 found that judges used the mere presence of diversity structures as evidence of compliance with civil rights law, rarely questioning whether organizations actually provided protection or fairness.[40] Similarly, in studies with fictional descriptions of firms and lawsuits, the sheer existence of diversity policies in companies hampered women's ability to detect sexist practices and led racial/ethnic minorities to regard discrimination claims from co-ethnics as less valid.[41]

Providing employers with compelling evidence of the discrimination they indulge in is expected to be more effective at pushing them to step up efforts to discriminate less. This mechanism is especially likely if evidence of discriminatory practices is made public, in which case employers should be strongly motivated to rectify these injustices to maintain high levels of attractiveness. Many job candidates, employees, customers, and suppliers prioritize engaging in socially responsible business relationships, making it crucial for employers to foster nondiscriminatory environments. Although this chain reaction still needs to be documented in the labor market, it has been observed in other fields. For example, in 2002, two U.S. economists, Joseph Price and Justin Wolfers, published a study demonstrating the existence of racial discrimination during National Basketball Association (NBA) games: Black players were more likely to be punished for fouls when the referee was white, and vice versa.[42] In 2007, these findings attracted extensive media coverage, including the front page of the *New York Times* and commentary by American basketball stars on television and radio. Price, Wolfers, and their colleague, Devin Pope, showed that this coverage put an end to racial discrimination initially documented. Having persisted from 2003 up until 2007, it completely disappeared thereafter.[43] The change was unrelated to any reforms in the NBA, such as antidiscrimination training for referees. It was tied instead to enhanced vigilance by referees regarding their own decisions.

Similarly, in a French university where evidence of gender biases in student evaluations of teaching was previously found, a field experiment was conducted to assess the impact of two awareness-raising campaigns aimed at reducing such gender discrimination.[44] In the first campaign, students were given a normative statement reminding them not to discriminate during their evaluations. In the second, the normative statement was supplemented with specific information about past instances where students, particularly males, had discriminated against female teachers. While the stand-alone normative statement showed no discernible impact, the additional information significantly narrowed the evaluation gap between female and male teachers. This change was primarily driven by how male students revised their evaluations of female teachers.

### Monitoring Employers' Career Management Behavior

The monitoring of employers' career management behavior to mitigate gaps in the labor market trajectories of men and women is increasingly widespread. Over half of OECD countries mandate that private employers report gender wage gaps in their organization, with many of these pay-reporting rules also applicable to the public sector.[45] This share should further increase, following the approval on March 30, 2023, of the new EU Pay Transparency Directive by a large majority in the European Parliament as member states have three years to enact the directive into national legislation.[46]

Pay transparency policies limit the possibility for employers to indulge in discrimination toward their female employees, whether through wage discrimination (offering women lower wages for work of equal value[47]) or discrimination in promotion (offering women lower access to high managerial positions, ceteris paribus). Indeed, these policies are typically accompanied by financial penalties should employers not report their gender wage gap or should their gender wage gap not improve over time when it was high to start with. Pay transparency policies also limit the capacity of firms to exploit the wage-setting power they have over women since the enduring unequal sharing of unpaid work within heterosexual couples constrains women to search for a job or consider exit options within firms located at a short commute distance. Field experimental evidence shows that, when female candidates are informed about the median wage offered by firms to similar (male and female) candidates, they revise the wage they ask upward, thereby driving the gender ask gap to zero.[48]

It is important to reflect on how best to extend tools aimed at monitoring employers' career management behavior toward women to other groups at risk of being discriminated against, including young and older employees, racial/ethnic minorities, and LGBTIQ+ hires. However, it appears unrealistic to expect that employers would collect this information themselves because of the administrative burden this practice would entail but also because racial/ethnic identity, sexual orientation, and gender identity are viewed as sensitive personal information that require high confidentiality and privacy standards unlikely to be met by employers (see the General Data Protection Regulation that prevails across the EU).[49] Rather, a state public body could be entrusted with the responsibility of computing firm-level gaps between majority and minority groups and publishing them on media available to both employees and the public, based on administrative data. This novel approach in international perspective has already been implemented in Lithuania in the field of gender equality: the country's Social Security Fund is responsible for reporting gender-disaggregated labor earnings in firms where the number of insured persons is at least eight (of whom more than three are women or more than three are men). It is also being implemented in Estonia.[50] On top of increasing buy-in among employers by shielding them from red tape, this approach would ensure that the figures produced are accurate and comparable across employers. This outcome would in turn increase the probability that the monitoring of employers' career management behavior reached its target and thus improved the situation of minority employees by mitigating the discrimination they might be exposed to. In the absence of an independent stakeholder in charge of assessing gaps between majority and minority employees, the evidence suggests that employers provide information that underestimates those gaps and thus reduces incentives to reduce disparities.[51]

Of course, the strategy of tasking a state public body with computing and publishing pay gaps will require more countries to collect in their census information that allows identifying LGBTIQ+ people or racial/ethnic minorities (e.g., based on a racial/ethnic self-identification question, or, as suggested by Thomas Piketty,[52] based on the region of origin of the respondent's ancestors, and to combine this information with linked employer-employee data. To achieve this objective, countries will need to step up efforts to address confidentiality concerns and build trust around the data collection process.[53]

### Monitoring Employers' Hiring Behavior

Monitoring employers' behavior should also entail observing their recruitment decisions because hiring discrimination remains widespread. Moreover, if employers' recruitment behaviors are not scrutinized, there is a high risk that tools aimed at monitoring employers' career management practices will generate perverse effects. For instance, pay transparency policies may create incentives for employers to refrain from hiring women in job categories (e.g., top management jobs) with the largest gender pay gap: owing to justified confidentiality and representativeness concerns, employers typically are not required to report gender pay gaps in job categories where the number of employees of either gender falls below a given threshold.

Unfortunately, monitoring employers' recruitment behavior is not a given. As mentioned earlier in this chapter, the share of jobs that minorities would hold in the absence of discrimination is unknown. In other words, it is not possible to use the composition of the workforce by ground protected by antidiscrimination laws as an indicator of whether employers discriminate during the hiring stage. For instance, although educational settings in OECD countries formally commit to providing equal opportunities for boys and girls, boys are still much more likely than girls to sort into studies related to information and communication technology (ICT) rather than education, health, and welfare (EHW) fields, thereby leading women to be concentrated in "5 Cs" jobs (cleaning, catering, cashiering, caring, and clerical work). Consequently, many jobs are characterized by an unequal gender distribution without this situation flowing primarily from employers' discriminatory practices but rather from mechanisms upstream of the labor market. Unquestionably, action should be taken to put an end to the horizontal segregation of men and women. But this won't happen by obligating employers to have a gender-balanced workforce. Rather, efforts should be stepped up to tackle the deeply ingrained social expectations about the roles of men and women that lead boys and girls to sort into different fields of study.

A straightforward alternative to monitoring employers' recruitment behavior via the composition of the workforce would consist in running large-scale correspondence studies. The aim would be to identify employers that engage in hiring discrimination and fault those that do not engage in corrective actions. France is a pioneer in this field. Between April and July 2016, at the request of the French Ministry of Labor, fictitious CVs and letters of applications of French applicants of French and North African origin were sent in response to real job openings published by forty French companies with more than one thousand employees. Each company was tested thirty to forty times (i.e., the pair of fictitious applicants was sent to thirty to forty job vacancies advertised by the company) to allow inferring, with sufficient confidence, whether the company engaged in hiring discrimination against the ostensibly minority candidate. The findings confirmed significant discrimination against the French applicant of North African origin in twelve of the forty companies tested.[54] The twelve discriminating companies were invited to submit an action plan to the Ministry of Labor to eradicate discrimination in their midst. Only the names of companies that did not notify the ministry of remedial actions within a year following the correspondence study were made public. This initial CV testing campaign was repeated in 2019 with the 120 largest French companies, with the objective of sending them fictitious applications up until late 2021 at the rate of forty companies tested per year.

Yet, while it may first appear enticing, CV testing campaigns suffer from several limitations. First, correspondence studies are suitable for exploring the recruitment behavior of large employers, that is, those that generate a sufficient volume of job ads to allow for the identification of any hiring discrimination. For others, the lower frequency of job openings must be compensated for by sending several applications of the majority and of the minority fictitious candidates in response to the *same* job ad, which entails a risk of detection. As stressed by Patrick Kline and Christopher Walters, with only two white and two Black applications per job, it is difficult to reliably identify discriminating employers. A minimum of ten applications is necessary to ensure a very low type 1 error rate (the false positive rate). However, despite its significance, this volume of applications would only allow for the identification of between 7 percent and 10 percent of discriminatory jobs with a reasonable level of certainty.[55] A second major shortcoming of CV testing campaigns is that they do not allow for the observation of job interview outcomes. Yet in a context where employers increasingly rely on automated CV screening tools, it is during the job interview that hiring discrimination is the most likely to emerge.

Despite their limitations, CV testing campaigns can effectively identify large firms that routinely engage in discriminatory hiring practices. For example, a comprehensive correspondence experiment conducted by Patrick Kline and his coauthors involved sending over 83,000 fictitious applications to jobs across the United States, posted by 108 of the largest employers.[56] The results revealed, with high confidence, that twenty-three of these firms discriminated against Black applicants. Building on this, the researchers developed an innovative statistical methodology to grade the racial callback gaps of major U.S. employers.[57] Their findings indicated that firms with the worst grades favored white applicants over Black applicants by 24 percent, whereas those with the best grades showed a much smaller disparity of only 3 percent.

For an alternative monitoring of employers' recruitment behavior, an alternative could entail observing how employers and job seekers interact in the labor market, and particularly on job boards, which are among the top channels people use to look for new jobs.[58] Tracking the search behavior of employers can be achieved through machine learning, as shown by Dominik Hangartner, Daniel Kopp, and Michael Siegenthaler.[59] In collaboration with the Swiss government–affiliated online recruitment platform Job-Room, these economists and political scientists analyzed the probability that employers contact "majority" and "minority" job candidates with similar profiles. The investigation focused on instances where employers searched for a specific occupation and location matching the job vacancy they sought to fill, and subsequently received a list of potential candidates. More precisely, the search generated a ranked list of candidates from which recruiters selected the profiles they believe to be best suited (based on detailed productivity-related information akin to a standard CV about the education, work experience, and skills of the job seekers, along with gender and markers of race/ethnicity, including the job seeker's language skills, and, for registered recruiters, their first name, last name, and nationality). Whether employers finally reached out to candidates whose profiles they consulted (presumably to invite them to a job interview) was proxied by the probability that they clicked on a button to obtain their contact information. In addition, because they linked the profiles of job seekers to the unemployment register, the researchers were able to investigate the probability of majority and minority candidates being hired, conditional on being contacted by the employer. Overall, from March to December 2017, the authors collected data on 43,352 recruiters, 452,729 searches, 17.4 million profiles that appeared in the search lists, and 3.4 million profile views. The results revealed that recruiters treat otherwise identical job seekers who appear in the same search list differently depending on their racial/ethnic identity: except for job seekers from southern Europe, individuals with a recent immigrant background faced a substantially lower contact rate compared to native Swiss citizens. The contact penalty reaches 13.5 percent for those from the Middle East and North Africa (MENA) region, 17.1 percent for those from sub-Saharan Africa, and 18.5 percent for those from Asia. The researchers also showed that these differences are consequential in terms of employment rate: every click on the contact button increased the probability that an individual would leave unemployment in the next three months by 2.1 percent.

This unprecedented research effort emphasizes the possibility of monitoring employers' recruitment behavior on online job boards, thanks to machine learning algorithms. Of course, to avoid discriminating employers using unmonitored job boards, the regulation should seek to cover all the main online recruitment platforms used in each country, including those managed by private companies. In the latter case, governments could set up partnerships with the companies, for instance in the framework of the companies' antidiscrimination policies, to access statistics on employers' search behavior and possibly on the identity of job seekers enrolled on their platform to link those data with administrative data. To create incentives for employers to continue using job boards that are monitored, governments could publicize the share of their hires that were contacted through these platforms as a signal of their efforts to combat discriminatory hiring practices.

## *Effective* Action Requires Information on the Prevalence of Discrimination and What Works to Remedy It

Public reporting of indicators aimed at spotting discriminatory practices at the hiring and career management stages should induce employers to take remedial action whenever the presumption of discrimination is strong enough. However, these transparency efforts will do little good if employers are not concomitantly provided with support on how to effectively combat discrimination. Across OECD countries, the lack of guidance in this area is widespread and may help to explain why, in the rare instances when pay transparency policies have led to reductions in the gender wage gap, this change has been induced by a slowdown in the growth of men's wages rather than by an increase in women's wages.[60] In France, for instance, the Equality and Citizenship Act of January 27, 2017, requires all staff in charge of recruitment to undergo training in "nondiscrimination in recruitment" in companies with more than three hundred employees. This law is a step in the right direction as evidence shows that multi-establishment companies that select candidates for recruitment through a centralized HR department (where the staff are typically trained in nondiscrimination) are less likely to discriminate than multi- establishment companies in which selection is made at the level of the establishment seeking to hire (where staff are generally less sensitized to discrimination issues).[61] It is surprising, however, that this training obligation is not accompanied by support to help companies identify the right training service providers, for instance by certifying those who comply with a set of terms of reference. There are many nondiscrimination training programs, but the content is very heterogeneous and does not necessarily provide the keys to making recruitment and management nondiscriminatory.

### Unconscious Bias Training Should Not Be Used as a Quick Fix but as a Step toward Broader Change

Diversity training, defined as any program designed to facilitate positive intergroup interaction, has been the most popular approach used by employers to reduce prejudice, stereotyping, and discrimination. In the United States, for instance, more than half of midsized and large employers offer diversity training to their employees.[62] Such training typically consists in a one-off intervention organized around three steps that have proved to be effective in the context of a laboratory experiment:[63] (1) informing participants about (un)conscious bias that underlies prejudice and stereotyping, and how this bias can result in discriminatory behavior and thus inequity; (2) having participants complete an implicit association test (IAT) and debriefing them about their results in a nonjudgmental way. In particular, while also emphasizing individuals' responsibility to take action, the training should explain how easily stereotypes can be absorbed, even by well-intentioned people; (3) learning about strategies to reduce bias, such as prejudice-reduction techniques that are aimed at narrowing the perceived distance from the outgroup (these techniques are reviewed in greater details in the next section of this chapter). For instance, a group of social psychologists have shown that the benefits of a diversity training offered to incoming freshmen at a U.S.-based university are enhanced when steps 1 and 2 are combined with a perspective-taking exercise in which participants are asked to write a short narrative on what a typical day would be like for a member of a marginalized minority group.[64] The authors found that, eight months after its completion, the intervention was still positively influencing self-reported behaviors toward minority individuals.

Yet scientists have had a hard time generalizing to the workplace results obtained in laboratory settings or equivalent. The randomized controlled trial conducted by Edward Chang and his coauthors is the only one to test a diversity training organized around the aforementioned three steps.[65] The training consisted of an hourlong online course meant to educate people about sexist bias and its consequences and was taken on a voluntary basis by more than three thousand employees in a large corporate employer. Although the researchers did their best to design an intervention that would be effective, the results suggest that the sorts of one-off trainings that are commonplace in organizations are not particularly powerful at leading to lasting change, especially among groups whose behaviors policymakers are most eager to influence: for groups whose average attitudes without the diversity training were relatively less supportive of women than other groups (though still supportive of women), the diversity training successfully produced attitudinal change up to twenty weeks post-intervention but no behavioral change.[66]

At least two reasons could explain this upsetting outcome. It may be that the standard diversity training is simply too brief to have the desired impact. Furthermore, the training is rarely preceded by data collection that would provide evidence that discriminatory behaviors were at play. Participants may thus consider that (un)conscious bias is not something they need to work on since they lack any data showing there is an issue to be solved in their organization.

All in all, to be effective, diversity training should not be considered as the alpha and the omega of antidiscrimination policies but as step one of a long series of actions to be implemented *once* a specific problem with diversity, equity, and inclusion is accurately diagnosed at the level of the organization, chiefly in the form of unequal treatment of equally productive job candidates and employees.

### The Need for Human Resources Strategies That Deny Conscious and Unconscious Bias a Chance to Operate

Unconscious bias training aims to make participants aware of their own biases and introduce them to prejudice-reducing techniques, with the hope that this combined effort will promote positive attitudinal and behavioral changes toward the outgroup. However, to ensure progress, it is important to surround and complement this challenging objective with less ambitious goals, such as teaching strategies to manage (un)conscious bias rather than aiming to eliminate it entirely. Managing unconscious bias is particularly crucial in fast-paced settings where stakeholders face tight deadlines, a typical environment for HR staff and managers. In such high-pressure situations, individuals might inadvertently resort to their "system 1" thinking, which is characterized by quick, automatic reactions, often rooted in ingrained stereotypes or prejudice. This phenomenon has been confirmed by researchers. In one study, students were tasked with selecting the top fifteen candidates from a pool of fifty CVs.[67] White and African American applicants' names were randomly assigned to these CVs, ensuring that the average quality of CVs within each group was consistent. The results revealed that participants who felt pressured during the selection process were less likely to choose CVs of African American applicants than were participants who were more relaxed while engaged in the task.

Regarding recruitment, strategies that deny conscious and unconscious bias a chance to operate include the following: (1) drafting a job profile that clearly describes the tasks related to the position to be filled (which is preferable to a long list of skills and requirements that may intimidate minority candidates); (2) selecting applications based on an assessment grid that focuses on the skills needed for the tasks described in the job profile; and (3) formalizing the conduct of the job interview. This formalization implies that the same questions be posed to all candidates, in the same order and by the same interviewer(s), with the sole purpose of determining whether candidates have the required skills. Without a consistent protocol, recruiters tend to let their prejudices and stereotypes become self-fulfilling: when their bias is positive, recruiters are more likely to begin the interview with the candidates' strengths, which increases candidates' chances of excelling, and vice versa. Several studies confirm that an inconsistent interview protocol fails to ensure skills-based recruitment.[68] For example, students' performance at the end of their first year in a U.S.-based university is not correlated with their entry ranking when this ranking is based on an oral admissions procedure that varies across panels. More specifically, the results show that a nonstandardized interview is no more effective than a selection procedure based on random selection of eligible students.[69] Last but not least, to make it easier for recruiters to resist their system 1, it is important not to schedule job interviews for the late morning or late afternoon. At these times of day, recruiters' intellectual sharpness tends to be low (not least because they are tired), as has been shown by Shai Danziger, Jonathan Levav, and Liora Avnaim-Pesso.[70] The researchers looked at judges' rulings regarding requests from prisoners, such as applications for parole or transfer. They found that the likelihood of judges refusing these requests, and thus endorsing the *status quo*, increased with the time elapsed since their last meal, owing to the increasing difficulty of mobilizing their intellectual abilities. Dominik Hangartner, Daniel Kopp, and Michael Siegenthaler have recently shown that these findings are transposable to the labor market: their reliance on machine learning to monitor hiring discrimination through online recruitment platforms revealed that minority racial/ethnic groups experienced penalties that were about 20 percent larger later in the day.[71] More precisely, these penalties increased from 11.5 percent between 9 a.m. and 10 a.m. to 13.4 percent between 11 a.m. and 11:59, reset to 11.5 percent after the lunch break, then rose again to 13.6 percent (4–5 p.m.) and 14.7 percent (5–6 p.m.).

These strategies to keep unconscious bias under control during recruitment could be combined with efforts to broaden the recruitment pool. The wording and imagery used in advertisements and job descriptions can influence who applies for a role. Field experiments have shown the importance of writing job ads in an inclusive way to diversify the profiles of job applicants. For instance, signaling employers' interest in employee diversity more than doubles the application of candidates of racial/ethnic minority background.[72] Similarly, explicitly stating that both men and women are expected to apply when the job ad concerns a position that is typically male-dominated allows significantly increasing the share of female job applicants.[73]

How about approaches aimed at making career management less subject to unconscious bias? A growing literature is providing critical insights into strategies to limit discrimination in performance assessment and/or promotion to high managerial positions. For instance, changing the scale of a quantitative rating of performance from a 1–10 to a 1–6 scale hinders managers' tendency to give men higher performance ratings than women, even when their qualifications and behaviors are identical.[74] Indeed, individuals are less likely to associate a 6/6 rating with extraordinary performance than they are a 10/10 rating, which means, in a context where sexist norms lead to reserving labels like "superstar" and "genius" for men, that the six-point scale limits the expression of gender bias more than the ten-point scale does.[75] Similarly, a longer shortlist increases the consideration of female candidates for executive-level positions.[76]

Last, in a context where algorithms increasingly influence hiring and career management, it is critical to train employers on responsible artificial intelligence (AI) use.[77] Machine learning algorithms rely on training data sets to build models that capture relationships between individual factors and specific outcomes. For instance, these models can predict the likelihood of an applicant being hired after an interview or assess an employee's job performance once hired. Once established, the model can then be applied to forecast outcomes for new applicants.

Some observers believe that AI can serve as a powerful tool to reduce discrimination. By uncovering predictive patterns, AI can potentially enable employers to identify high-quality candidates that human recruiters, susceptible to biases, might overlook.[78] However, this benefit only holds if AI models are trained on unbiased data; otherwise, automated methods risk reinforcing existing biases.[79] In an illustrative case, Bloomberg used GPT to generate eight different résumés with identical educational attainment, job titles, and work experience.[80] The only variation was in the names, which represented different demographic groups: men and women who were Black, white, Hispanic, or Asian. Names were randomly assigned to each résumé, and GPT was prompted to rank candidates for a real job opening at a Fortune 500 company. Even though all résumés were equally qualified, GPT ranked one candidate highest. After one thousand iterations with various names and combinations, the results revealed clear evidence of name-based discrimination. Ideally, each of the eight demographic groups would be ranked as the top candidate 12.5 percent of the time. Instead, names associated with Black Americans were consistently the least likely to be selected for a financial analyst role.

Such bias is particularly likely given that most modern hiring algorithms rely on "exploitation," which focuses on identifying the characteristics of applicants that historically have predicted success. This approach, known as supervised learning, works well when firms have extensive data on past applicants and when past success predictors remain relevant over time. However, these assumptions often fall short. Candidates from nontraditional backgrounds may be underrepresented in the training data precisely because of discrimination, hindering accurate performance predictions. Additionally, skill demands evolve, as demonstrated by the emphasis on remote work capabilities during and in the immediate aftermath of the COVID-19 pandemic.

To counteract this issue, a team of researchers tackled hiring as a dynamic learning problem by assessing candidates based on their potential or "option value."[81] Their algorithm introduced an "exploration bonus" that prioritizes candidates about whom the firm has limited data. These individuals might be rare because of their educational attainment, work history, or demographics, but their potential offers valuable learning opportunities. This concept, known as "hiring as exploration," encourages firms to take a chance on lesser-known applicants. Using data from a Fortune 500 firm's professional services recruitment, the research team demonstrated that incorporating an exploration approach into hiring algorithms improved candidate quality (as measured by eventual hiring rates) and increased demographic diversity compared to the firm's existing practices. In contrast, algorithms based on exploitation improved hiring rates but resulted in significantly fewer Black and Hispanic applicants being selected. Specifically, the exploration approach yielded more than three times as many Black and Hispanic candidates as traditional résumé-screening algorithms.

## Eradicating Discrimination in the Labor Market Also Entails Educating Society at Large

Addressing prejudice toward outgroups necessitates a two-pronged approach. First, schools play a pivotal role in molding individuals' values from a young age. It is imperative that prejudice-reduction training be woven into the curriculum beginning in the earliest school years and continuing consistently throughout a student's entire educational journey. Second, efforts to combat prejudice shouldn't cease on graduation. It is equally crucial to implement and support such training outside the educational system, to guarantee that individuals remain engaged with positive intergroup interactions even after their formal schooling concludes.

### Combating Prejudice and Stereotypes at School

Twenty-first-century students live in a world that is more globalized and diverse than ever before. Young people today must learn not only to navigate an interconnected world but also to appreciate and benefit from interactions with diverse groups. This ability is what the OECD terms "global competence."[82] In several countries, targeted classroom sessions are designed to enhance students' capacity for positive interactions with outgroups.

Achieving this objective involves using techniques aimed at reducing prejudice and stereotypes against these groups. Evidence indicates that not only the substance but also the format of these techniques matters: they are most effective when used in interpersonal conversations that allow for nonjudgmental exchanges of narratives.[83] On the substance, three distinct techniques are commonly employed, all seeking to narrow the perceived distance from the outgroup.[84]

The foremost among these is education. This method revolves around presenting fact-based information about the outgroup, thereby debunking common misconceptions that arise from negative biases. A particularly effective example of this technique is "counterstereotypic imaging." Participants are encouraged to reflect on members of both their own group and the outgroup who defy prevalent prejudice and stereotypes. The objective is to highlight that such counterexamples are far from rare, challenging the ingrained positive perceptions of the in-group and negative views of the outgroup. For instance, a team of psychologists exposed white students to images of highly respected African Americans (e.g., the actor and director Denzel Washington) juxtaposed with images of widely disliked white individuals (e.g., serial killer Jeffrey Dahmer).[85] Using an IAT, the researchers demonstrated that this exposure substantially reduced the students' negative bias toward African Americans, with the effect persisting even twenty-four hours after the experiment.

However, presenting fact-based information about an outgroup might not always negate deeply entrenched negative prejudices and stereotypes. For example, a team of economists studied the effectiveness of fact-checking in counteracting misleading statements made by politicians.[86] Using an online randomized experiment during the 2017 French presidential election campaign, they surveyed nearly 2,500 French voters. While the exposure to accurate facts about the European refugee crisis improved voters' knowledge, it did not diminish their support for the extreme-right candidate, Marine Le Pen, even though she perpetuated several myths about the crisis. Given these findings, it is essential to supplement the "education" approach with techniques that can better ignite individual empathy and foster a deeper connection with the outgroup.

One such complementary technique for reducing prejudice and stereotypes is "perspective taking" or "perspective giving." Perspective taking seeks to foster empathy by prompting participants to walk a mile in the shoes of outgroup members. In a landmark study, students were randomly divided into two groups. Both groups were shown a photograph of a young African American man and tasked with writing a brief essay about a day in that individual's life. However, there was a twist: students in the treatment group were instructed to vividly imagine the target person's thoughts, feelings, and experiences, adopting his perspective, while the control group was encouraged to remain objective and detached. The results were illuminating. Those in the treatment group displayed not only reduced bias on a subsequent IAT but also demonstrated more amicable body language toward African Americans they interacted with during the experiment. They smiled more frequently, maintained prolonged eye contact, and leaned in, as opposed to maintaining a distant posture.[87] Empathy can also be activated through perspective giving. For instance, a session aimed at raising awareness about the importance of greater LGBTIQ+ inclusion might feature prerecorded testimonials from victims of anti-LGBTIQ+ harassment or a coming-out story from one of the session facilitators. These personal narratives often provide poignant accounts of the challenges faced in self-acceptance and gaining acceptance from family and friends, deeply resonating with the audience.

The final key technique to counter prejudice and stereotypes is known as "social (re)categorization." This strategy encourages participants to perceive members of the outgroup as part of their own in-group. It aims to highlight shared commonalities, fostering a sense of unity. A telling laboratory experiment among university students in the UK underscores the impact of erasing perceived intergroup boundaries.[88] In the treatment group, participants identified and elaborated on five shared characteristics between white and Black individuals. Meanwhile, the control group listed commonalities between cars and bicycles. Results illustrated the efficacy of the social (re)categorization approach: students in the treatment group exhibited significantly reduced biases against Black individuals compared to those in the control group.

The efficacy of lab-tested techniques in school settings was scrutinized by the OECD.[89] In its efforts to promote LGBTIQ+ inclusion, the organization conducted the first ever large-scale randomized controlled trial, involving over 10,000 students aged thirteen to eighteen years, to evaluate the impact of school-based interventions aimed at combating homophobia and transphobia. Of note, these interventions have the distinct advantage of leveraging the three previously discussed prejudice-reducing techniques. The results are encouraging. Just two hours of structured, open discussion can significantly enhance students' receptiveness to LGBTIQ+ inclusion. These findings allow debunking two widespread myths: first, the belief that such brief sessions cannot produce meaningful change, and second, the concern that they might backfire owing to the possibility of hateful remarks being made against outgroups. While it is true that negative group dynamics can emerge, they neither consistently arise nor are powerful enough to overshadow the positive effect of these school-based interventions.

It is important to note that the role of schools in combating prejudice and stereotypes extends beyond formal training sessions. Day-to-day interactions with classmates from different backgrounds are paramount in fostering less prejudiced intergroup relations in adulthood. To underscore this point, a study led by economists revealed that early exposure to racial diversity for white students leads to more positive attitudes and behaviors toward Blacks later in life.[90] Using the random variation in the proportion of Black students across U.S. school cohorts, the researchers determined that white adults who had greater interactions with Black peers of the same gender during their formative years reported lower levels of prejudice against Blacks. Consequently, they were more likely to be in romantic relationships with Black individuals. The researchers were diligent in emphasizing that this effect wasn't merely due to an increase in opportunities for indirect meetings, such as encountering a romantic partner through school acquaintances. If that were the primary reason, one would anticipate a stronger impact of racial diversity exposure on interracial romantic relationships formed during school years or involving a partner in the vicinity of the school. However, the study yielded no evidence supporting such a differential effect. Overall, these findings highlight the need to step up efforts to limit racial segregation in schools.

## Combating Prejudice and Stereotypes Outside School

Nonjudgmental exchanges of narratives that build on established prejudice-reduction techniques have proved to be effective outside schools. This evidence was observed during a door-to-door operation in Florida in 2014. Following passage of an ordinance by a local authority that protected transgender people from discrimination in housing, employment, and public accommodations, there were fears that this decision might be put to a citizens' vote and subsequently repealed. In response, LGBTIQ+ associations embarked on a voter education campaign.

To gauge its impact, they partnered with two political scientists, David Broockman and Joshua Kalla.[91] In this study, 501 electors were randomly divided into two groups. Investigators visited them with the aim of raising awareness on one of two topics: household waste recycling (for the control group) or protection of transgender people (for the treatment group)—all within a brief ten-minute window. The strategy used for the treatment group aimed to bridge the perceived gap between voters and the transgender community. Specifically, voters were encouraged to reflect on a time when they felt ostracized because of their differences and to consider the parallels between their experiences and the discrimination faced by transgender individuals (a mix of perspective taking and social (re)categorization technique). Remarkably, even with its short duration, the intervention proved highly effective. The results indicated that participants became significantly more accepting of transgender individuals and more supportive of decisions that prohibited discrimination against them. These effects were still present three months post-intervention.

Yet, scaling up nonjudgmental exchanges of narratives centered on prejudice reduction to curb exclusionary attitudes and behaviors is a challenge. Several alternatives have thus been tested, notably in the framework of antiracism public campaigns. One approach involves urging the public not to discriminate, while another adopts a humorous angle, poking fun at the prejudice or negative stereotype in question to invalidate it.[92] Take, for instance, the injunctive slogan "*Touche pas à mon pote*" ("Hands off my pal"), introduced in 1984 by the organization SOS Racisme, a French NGO dedicated to combating racism. Another example is the poster campaign conducted in the early 2000s by Adia, a temporary employment company now operating as Adecco. A poster from this campaign featured a young man of African descent, pictured in profile, with a hood covering his head.

Boldly emblazoned across his chest are the words, "This young man is a breaker." Beneath it, in smaller print, the text reads: "of received ideas. You might see someone wasting hours in training, assuming he lacks skills. Yet, with Adia, he is constantly exploring new experiences. You might picture him breaking into cars, but to his employers, he epitomizes respect." The poster concludes with a commanding message: "Don't be fooled by appearances, trust in skills."[93]

The effectiveness of these approaches remains debatable, however. Abdelatif Er-rafiy and Markus Brauer compared these two approaches with each other and with one of the established prejudice-reducing techniques, social (re)categorization.[94] To operationalize this technique, the researchers created a poster intended to highlight the diversity intrinsic to any group. This was aimed at showcasing that the outgroup exhibits a variety of characteristics, much as the in-group does, thereby promoting a sense of shared identity. The poster presented twelve portraits of individuals of North African descent, each accompanied by a caption indicating their name, age, and a specific trait or aspiration. These traits ranged from clearly positive to neutral or mildly negative, such as "Ilham, 18, chess champion"; "Samir, 34, talkative"; "Aisha, 30, frugal"; "Said, 42, skilled handyman"; and "Abdel, 28, aspiring comedian." Concluding the poster was a striking message: "Our shared trait: diversity."

The authors demonstrated that participants randomly exposed to the latter poster had lower scores on McConahay's modern racism scale compared with participants exposed to the straightforward directive, "Discrimination . . . STOP!" or to a poster designed after the Adia campaign.[95] Moreover, those in the social (re)categorization group were less prone to associating the North African population with negative stereotypes. They were also more receptive to generously offering their assistance to an association fostering intercultural dialogue between the French and North Africans.

Overall, abundant evidence underscores the efficacy of prejudice-reducing techniques that foster a sense of closeness to outgroups. While ideal implementation would involve direct, nonjudgmental interpersonal interactions, this isn't feasible for large-scale public campaigns because of the exorbitant costs. However, there is cause for optimism. As exemplified by the poster designed by Er-rafiy and Brauer, it is possible to craft content that both applies the spirit of these techniques and is suited for mass media dissemination—whether through print, broadcast, and digital media or through billboards, posters, and electronic displays in public spaces. Personal perspectives or narratives from outgroup members that provide a human face and convey their experiences in their own words stand out as promising content.[96] Not only is this approach low-cost and scalable (since the narratives can easily be prerecorded or transcribed for mass dissemination), it has also been shown to diminish negative attitudes toward the outgroup, whether in high-income or lower-income countries.[97]

For instance, given the current heightened public backlash against immigration—especially toward Muslims in Christian-majority countries because of their perceived association with global terrorism—a team of political scientists sought to explore the potential of personal narratives in reducing hostility against immigrant outgroups.[98] They zeroed in on the Somali population in Kenya, which includes both refugees and long-time citizens. This group faces increasing prejudice owing to the surge of terrorist attacks in Kenya by al-Shabaab, a militant group originating in southern Somalia. In this context, the researchers assessed the influence of prerecorded personal narratives on perceptions of immigrant outgroups through a representative public opinion survey in Nairobi. Two narratives were created: one, voiced by a Somali refugee, was designed to evoke empathy, highlighting the struggles of refugees and expressing gratitude to the Kenyan public. The second, meant to underscore civic-mindedness and a shared sense of Kenyan nationality, was delivered by a Kenyan of Somali descent, emphasizing the widespread opposition to Islamic terrorism among Muslim Somalis in Kenya, comparable to the opposition prevailing among Christian Kenyans.

The study revealed that both prerecorded personal narratives significantly improved Kenyan attitudes toward Somali refugees and Kenyan Somalis. For instance, the narrative detailing refugee hardships increased the proportion of refugees deemed eligible for citizenship by seven percentage points. It also bolstered support for keeping Dadaab, the primary camp housing Somali refugees, open—opposing the forcible repatriation of its residents—by seventeen percentage points. Meanwhile, the antiterror narrative elevated perceptions of Somalis as peaceful by ten percentage points and resulted in a fourteen percentage point uptick in the belief that Kenyan Somalis should retain their citizenship rather than be sent back to Somalia. Remarkably, these effects were consistent across various demographic groups, including those initially holding more negative views. In summary, this research underscores the power of simply hearing a prerecorded personal narrative from an immigrant outgroup member. Even without direct interactions or other interventions, such narratives can effectively counteract negative intergroup perceptions, even among those with the strongest preexisting biases.

## Empowering Minorities to Defy Stereotypes Associated with Them

All minorities face negative stereotypes that contribute to statistical discrimination against them. This is evident among such groups as women and racial/ethnic minorities. Even though these stereotypes are deeply rooted in misconceptions and distortions, it is essential to actively confront and debunk them, ensuring they never gain a semblance of validity.

### Women

Chapter 5 detailed the challenges women face in maintaining consistent career involvement relative to men, since social norms still result in women doing the bulk of domestic and family work. This disproportionate burden leads to statistical discrimination against women of childbearing age when seeking employment in high-paying firms or pursuing senior managerial roles within firms. Unequal sharing of unpaid work between men and women also negatively affects women's bargaining power, limiting them to job opportunities within close commuting distances. Limiting statistical discrimination against women would thus require ensuring a more equal involvement of men and women in paid work, on the one hand, and domestic and family work on the other. A promising strategy to promote gender balance revolves around extending paternity leave and boosting its uptake through mechanisms such as a "father quota" (a period of leave exclusively for fathers) or a "bonus period" (extra paid leave provided if fathers commit to a certain leave period). Substantial evidence indicates that fostering equal caregiving around a child's birth leads to a ripple effect of gender-balanced parenting as the child grows. This effect, with varying intensities, is observed in Australia, Canada, Denmark, France, Germany, Spain, Sweden, the UK, and the United States.[99] Specifically, when fathers take extended leave, they become more involved in childcare and domestic tasks. The longer the leave, the more profound and lasting these effects are, persisting even after the leave ends. Such behavioral shifts can even influence the next generation. For instance, in Spain, researchers found that an additional thirteen days of paternity leave introduced in 2007 (on top of only two days before the reform) not only achieved the immediate goal of fathers spending more time at home during their children's infancy but also left a lasting impact on subsequent generations.[100] Children born after the policy change exhibit more gender egalitarian attitudes. They are also more likely to engage in counterstereotypical day-to-day behaviors and to deviate from the conventional male-as-breadwinner model in their adult lives.

The example of Sweden, however, indicates that efforts to increase fathers' parental leave and foster its uptake must be gradual, otherwise they will be counterproductive. The initial 1995 reform was notably abrupt, introducing thirty days of paternity leave while proportionally reducing maternity leave. This reform was detrimental to women in the short term since they compensated for the decrease in paid maternity leave by taking additional unpaid time off work, resulting in a decline in total household income.[101] The policy also led to an increase in divorce among couples where women were the least involved in the labor market and where traditional gender norms were therefore most entrenched. These adverse effects did not, however, arise in the case of the second reform of Swedish parental leave in 2002.[102] Although it extended paternity leave by another thirty days, the reform was nonetheless perceived as less radical than the first. By then, most fathers had already become accustomed to having thirty days' paid leave following the birth of a child.

To fully reap the benefits of fathers' parental leave reforms, it is crucial not only to introduce these reforms gradually but also to implement them in environments where the parental leave benefits are sufficiently generous. Two economists analyzed the outcomes of a 2015 reform in France that allocated up to twelve months of paid leave exclusively for fathers.[103] At the same time, it reduced the maximum paid leave for mothers by the same duration. Despite these changes, there was a negligible rise in the number of fathers taking parental leave. Prior to the reform, only about 2.4 percent of fathers availed themselves of such leave. After the reform, while mothers experienced a twenty-five percentage point decline in their participation rate because of the reduced leave, the rate of fathers taking leave increased by less than one percentage point. A potential reason for this minimal impact could be the reform's unchanged low parental leave benefit, equivalent to one-third of the minimum wage. Only regions with less traditional gender norms saw a more significant effect from the reform.

### Racial/Ethnic Minorities

In the majority of OECD countries, racial/ethnic minorities primarily consist of immigrants and their immediate descendants, especially when they come from regions different from that of the host country (e.g., individuals of non-European origin residing in Europe). However, their integration is not guaranteed, as they often face negative stereotypes. First, it is believed that immigrants may have limited proficiency in the language of the host country. Moreover, there is fear that they might be unfamiliar with—and therefore might not adhere to—the laws and institutions of the host country. It is also sometimes assumed they bring values that clash with those of the host society.

To minimize the likelihood that immigrants conform to these stereotypes, several European governments initiated so-called civic integration policies in the late 1990s. In practice, they condition entry, permanent residence, or citizenship on acquiring language and civic skills, which include learning about the host country's history, laws, and institutions, as well as values. Key principles emphasized are gender equality and the freedom of religion and belief. This means an individual's right to believe (or not) as they see fit and to practice (or abstain from practicing) their religion, as long as this right doesn't infringe on others' fundamental rights or jeopardize public safety. The Netherlands was the first, in 1998, to introduce a twelve-month integration course for newcomers. Austria, Belgium (Flanders), Denmark, Germany, and France soon followed suit, implementing similar mandatory integration requirements in the early 2000s. Today, at least sixteen European countries have established clear criteria for fulfilling integration contracts or agreements.[104]

Despite the popularity of these policies in Europe, evidence as to whether civic integration policies help integration is relatively thin. So far, only three research projects have specifically addressed this topic. Each of these studies looked at the impact of France's free-of-charge integration contract, initially termed *Contrat d'accueil et d'intégration* in 2003 and later renamed

*Contrat d'intégration républicaine* in 2016. The results are disappointing. They show that the language training of the French integration contract had no effect on the probability of finding employment.[105] It did, however, have an impact on the intensive margin: for employed immigrants, a longer duration of training significantly increased their chances of having a formal sector job and a permanent employment contract.[106] A potential reason for these lackluster results could be the training's target demographic. It was proposed only to immigrants who failed at a test gauging skills at an A1.1 level (deemed a "survival" level). This suggests the training's goals might have been too conservative. It aimed at merely imparting a survival level of proficiency, while a foundational level would have been more apt to increase employers' inclination to hire individuals who had been through the training.

Concerning the civic training component of the French integration contract, a team of political scientists has demonstrated that it didn't revolutionize the integration of immigrants either.[107] The team's findings revealed that, although there was a notable increase in the likelihood of employment within a year of arrival, this effect vanished in the medium to long term. Such an outcome suggests that the policy simply bolstered immigrants' onboarding into the labor market by a few months. A key factor in this acceleration appeared to be the information exchange that occurred before, during, and after the classes. Participants and instructors utilized this time to share their experiences in France and offer valuable insights into French life and the labor market.

However, this modest impact of the civic training should be interpreted with caution. The structure and organization of the training might not have been conducive to eliciting significant change. First, the renewal of residency permits was based on attendance at the civic training, not on passing a test that ensured participants had gained a minimum level of knowledge. As a result, participants might not have been fully engaged with the content. Second, the authors' assessment pertains to a period when France offered one of the shortest civic training durations in comparison to other regions. Specifically, the civic training in France lasted eight hours, whereas it was thirty hours in Germany, sixty hours in Flanders, and seventy-five hours in Austria. Evaluating the impact of the current civic training, as structured within the *Contrat d'intégration républicaine*, might produce more favorable results since the duration of the civic training has now been extended to four days, totaling forty hours.

It is important to highlight that the authors found no evidence of integration contracts causing any backlash. One might assume that by requiring that immigrants learn about the host country's values and customs, these contracts could inadvertently alienate them. This is because such mandates might implicitly suggest that the immigrants' own values and customs are deficient or less acceptable. However, the authors found no evidence that specific subgroups of immigrants, such as those from Muslim-majority countries, who might feel especially targeted by these policies, were affected differently by civic integration policies compared with immigrants from other countries.

Finally, it is essential to ensure that immigrants and their families are settled in areas with optimal economic prospects. This would prevent the all-too-common scenario of them ending up in underprivileged neighborhoods, a pattern that helps perpetuate stereotypes associating immigrants with unemployment (and thus economic burden) and even criminality.[108] In this setting, data-driven algorithmic assignment seems very promising. Kirk Bansak, an assistant professor of political science at the University of California, Berkeley, and his coauthors relied on a combination of supervised machine learning and optimal matching to discover and leverage synergies between refugee characteristics and resettlement sites.[109] The authors then tested the resulting algorithm on historical registry data from two countries with different assignment regimes and refugee populations, the United States and Switzerland. Relative to current assignment practices, their approach led to gains of roughly 40 to 70 percent, on average, in refugees' employment outcomes.

* * *

The two commonly lauded antidiscrimination strategies in the labor market, affirmative action and blind job application procedures, often fall short of their intended outcomes. To truly motivate employers to combat discrimination, it is essential to establish mechanisms that monitor their hiring practices and career management behaviors. Yet monitoring alone isn't sufficient. For meaningful action against discrimination, employers need to be aware not only of its prevalence within their organizations but also of effective remedies. Relying solely on unconscious bias training is inadequate; while it can serve as a foundational step, it should be part of broader organizational change, including the implementation of human resources strategies that deny conscious and unconscious bias a chance to operate. Eradicating discrimination in the labor market also entails educating society at large. This calls for the integration of prejudice-reduction training both within and outside the educational system. Finally, it is vital to empower minorities to defy stereotypes associated with them, and thus make sure those stereotypes never gain a semblance of validity.

# 12 Ensuring Equal Opportunities Upstream of the Labor Market

Research leaves little doubt that prejudices and stereotypes—indeed, hostility and outright hatred—are vectors of discrimination against women and many minorities. But discrimination can operate more insidiously, even before entry into the labor market.

When potentially affected individuals expect that they will encounter hostile behavior, they may have to change their education or career choices: as examples, women may avoid engineering courses and gay men may avoid applying to jobs in industry, the police service, or the army. The negative expectations associated with discriminated groups can even adversely affect their skills, especially when those expectations are expressed by teachers or parents. As examples, girls are commonly deemed to be less good at math and boys to be more competitive, while children from an immigrant background are supposed to have more trouble in class. Equally marked—and not always conscious—are the expectations about the chances of academic success for young people from disadvantaged backgrounds. Minorities internalize these stereotypes and suffer the stress they generate.

In the end, minority groups will not be working in the same sectors or with the same type of employer as the majority group, and will not have the same skills. This will lead to differences in wages or access to employment when they enter the labor market. Admittedly, these differences may be related to "objective" factors such as preferences, psychological traits, or mathematical abilities that differ from one group to another. But this does not mean that there is an absence of discrimination. In fact, it will be expressed upstream of the labor market. It is therefore essential to counter these self-fulfilling mechanisms that hamper people's development and achievement.[1]

## Preferences That Matter in Terms of Risk, Competition, and Negotiation

As stressed in chapter 5, a liking for or, conversely, aversion to risk-taking can strongly influence wage progression. Risk-averse individuals tend to prefer jobs that ensure a more stable income but that are also less well remunerated on average. This link is statistically well attested. Using the German socioeconomic panel, which has tracked thousands of individuals over the last three decades and includes a question on attitude toward risk, we find that people who are more risk-averse are also more likely to work in occupations where earnings vary and do not increase much over time.[2] And, according to this German survey, women as a group are the least likely to take risks.[3]

Attitudes toward competition are also gender dependent and likewise affect earnings. Many high-paying professions have highly competitive working environments, in which women tend to feel less comfortable. In a laboratory experiment conducted in the United States, the economists Muriel Niederle and Lise Vesterlund asked participants to solve arithmetic problems.[4] While men and women performed equally well in both non-competitive and competitive environments, men were more likely to opt for competition when given a choice of their working environment: three quarters of them preferred a tournament-style competitive framework, compared to only one-third of women.

The discrepancy cannot be explained by differences in numeracy because women perform as well as men. Rather, men choose the knock-out format simply because they are more confident than women of winning. This expectation is sometimes self-fulfilling, as the economists Evren Örs, Frédéric Palomino, and Eloïc Peyrache have demonstrated.[5] On the basis of the performances of nearly six thousand students who passed the highly selective entry examination to the Paris-based HEC business school, the authors showed that male candidates did better than female candidates on both the written and the oral components. On the other hand, their performance was weaker both two years earlier, at the *baccalaureat* level (high school diploma) and, for the subsample that passed the entrance exam, at the end of their first year at HEC. The findings did not stem from a greater propensity among boys to focus on high-powered subjects at the time of the entrance examination since the disparity in their marks on the exam was the same as that of girls. Rather, the results suggest that girls are less amenable to competitive environments, even though they do better than boys in the absence of competition.

Unequal bargaining skills can also explain some of the wage gap between men and women. In a pay negotiation game in a laboratory setting in which the 122 participants played the role of employees, German researchers found that men consistently asked for higher salaries than women.[6] And when the participants negotiated as employers, men made higher initial salary offers to men than to women, whereas women treated employees of both genders on an equal footing. In other words, the behavior of employers does not compensate for women's lower propensity to negotiate a high salary. But it is possible to give women a boost, for example in the wording of the job offer. Thus, in a field experiment, Andreas Leibbrandt and John List published real job offers in nine U.S. cities, some of which explicitly mentioned that wages were negotiable while others did not.[7] Nearly 2,500 applicants responded to the offers. The authors show that women are 23 percent less likely than men to negotiate a higher salary than specified in the advertisement, when it is not explicitly described as negotiable. But the reverse is the case when it is clear that the salary is negotiable: women are then 8 percent more likely than men to negotiate a higher salary. These findings suggest, therefore, that women need to be encouraged to enter into negotiations because otherwise some of them "do not dare."

## Conforming to Stereotypes

These psychological traits depend less on innate preferences than on pressure to conform to stereotypes that are established at an early age, as has been shown by two, respectively British and Australian economists, Alison Booth and Patrick Nolen. In an experiment conducted in 2012, they asked students aged eleven to fifteen years from eight mixed-sex and single-sex schools in the UK to play a lottery with two options: either to get £5 with certainty or to toss a coin and get £11 if it came down heads and £2 if it came down tails. Before deciding, the boys and girls from the various schools were randomly allocated to different groups: girls only, boys only, and mixed. By comparing students with similar educational and family backgrounds, the researchers were able to show that girls attending girls' schools chose the risky option as often as boys, unlike their counterparts from mixed-sex schools. However, the latter were more likely to choose the risky option when allocated to the girls-only group rather than a mixed group.[8]

But that was not all. The researchers also asked the girls and boys in each group to solve maze puzzles in a limited amount of time, with payment depending either on the number of mazes individually solved or on their performance-based ranking within the group. When they were given the choice of payment, girls from girls' schools behaved more like boys in that they were much more likely to choose the competitive option. This was not the case, however, for girls from mixed schools. Furthermore, there was no difference between boys from mixed schools and boys from boys-only schools.

As already mentioned in chapter 2, negative stereotypes regarding a minority group can affect the performance of its members simply by mentioning that they belong to that group. Pioneering studies on the effect of social identity in the United States have shown that getting students to tick a box specifying their ethnic origin prior to giving them an aptitude test is enough to reduce the performance of African American students compared to the performance of white students.[9] The stress produced by the mere mention of the stereotype causes participants to lose time and concentration. While these findings suggest that stereotypes can influence people's behavior from an early age, there is nonetheless nothing inevitable about such behavior. Indeed, it is possible to change the situation by influencing the educational and family environment on a lasting basis.

## The Golem and Pygmalion Effects

Similarly, young (and not so young) people also tend to conform to prejudices about their chances of success. The "Golem effect" is a well-known psychological phenomenon in which lower expectations of an individual's performance actually lead to failure. The term is derived from the Jewish legend that a clay creature, the golem, is brought to life by its creator, but eventually becomes an uncontrollable monster that must be destroyed. The "Pygmalion effect" is the opposite. In the Greek myth, Pygmalion carves an ivory statue, Galatea, representing his ideal of beauty. His love for her brings her to life. In other words, simply believing that someone will succeed can actually improve their chances of success. Both these effects are examples of self-fulfilling prophecies.

The Pygmalion effect was the first of these two phenomena to be studied in the framework of social psychology. In a famous experiment carried out in the United States in the late 1960s, two American psychologists, Robert Rosenthal and Lenore Jacobson, sought to influence teachers' views of their students at the beginning of the academic year.[10] Rosenthal and Jacobson made the teachers believe that some students had greater intellectual potential than others because of their higher IQ test results. In fact, these students were randomly selected, and their IQ test results were manipulated. However, the students with the supposedly higher IQs scored 50 percent more points than their peers on an IQ test—a genuine one this time—carried out later in the year. The two researchers proposed these students' better performance was due to the greater attention paid to them by the teachers. In other words, teachers' beliefs, whether true or false, about certain groups of young people can strongly influence their academic performance and thus their professional future.

This experiment has been replicated on many occasions.[11] The early ones, however, were based on small samples, which may have led to either underestimation or overestimation of the Pygmalion effect because of the inaccuracy of the findings. A review of the recent literature concludes that there really is a Pygmalion effect in the classroom, though probably more modest than suggested by Rosenthal and Jacobson.[12] Complementary work shows that self-fulfilling expectations are not confined to teachers but are also found among managers, as revealed by two Israeli psychologists, Dov Eden and Abraham Shani, in a replication of the original Rosenthal and Jacobson experiment in the Israeli armed forces.[13]

There are fewer studies of the Golem effect, probably because it is more difficult to create a belief in people's limitations rather than in their potential. Not only is this the case in practical terms, people's limitations being easier to observe than their potential, but also from an ethical standpoint, since inducing teachers or managers to lower their expectations about someone can be very penalizing for the individual concerned.

But the Golem effect seems to be as much at work as the Pygmalion effect. In one study of the expectations of twenty-six physical education teachers regarding the athletic potential of more than two hundred students, it was found that students with the lowest teacher expectations performed worst, and vice versa.[14] Furthermore, when the teachers were induced to believe that some students had greater sports potential than others, they paid them more attention, thereby enabling them to improve their performance, to the detriment of the other students' performance.

Teachers' expectations may also result in systematic, and not always conscious, bias in terms of marking. Two Israeli researchers, Victor Lavy and Edith Sand, identified such biases by following three cohorts of schoolchildren in Tel Aviv, from primary through to secondary level.[15] They compared the grades the teachers gave to boys and to girls according to whether or not the exercise was anonymous. They found that the teachers tended to mark boys higher, with long-term effects on the students' performance. For example, a boy who early in school is assigned to a teacher displaying gender bias will do better than others. The reverse is the case for girls. In particular, when the biased teacher happens to teach math, girls are less inclined to choose mathematics from among the optional courses offered at the high school level. In the Italian context, Michela Carlana found similar results for gender-biased math teachers.[16] She showed that being exposed to these teachers lowers self-confidence among girls as to their ability in math. This suggests that teachers' behavior in the early stages of schooling can have long-run implications for occupational choices and earnings in adulthood. For instance, barriers to women's participation in mathematically intensive academic science fields are now probably more influenced by what happens in middle school and high school than by discriminatory behaviors in universities.[17]

Unconscious bias can also alter the evaluation of young migrants by teachers. Based on a randomized experiment in Northern Italy middle schools, Alberto Alesina, Michela Carlana, Eliana La Ferrara, and Paolo Pinotti from Harvard University and Bocconi University found that, with performance on standardized, blindly graded tests held constant, immigrant students tend to receive lower grades than natives when they are graded by their teachers in a nonblind way.[18] This grading gap is correlated with teachers' results from an implicit association test (IAT), especially for high-performing immigrants. Indeed, about 70 percent of teachers involved in the experiment exhibited moderate to severe stereotypes based on such tests. Hopefully, this grade gap can be reduced through the use of debiasing techniques. The researchers showed that revealing to teachers their IAT results before the teachers assign grades reduces the native-immigrant grade gap. They also showed that using such individualized tests is more effective for severely biased teachers than just making them aware of the generic existence of conscious and unconscious biases and the potential consequences of such biases for students' educational attainment.

These effects may in part be transmitted through young people's aspirations. The economists Nina Guyon and Elise Huillery followed 3,400 young people at the end of intermediate schooling in fifty-nine schools in the Paris region.[19] They showed that for a given school, and with similar family backgrounds and academic records, fourteen-year-olds who aspire less to join the general stream of high school (preferring to take vocational training or an apprenticeship) also have poorer academic results a year later. Yet aspirations are strongly dependent on social origin. Children from underprivileged backgrounds aspire less often than others to complete high school and go on to higher education. One of the reasons for this relative lack of ambition is that they are less well informed about educational pathways and the opportunities they offer. But they also have lower self-esteem, and are more pessimistic about their capacity to succeed. These factors undermine aspirations, even among the best students from disadvantaged backgrounds. Measures to raise aspirations and enhance self-confidence could therefore have a positive impact on their academic and professional trajectories.

## Ways of Strengthening Aspirations to Study and Work

Brief, inexpensive interventions can have lasting effects, provided they take place early enough, upstream of the labor market. For example, interacting with "success stories" can help young people imagine new possibilities and reinforce their feeling of self-efficacy—that is, their sense that they can influence the course of events through their own actions.[20]

Mentoring programs have demonstrated their potential, but they are still unusual, especially at a large scale. In the United States, the largest and oldest of such programs, Big Brothers Big Sisters (BBBS), aims to create a lasting link between young people from disadvantaged backgrounds and well-placed adults in the labor market. Far from simply being a platform for putting young people in touch with adults wanting to be involved, it is a highly organized social enterprise that monitors, orients, and trains mentors in their role and counsels them throughout the relationship they forge in their meetings with the child. Based on a controlled experiment in the United States, where more than one thousand young people were randomly assigned either to a BBBS program or to a control group and interviewed eighteen months later, Jean Grossman and Jean Rhodes evaluated the impact of BBBS on self-esteem, academic performance, and various social indicators, such as the perception of welfare, violent behavior at school, and drug use.[21] They found that the adolescents whose mentoring relationships lasted at least a year did better in school, were less violent, and used drugs less; they also attended school more regularly. Older teens and those experiencing violence had shorter mentoring relationships and underwent little improvement. The program, however, had no impact on school grades. The positive impact of mentoring on educational outcomes depends largely on the quality and strength of the relationship between the young person and the mentor, as well as on appropriate targeting regarding at-risk youth.[22] The quality hinges on the appropriate matching of mentors and mentees based on traits and attributes, but also on mentor emotional engagement and support, and the duration of the relationship.[23] The promotion of well-structured programs such as BBBS can thus have a significant and lasting impact by providing young people with a role model and aspirations that they may not find at home.

Role models in schools can also influence the course of student's life, either by directly counteracting certain stereotypes, or by affecting students' preferences for some disciplines, or by changing their beliefs regarding certain types of occupations. A significant literature has studied the influence of teachers' gender and ethnic membership on student behavior and performance.[24] For instance, female science teachers in high schools and female professors in universities can contribute to support female students' academic achievement and the chances that they enroll in science, technology, engineering, and mathematics (STEM) disciplines. But role models can also be found outside the faculty and still have a lasting influence on young females' educational and career choices, even when they involve relatively short interactions.[25] Thomas Breda, Julien Grenet, Marion Monnet, and Clémentine van Effenterre have evaluated the impact of a one-hour school-based intervention called "For Girls and Science" launched in 2014 by the L'Oréal Foundation whereby young female scientists share their experience and career path with the students.[26] The evaluation involved about 20,000 students from grade ten to twelve in ninety-eight high schools located in the Paris region who were randomly assigned to either treatment or control groups. The researchers found that this intervention significantly influenced the choices of high-achieving girls, who became more likely to enroll in selective and male-dominated STEM programs in college: the increase in the probability of enrolling in STEM programs was 28 percent for selective program (from a baseline rate of 11 percent) and 20 percent in male-dominated STEM programs (from a baseline rate of 17 percent). Thanks to a postintervention survey, they also identified through which channel this effect was mediated. The intervention had no significant effect on students' taste for science subjects or academic performance, but it significantly improved students' perceptions of science-related jobs and helped mitigate some of the stereotypes typically associated with STEM occupations (such as being hard to reconcile with family life).

The media can also play a major part in projecting role models. Women's place in economic and political life can be influenced by TV programs. Telenovelas (soap operas), mainly featuring women without children, have played an important role in bringing down the fertility rate in Latin America in recent years. To demonstrate the impact, three economists, Eliana La Ferrara, Alberto Chong, and Suzanne Duryea, focused on Brazil. In their study, they exploited the fact that while telenovelas are almost all produced and broadcast by Globo, this TV channel became available in the different regions of Brazil at different times.[27] The authors compared changes in the fertility rate in the areas where telenovelas were broadcast with the fertility rate in areas where they were not. They found that the rate was much lower in the former than in the latter, whereas this trend was not apparent before telenovelas began to be broadcast. The decline has been particularly marked among women viewers of a similar age to that of the lead female actors—thus those who were most likely to identify with the characters on screen. The authors estimate that the impact of telenovelas on the Brazilian fertility rate was equivalent to an increase of two years in women's education, with the rate falling by 11 percent on average among women aged between thirty-five and forty-four. Organizations such as BBC Media Action have learned the lessons of this type of work and are using radio and film as development tools around the world, tackling issues as diverse as improving the lot of migrants, using protection during sex, and the prevention of health problems.

In the same way, films or TV series that portray gay, lesbian, bisexual, or transgender characters in a positive light can inspire LGBTIQ+ people, especially young ones, to change the perception of their identity and help them fight against discrimination. Such films as the Canadian director Xavier Dolan's *Laurence Anyways*, Gus Van Sant's *Milk*, Todd Haynes's *Carol*, and the Chilean director Sebastián Lelio's *Una Mujer Fantàstica* convey positive images that can inspire LGBTIQ+ people to come to terms with their identity more easily. Media are part of the cultural context that contributes particularly to the LGBTIQ+ identity development and as such can influence self-realization and coming-out decisions by providing role models.[28] Being exposed to gay characters or personalities can also change how these groups are perceived by the general public.[29] A survey in the United States suggests that non-LGBTIQ+ people who have been exposed to LGBTIQ+ people in the media over the previous three months are more likely than those not so exposed to experience increasing levels of acceptance and comfort with homosexuality, bisexuality, and transgender people, to be more supportive of equal rights, and to be more comfortable in dealing with LGBTIQ+ people in their daily lives.[30]

### Countering Beliefs That Lead to Failure

Building self-esteem and a sense of belonging to the educational institution can improve the academic performance of students from disadvantaged groups. Because they know they belong to a group that is less successful than others, on entering secondary school or university many of these young people think it is not for them, that they don't fit in, or that they will be unable to surmount the difficulties ahead. An experiment was conducted in the United States with a representative sample of 10,000 high school students from disadvantaged backgrounds (mostly African American or Hispanic) newly admitted to university.[31] A random selection of these students took part in an online teaching module designed to reassure them (the treatment group) while the remainder were assigned to a placebo module (the control group). The treatment group module sought to reinforce the idea that these students were in no way out of place at university, making them understand that everyone encounters problems from time to time and that they were no less equipped than anyone else to deal with them. The results were revealing: a year later, 45 percent of the students in the treatment group were still at university and studying full-time, compared to 32 percent in the control group. In addition, the performance gap between these university students and the rest of their year was a third lower in the treatment group. Follow-up surveys also showed that those in the treatment group more often took the suggested support classes. Overall, their involvement in campus life and their sense of belonging to the educational institution were much greater.

Building confidence and self-esteem can also be achieved with lasting effects through specific, relatively short exercises. One technique that has been replicated in various contexts is to ask young people from minority or disadvantaged groups to reflect on their values. The aim is to restore their sense of personal integrity, thereby helping them overcome their anxiety at belonging to a group that may be deemed less successful than others. Four American psychologists, Geoffrey Cohen, Julio Garcia, Nancy Apfel, and Allison Master, invited randomly drawn twelve- to fourteen-year-olds to spend fifteen minutes writing an essay about the personal value that mattered most to them (the treatment group).[32] The essays were then given to their teachers to read, without revealing the names of the students who wrote them. A term after this intervention, the academic performance of the treatment group was much better than that of the control group (also comprising randomly selected twelve- to fourteen-year-olds, but who had not been asked to write an essay). The difference between the two was particularly marked for students from groups at high risk of dropping out of school: the proportion of African American students getting a D or F (the lowest grades) in the treatment group was only half that of the control group. More surprising was that these positive effects persisted over the two years following the intervention, without any need to repeat it.[33]

Another way of countering the internalization of expectations is to teach young people that intelligence is malleable rather than innate and set in stone. There is no doubt about this, even if psychologists debate the exact degree of malleability. Whatever the truth of the matter, research shows that young people's beliefs about the malleability of intelligence influence their performance. In a landmark study, the American psychologists Joshua Aronson, Carrie Fried, and Catherine Good tested the impact of training that demonstrates that intelligence is polymorphic and can progress over a person's lifetime. The training consisted of three one-hour sessions given to a hundred African American students recently admitted to Stanford University.[34] Each of them was then asked to convey in writing what they had learned to another student at risk of dropping out of school. Compared to a control group, the intervention resulted in an increase in the proportion of African American students convinced that intelligence is malleable. It also increased their enjoyment of study, their belief that higher education is important, and their academic performance.

Interventions of this kind are also effective on a large scale for more heterogeneous populations. Psychologists at Stanford University and the University of Texas produced two forty-five-minute videos and showed them to nearly 1,600 students in thirteen geographically diverse U.S. high schools.[35] The first video conveyed the idea that intelligence is malleable, and was followed by a discussion. The second video, also followed by a discussion, encouraged students to realize the importance of involvement in their studies for success in life. Even though a third of those in each group were at risk of dropping out of school, both these interventions significantly improved the students' academic performance in English and mathematics throughout the following year, compared to students in a control group. Further to this experiment, a group a psychologists and sociologists led by David Yeager designed an even larger scale, nationally representative, randomly controlled trial involving no less than 16,000 ninth grade students in seventy-six schools in the United States.[36] The intervention consisted in reading and listening to materials describing scientific evidence about how the brain works and why people can grow their intellectual abilities over time. The program also encouraged students to think about why they might want to develop their cognitive skills in order to make a difference in something that mattered to them. Then students were asked to write an essay in which they advised future ninth-graders how to ease the transition to high school, as a way to reflect on and synthesize what they just learned. The researchers showed that even this short (less than one hour), online growth mindset intervention improved grades among lower-achieving students and increased overall enrollment in advanced mathematics courses.

These results show that low-cost interventions can have considerable effect. Similar interventions are now being carried out on a large scale by the World Bank in various countries. In France, the Energie Jeunes association has set up a training program in the same vein, consisting of twelve one-hour sessions. The training is offered every year, from grade six to grade nine, for pupils aged from eleven through fifteen, in disadvantaged middle schools. The goal is to encourage pupils' perseverance, self-discipline, self-esteem, and motivation. The various exercises include making personal commitments, creating a personal report book and video testimonials, and participating in classroom discussions. The program has been evaluated by approximately 23,000 students in some one hundred schools throughout France and by randomly assigning classes to either the treatment or the control group. The program has had a positive impact on pupils' grades, with a median effect of 0.05 standard deviations on grade point average at the end of middle school, which is significant in view of the program's limited intensity and cost (about $75 per pupil). This was achieved by making students more optimistic about the possibility of improving their intelligence and academic abilities through effort, which in turn improved class attitude and optimism and reduced absenteeism and social fatalism.[37] However, even if the approach seems effective, such interventions run by external providers yield relatively limited improvements overall, suggesting that directly training teachers and parents who are in daily contact with students on how to develop their perseverance and conscientiousness may be necessary to achieve more substantial outcomes.[38]

### Learning How to Set Goals and Plan Work

A complementary approach to this work on beliefs and self-esteem involves helping young people set themselves goals and stick to them. In this respect, coaching can help struggling students determine what they want and make action plans to achieve it, and can then track their progress toward the goal on a day-to-day basis. A private U.S. provider, InsideTrack, offers this type of coaching to students enrolled in university. A study carried out on 14,000 students showed that this approach reduces the risk of dropping out compared to the dropout rate of students in a comparable position who have not had coaching, and that the positive effects persist for at least a year after the coaching ends.[39] The fact that the beneficial effects persist suggests that the students continue to apply the planning method they have learned.

The method can be applied from an early age in a school setting. As well as helping pupils define their goals, it also shows them how to handle difficulties by developing a complete action plan specifying the decisions to be made in the event of success or failure. This "WOOP" (wish, outcome, obstacle, plan) approach has been tested by American psychologists on eleven-year-old pupils from disadvantaged backgrounds.[40] The pupils were first asked to write down the most important academic goal they wanted to achieve in "the weeks or months to come," then to explain how that goal would change their lives if it were achieved. They were then divided into two groups on a random basis. Children in the first group were asked to imagine an obstacle that could compromise the realization of their goal, and to think of a way of overcoming it ("if . . . , then . . ."). In the second group, they were simply asked to imagine a second positive consequence if the goal were achieved. During the following year, the first group performed better than the second, and also distinguished itself by greater participation in class.

### Reducing Class Size in Disadvantaged Areas Where Minority Children Live

Counteracting stereotypes and setting aspirations may not be enough for children from minority groups to succeed in school. They usually come from disadvantaged family backgrounds, which also bears on their cognitive abilities—in reading or math—and noncognitive skills from an early age. Additional educational resources may be needed to fill these gaps.

Intervening early is key because skill acquisition is more fluid at an early age. Besides, family disadvantages are easily transmitted if not counteracted and influence the development of adults. As noted by James Heckman, winner of the Nobel Prize in Economic Sciences, skills beget skills and motivation fuels motivation. The opposite applies if capabilities are adversely affected early in life. A study by Flavio Cunha and James Heckman shows that in American society, about half of income inequality in life is attributable to factors determined before the age of eighteen.[41]

Launched in 1965, Head Start is one of the oldest children's programs in the United States targeted at disadvantaged, very young children, the overwhelming majority of whom are Black, Hispanic, or Native American. It was inspired by research in education, and especially by the famous 1960s Perry Preschool Pilot program.[42] This nationwide program is currently funded by the federal government and has helped nearly 40 million children since its inception. Head Start is delivered by about 1,700 public agencies, nonprofit organizations, or private, for-profit companies. The program takes place on a daily basis and lasts a half day (four hours) or whole day, four or five days a week, and potentially for several years, until the children reach the age of five. Over 70 percent of the teaching personnel are university graduates or have a higher degree. Importantly, the teacher-child ratio is 1:4 until the children are aged three and 1:10 thereafter. Class size is limited to eight children before age three. It is easy to understand why programs for toddlers require such high supervision rates. In many cases they need to compensate for family deficiencies and teach children on a day-to-day basis to control their emotions and improve interaction with their peers. It is also a matter of helping the children catch up and overcome their difficulties at all stages of learning. All this calls for close observation of individual behavior and personalized and repeated responses from teachers in the framework of small groups.

Researchers have demonstrated the major impact of Head Start on cognitive skills (less so on noncognitive skills) among the most disadvantaged groups: Hispanics, those who are not proficient in English, and young people with weaker cognitive skills.[43] But the favorable results of the program do not persist after primary school for all groups, notably for African American pupils.[44] Besides, children who enter Head Start at age three have higher reading and math test scores than children who join at age four.[45] Intervening as early as possible and over a sufficiently long period of time is thus essential. Very early interventions need to be followed by targeted support in primary and secondary schools.

Indeed, reducing class size can have a substantial impact on performance even after kindergarten. Only a few studies have properly evaluated the impact of class size on test score results either through randomized controlled trials or natural experiments. One of the most famous is the STAR experiment in Tennessee, which reduced the size of some classes from twenty-two to fifteen students in the 1980s in a sample of 325 primary school classes (11,600 students) and randomly assigned pupils either to a normal-size or a small class. Those assigned to small classes had better grades in reading and math, were more likely to take the SAT college entrance exam, and achieved somewhat better test scores, especially among minority students.[46]. Students assigned to high-quality classrooms—proxied by test scores at the end of kindergarten capturing teacher and peer effects—also benefited from higher earnings later in life, probably thanks to improved noncognitive skills such as effort, initiative, and lack of disruptive behavior.[47] Evidence from France also suggests that the effects of reducing class size tend to be even larger when it benefits disadvantaged students.[48] Another compelling study uses the maximum class size rules in Swedish upper primary schools, which leads to splitting a class in two when the number of students in the grade exceeds thirty. Not only do smaller classes improve cognitive and noncognitive abilities in primary school, but this improvement lasts through high school and beyond. Smaller classes in primary school improve the chances of graduating from high school and increase earnings later in life.[49] Thus, from a cost-benefit point of view, the reduction in class size could be a viable option, especially if employed by schools with a high share of minority and disadvantaged students whose parents have lower capacity to help in the context of a large class.[50]

These evaluations suggest that dividing up a class of, say, twenty-four students (i.e. a decrease to twelve students per class) in primary school improves average performance of the students concerned between 20 to 30 percent of a standard deviation in math and reading test scores.[51] This finding led the French government, for instance, in 2017 to halve the number of pupils in first grade and second grade classes of elementary school located in disadvantaged areas (*priority education zones*).

### Innovative Teaching Methods That Make a Difference

Improving reading and math test scores among minority students is a matter not only of resources but also of methods. Some interventions use alternative approaches to improve specific cognitive skills. For example, Making Pre-K Count is a programmatic approach to teaching prekindergarten children the basics of mathematics. Based on the Building Blocks approach developed by researchers at the University of Buffalo, this method helps children make a connection between their senses and their knowledge of mathematical concepts. It was tested on children living in poverty in New York City. Indeed, early learning of mathematics is strongly predictive of better results not only in mathematics but also in reading during primary school. Researchers at MDRC, a New York City–based organization specialized in evaluations, found that when associated with supplemental math enrichment in small groups outside the regular class time, two years of treatment improve third-grade math test scores.[52]

Another older and better known example is Success for All, an approach for primary schoolteachers, the main purpose of which is to remedy deficiencies in reading. The program was developed in Baltimore by Johns Hopkins University from studies in education. Introduced into Baltimore public schools from 1987, it is now used in thousands of schools in very poor areas throughout the United States. The program is supported by the Success for

All Foundation.[53] Starting with children at age five, the program aims to improve their language proficiency, but also to boost their self-esteem. In primary school, it uses a structured reading learning method, focusing on phonetics in the context of the stories that are enjoyable to listen to. The children work in groups and learn to cooperate and help each other. For those who still have difficulties with reading, tutors—all of them certified teachers—take over and work one-on-one to help the children to catch up. Family support is also a key aspect of the program, with a dedicated team in every school. The effects of the program on reading have proved lasting and have been often replicated.[54]

To help high school students, Mastery Learning was developed in the 1960s. This method is based on working groups, with the pace of learning being slowed if necessary so as not move on to the next stage until certain objectives have been attained.[55]

### Allowing More Leeway for Schools in Disadvantaged Areas

Apart from these specific ad hoc interventions, a more general adaptation of teaching methods and the content of programs to the specific needs of minority pupils can also improve their academic success and cognitive test results. In particular, this approach implies greater institutional autonomy, especially with regard to the selection of teachers and the definition of a teaching project. Institutional autonomy is an underlying trend in OECD countries. For example, in thirteen of the nineteen most successful countries in terms of PISA cognitive testing scores—mostly Anglo-Saxon and Nordic—more than 80 percent of students are enrolled in schools that are responsible for recruiting their own teachers. In half of these countries, such schools are also free to dismiss them.[56] In Germany, empowerment has been a key element in the strategy to improve the performance of the educational system. The UK has been experimenting with autonomy since the early 2000s by encouraging the emergence of the independent but subsidized schools known as academies. Initially, academies tended to be located in less-favored areas, but they now account for more than a quarter of state-funded schools.

Another example is that of charter schools in the United States, introduced in 1991, which in the country as a whole now take in some three million pupils every year, which represents 6 percent of the U.S. public school student population. They exist in forty-four states, each of them having a specific legislation authorizing the schools to operate. Charter schools are publicly funded institutions located in disadvantaged neighborhoods that have signed a charter with the authorities so as to have a large autonomy in defining a pedagogical project adapted to the specific needs of their students. In this way they can manage their teaching staff more effectively and adjust programs and teaching time as they wish. In return, head teachers undertake to achieve a specified level on national proficiency tests. They are also required to produce reports on a series of performance indicators. These schools generally benefit from increased resources, thereby allowing them to increase teaching and support hours, reduce class sizes, and hire better qualified teachers for mentoring at-risk youth. Beyond the recruitment of high-quality teachers, they tightly monitor student progress and assign students to small-group tutoring sessions if necessary.[57]

Many studies have examined the impact of charter schools on the future of young people, particularly African Americans and Hispanics, their main beneficiaries. Indeed, for most of these schools, the number of applicants exceeds the number of places available, resulting in the random selection of new entrants by lottery. Selection in this way makes it possible to have two perfectly comparable groups, one of which has been subject to the impact of charter schools and the other not. The results show that these schools have a significant and lasting impact on students' skills in mathematics, reading, and writing and also on some noncognitive skills.[58] They also increase the chances of going on to higher education and of getting a job.[59] The improvements are even more marked among young people who were furthest behind in reading and writing when they first enrolled in the charter school.[60] In addition, six years after their admission, lottery winners are more likely to graduate on time and to enroll in college immediately after high school. Girls and young women also face lower risks of teenage pregnancy, while boys and young men are less likely to be incarcerated.[61]

Unsurprisingly, the approaches adopted by these schools often differ from one another, but some models have been particularly successful. For example, KIPP (Knowledge Is Power Program) charter schools have been set up in poor neighborhoods in major U.S. cities. Over the year they provide more teaching days than other public schools, including Saturday mornings and three additional weeks in July. The school days are longer (from 7:30 a.m. to 5 p.m.). Most of this additional time is used for mathematics and reading. Researchers at Mathematica, a company located in Princeton, New Jersey, and specializing in impact evaluations, has found significant effects on reading and mathematics test results. For example, admission to a KIPP school increased the average mathematics score by 0.24 student standard deviation units after two years, equivalent to a student going from the fortieth to the fiftieth percentile in the national test results. Similar improvements have been obtained in reading.[62] Besides, attending both a KIPP middle school and a KIPP high school has large and positive impacts on students' college enrollment and graduation rates.[63] For other charter schools, the long-term effects on tertiary education outcomes are mixed, depending on the operators and grade levels. The longer-term impact on the labor market outcomes of these schools is uncertain. For instance, another type of network called the No Excuses charter schools puts the stress on high behavioral expectations and stricter disciplinary codes, while offering extended school hours. While this network shows positive effects on both cognitive test scores and college enrollment rates, especially for minority students, these differences do not translate systematically into higher earnings later in life.[64]

One of the challenges in expanding this model is that students who would benefit most from this type of education are typically those who apply less frequently. Indeed, richer, higher-achieving students are more likely to apply to charter schools, but charter schools boost test scores more for poor students and low achievers.[65] This may stem from the fact that parents who invest more in their children's education are also more likely to seek out effective schools, or, on the other hand, from the fact that disadvantaged families are also less aware of the quality of schools and their potential impact on their children's future. This means that expanding charter schools further could lead to larger impacts than those measured based on successful lottery applicants, on the condition that this expansion be accompanied by substantial outreach efforts to enroll children from more disadvantage backgrounds. Interestingly, the expansion of charter schools may also benefit students who remain in public schools. Indeed, there is evidence that the latter tend to react to the competition from nearby charter schools when their curricula are not significantly differentiated.[66]

U.S. charter schools have inspired the creation of similar models in other countries. For instance, Sweden introduced "free schools" (*friskolor*) in 1992 in the form of a publicly funded voucher enabling private schools to attract students while retaining more freedom than public schools do, notably in setting their own curriculum. These schools enroll about 15 percent of all primary schoolchildren and 30 percent of upper secondary students. Similarly, in the UK, "academies" are publicly funded, nonprofit organizations that operate independently of the local authority. They have more autonomy than public schools in their curriculum, but their performance is closely monitored. Underperforming public schools can be forced to become academies, while underperforming academies can be forced to join groups of academies known as multi-academy trusts. Academies represent more than a third of primary schools. In line with the finding for U.S. charter schools, there is evidence that the initial program of academies, which targeted disadvantaged pupils enrolled in poorly performing schools, boosted performance on the exam taken at the end of compulsory school and had a positive impact on medium-term post-compulsory schooling outcomes. However, such improvements are not identified among schools that were created or became academies during the mass expansion phase of the program, which started in 2010, suggesting that this approach works best if targeted at disadvantaged areas and students.[67] In the absence of targeting, the widespread development of publicly subsidized private schools might just lead to more segregation based on the social and economic background of parents, with an overall uncertain impact on educational outcomes.[68]

## Affirmative Action in Universities

Even with these enhanced interventions and programs in the school environment, it is not easy to ensure the inclusion of minorities in higher education establishments, where they are in fact significantly underrepresented. One final strategy, therefore, is to introduce quotas or admission criteria to universities for high school graduates from minority groups. This approach would entail reserving a certain number of places at university for students from ethnic minorities and providing access for a certain percentage of women to scientific and technological institutions because enrollment in these establishments is selective.

This form of positive discrimination has been applied in higher education in the United States since the 1970s. The practice has increasingly been supervised by the Supreme Court so as not to harm meritorious nonminority students. In particular, in 2003 the court ruled that race could be used as one of several admission criteria (without an explicit quota, *Grutter v. Bollinger*), but that the system of admission by points with additional points for racial minorities was unconstitutional because it was too mechanical and did not sufficiently reflect individual merits (*Gratz v. Bollinger*). But in 2023 the Supreme Court (*Students for Fair Admissions v. Harvard* and *Students for Fair Admissions v. University of North Carolina*) overruled previous decisions, holding that the use of race as a factor in college admissions processes violates the equal protection clause of the Fourteenth Amendment of the Constitution. This decision does not prevent universities from continuing to pursue diversity goals. In fact, they can include in their selection process questions related to how race has affected applicants' life, to the extent that these questions remain focused on personal experience. This suggests that positive discrimination will not disappear altogether from American universities. Besides, this practice has become popular in other countries and can be found, in one form or another, in India and Brazil, as well as also in Europe, particularly in France.[69]

In the absence of such measures, ethnic minority students would today be significantly underrepresented in the most prestigious universities. The sociologists Espenshade and Chung have estimated that, for the year 1997, had there not been positive discrimination, the admission rates of African American and Hispanic candidates to elite universities would have been more than 50 percent lower.[70] Yet, even in the context of affirmative action, the higher achievers among disadvantaged students tend not to apply spontaneously to selective colleges despite being extremely likely to be admitted with substantial financial aid.[71] Simply providing them with the information about the chances of admission to and costs of attending various colleges and universities can have significant effects on the quality of the institution they eventually attend.[72]

Positive discrimination can also have perverse effects, however. By enabling minorities, whose cognitive skills are on average lower on leaving high school, to enter the best universities and schools, it can also encourage them to opt for the least demanding courses so as to increase their chances of obtaining a degree. The economists Peter Arcidiacono, Esteban M. Aucejo, and Ken Spenner have shown that although young African Americans prefer natural sciences, engineering, and economics, they tend not to choose these subjects when admitted to the best universities because it is more difficult to obtain good grades.[73] Hence positive discrimination could increase the proportion of minority students in nonscientific fields at the best universities, to the detriment of their following scientific curricula at less prestigious universities. As a result, the overall proportion of engineers and scientists in these minority groups is liable to be reduced.

Still, simply banning affirmative action in college and university admissions altogether would undo the progress made over the past decades in helping minority students access higher-quality institutions. This would lead to worse labor market outcomes, and perhaps also to less human capital investments by minority students since they would become less likely to be admitted to higher-quality institutions.[74] For affirmative action to effectively raise the quality of education among minority students without generating substantial mismatch or failure, colleges and universities need to set their diversity rules in line with their capacity to make disadvantaged students succeed, for instance through providing services targeted to these students.[75]

* * *

Intervening upstream of the labor market is crucial because of the significant impact discrimination has on marginalized groups from an early age, by perpetuating negative stereotypes and socioeconomic disadvantages. Early intervention is essential, particularly in the development of cognitive and noncognitive skills. But views and conceptions continue to be malleable right through the high school years, and interventions in the school environment can change career paths by limiting the risk of conforming to stereotypes. Training of school staff and targeted investments in evidence-based programs are essential to the success of these strategies.

# Conclusion

On July 17, 2018, the centenary of the birth of Nelson Mandela, former U.S. president Barack Obama addressed an audience of 15,000 gathered in Johannesburg. His lecture included the following poignant words.

> Now, it's surprising that we have to affirm this truth today. More than a quarter century after Madiba walked out of prison, I still have to stand here at a lecture and devote some time to saying that black people and white people and Asian people and Latin American people and women and men and gays and straights, that we are all human, that our differences are superficial, and that we should treat each other with care and respect. . . .
>
> It is a truth that lies at the heart of every world religion—that we should do unto others as we would have them do unto us. That we see ourselves in other people. That we can recognize common hopes and common dreams. And it is a truth that is incompatible with any form of discrimination based on race or religion or gender or sexual orientation. And it is a truth that, by the way, when embraced, actually delivers practical benefits, since it ensures that a society can draw upon the talents and energy and skill of all its people. And if you doubt that, just ask the French football team that just won the World Cup. Because not all of those folks—not all of those folks look like Gauls to me. But they're French. They're French.[1]

These words echo in a striking manner what the present book is about. Yes, discrimination is omnipresent, especially in the labor market, and it is sometimes extreme. The list of groups who are discriminated against is long. In OECD countries, women find it more difficult to get jobs when they are of childbearing age, and in full-time work they earn on average 11 to 12 percent less than men—a gender gap that is largely unaccounted for. Older people are 30–50 percent less likely than younger generations to be invited to job interviews in many professions—a disadvantage that may be experienced by those who are still only in their forties. The situation is even worse for LGBTIQ+ people, who are nearly 40 percent less likely than heterosexual and cisgender people with equivalent skills and experience to get an interview if they reveal their identity at the time of application. For some racial/ethnic minorities, the chance of getting offered a job can be up to twice lower than for white candidates, especially when they are Muslim (unless they emphasize that they are nonpracticing). But that's not all: people who are viewed as physically unattractive, obese people, and those of short stature suffer greatly from discrimination, especially in professions involving interacting with customers. And even though we have not addressed the specific issue of people with disabilities in this book, numerous studies point to employers' reluctance to take them on, regardless of their capacity to work.

Admittedly, employment and wage disparities continue to be found in the labor market at all skill levels and in all sectors. But no inequality is less acceptable than that resulting from discrimination because it does not recognize talent, effort, or even good fortune. On the contrary, discrimination discourages talent, disrupts effort, and reduces the chances of success. It generates an economic, human, and social cost that reduces a country's growth potential. It prevents diversity being used as a performance lever, undermines the self-esteem of its victims—and consequently their productivity—and instills in society the poison of mistrust.

What is more, discrimination exerts its influence well upstream of the labor market. It erodes the acquisition of key skills at school, thus accentuating the stress of belonging to a minority group. Such stress may stem from the stereotypes associated with one group or another—girls are not so good at math, immigrants have less potential—or from outright harassment—LGBTIQ+, less physically attractive, small, or overweight children are regularly abused in primary and secondary school, making it more difficult for them to learn. Their marks in school are adversely affected, they self-censure in areas where they could excel, and their potential for future development is sometimes permanently compromised.

Nevertheless—and this is the encouraging message of the present book—discrimination is not inevitable. It can be remedied, just as the cognitive biases that generate it can be attenuated. Examples of progress abound, including at the country level. In Ireland the 1861 law on the criminalization of homosexuality remained in force until 1993. Yet Ireland was the first country to put the legalization of same-sex marriage to a popular vote, and to approve it in 2015. The legal prohibition of discrimination is a necessary first step, but it is not sufficient. It needs to be complemented by a broad set of policies, including the establishment of mechanisms that monitor employer's hiring practices and career management behaviors, policies that complement bias training with awareness about human resources strategies that deny conscious and unconscious bias a chance to operate, the education of society at large, and means to change stereotypes about certain groups, such as the deep-seated belief that women with children cannot take up positions of responsibility. Actions upstream of the labor market, from school age on, to counter the tendency of discriminated groups to conform to the negative stereotypes that target them and lead to failure also are essential. Exploiting the full range of antidiscrimination policies is all the more important because the specter of discrimination is ever-present. The French team may have won the World Cup, but soccer, like the job market, is still contaminated by the primary impulse to reject difference—witness the cries of "monkey" hurled at players of African origin or homophobic insults such as "poofter" or "faggot" that a quarter of French fans acknowledge calling players during matches.[2]

Governments therefore need to engage in a ceaseless battle against discrimination of various kinds. Inaction or the exclusively punitive approach that currently characterizes policies in this area are no longer enough. Accordingly, the creation of a national strategy, together with an experimentation fund to assess on a large scale the effectiveness of the school, workplace, and awareness-raising policies outlined in this book, could make all the difference.

# Notes

*A complete bibliography for this book is available on the MIT Press website at https://mitp-content-server.mit.edu/books/content/sectbyfn/books_pres_0/13631/Carcillo_bibliography.pdf.*

## Introduction

1. Andrew Daniller, "Majorities of Americans See at Least Some Discrimination Against Black, Hispanic, and Asian People in the U.S.," Pew Research Center, March 18, 2021.

2. European Commission. Special Eurobarometer: "Discrimination in the EU," December 2023, https://europa.eu/eurobarometer/surveys/detail/2972.

## Chapter 1

1. See Susan T. Fiske, "Stereotyping, Prejudice, and Discrimination," in *Handbook of Social Psychology*, ed. Daniel T. Gilbert, Susan T. Fiske, and Gardner Lindzey (Boston: McGraw-Hill, 1998), 357–411; and P. R. Hinton, *Stereotypes, Cognition and Culture* (Hove, UK: Psychology Press, 2000).

2. Fiske, "Stereotyping, Prejudice, and Discrimination."

3. Daniel Kahneman, *Thinking Fast and Slow* (New York: Farrar, Straus and Giroux, 2011).

4. Sean P. Mackinnon, Christian H. Jordan, and Anne E. Wilson, "Birds of a Feather Sit Together: Physical Similarity Predicts Seating Choice," *Personality and Social Psychology Bulletin* 37, no. 7 (2011): 879–892.

5. Henri Tajfel, "Experiments in Intergroup Discrimination," *Scientific American* 223, no. 5 (1970): 96–102.

6. Michael Billig and Henri Tajfel, "Social Categorization and Similarity in Intergroup Behavior," *European Journal of Social Psychology* 3, no. 1 (1973): 27–52.

7. Morten Størling Hedegaard and Jean-Robert Tyran, "The Price of Prejudice," *American Economic Journal: Applied Economics* 10, no. 1 (2018): 40–63.

8. For example, based on a correspondence study (see chapter 4) carried out in France, economists Anthony Edo, Nicolas Jacquemet, and Constantine Yannelis identify an "ethnic homophily" with regard to the hiring decision: recruiters with European-sounding names are more likely to favor fictitious candidates of French origin over those of non-European origin, even when both groups present equivalent CVs. These authors also identify a "gender homophily" (although this latter result was not confirmed by economist Magnus Carlsson in the context of a correspondence study in Sweden). See Anthony Edo, Nicolas Jacquemet, and Constantine Yannelis, "Language Skills and Homophilous Hiring Discrimination: Evidence from Gender- and Racially-Differentiated Applications," *Review of Economics of the Household* 17 (2019): 349–376. See also Magnus Carlsson, "Does Hiring Discrimination Cause Gender Segregation in the Swedish Labor Market?," *Feminist Economics* 17, no. 3 (2011): 71–102.

9. For further insights into these mechanisms, see Kevin Lang and Ariella Kahn-Lang Spitzer, "Race Discrimination: An Economic Perspective," *Journal of Economic Perspectives* 34, no. 2 (2020): 68–89.

10. Devah Pager, "Are Firms That Discriminate More Likely to Go Out of Business?," *Sociological Science* 3 (2016): 849–859.

11. For similar evidence in the context of gender-based discrimination in the labor market, see Andrea Weber and Christine Zulehner, "Competition and Gender Prejudice: Are Discriminatory Employers Doomed to Fail?," *Journal of the European Economic Association* 12, no. 2 (2014): 492–521.

12. For a review, see Guilherme Hirata and Rodrigo R. Soares, "Competition and the Racial Wage Gap: Evidence from Brazil," *Journal of Development Economics* 146 (2020).

13. To the best of our knowledge, Abu Siddique, Michael Vlassopoulos, and Yves Zenou are the only authors who study a market that is competitive enough for discriminators to be driven out. They analyze not the reaction of employers to different job candidates in the labor market but the reaction of buyers to different sellers in a product market, the rice market in Bangladesh. The authors show that, although ethnic-majority buyers share the same distaste for transacting with ethnic-minority sellers, whether they act according to this distaste hinges on the degree of competition in the rice market where they operate. Ethnic-majority buyers who operate in nearly perfectly competitive rice markets do not discriminate: they quote the same price for rice sold by ethnic-minority and ethnic-majority sellers. By contrast, ethnic-majority buyers who have a local monopsony power do discriminate: they quote a lower price for rice sold by ethnic-minority sellers (relative to the price of rice sold by ethnic-majority sellers). See Abu Siddique, Michael Vlassopoulos, and Yves Zenou, "Market Competition and Discrimination," *European Economic Review* 152 (2023).

14. See, for example, Dylan Glover, "Job Search and Intermediation under Discrimination: Evidence from Terrorist Attacks in France," Chaire SPP Working Paper no. 2019-02 (2019).

15. Felipe Goncalves and Steven Mello, "A Few Bad Apples? Racial Bias in Policing," *American Economic Review* 111, no. 5 (2021): 1406–1441.

16. Mario L. Small and Devah Pager, "Sociological Perspectives on Racial Discrimination," *Journal of Economic Perspectives* 34, no. 2 (2020): 49–67.

17. Direct discrimination occurs when an individual is treated less favorably than others under similar circumstances due to a protected attribute such as race/ethnicity, gender, or age. For instance, a hiring manager who decides against employing someone because of their race/ethnicity is engaging in direct discrimination. Indirect discrimination, on the other hand, involves policies, practices, or rules that, while appearing neutral, disproportionately impact certain groups.

18. Kenneth J. Arrow, "What Has Economics to Say about Racial Discrimination?," *Journal of Economic Perspectives* 12, no. 2 (1998): 91–100.

19. Steven Pinker, *Rationality: What It Is, Why It Seems Scarce, Why It Matters* (New York: Viking, 2021).

20. This code of conduct has inspired several prominent thinkers, including Spinoza ("Men who are governed by reason—that is, who seek what is useful to them in accordance with reason—desire for themselves nothing, which they do not also desire for the rest of mankind, and, consequently, are just, faithful, and honourable in their conduct"), Kant ("Act only according to that maxim whereby you can, at the same time, will that it should become a universal law"), and Rawls ("The principles of justice are chosen behind a 'veil of ignorance'").

21. Henri Tajfel, "Cognitive Aspects of Prejudice," *Journal of Social Issues* 25, no. 4 (1969): 79–97.

22. Pedro Bordalo, Katherine Coffman, Nicola Gennaioli, and Andrei Shleifer, "Stereotypes," *Quarterly Journal of Economics* 131, no. 4 (2016): 1753–1794.

23. Amanda Agan and Sonja Starr, "Ban the Box, Criminal Records, and Racial Discrimination: A Field Experiment," *Quarterly Journal of Economics* 133, no. 1 (2018): 191–235.

24. Similarly, Alexander Bartik and Scott Nelson find that banning the use of a credit report in hiring is detrimental to Black job seekers as well as employees, rather than beneficial to them: in the United States, this ban decreases job-finding rates for Black applicants by 2.4 percentage points and increases involuntary separations for Black employees shortly after being hired by three percentage points. Alexander W. Bartik and Scott T. Nelson, "Deleting a Signal: Evidence from Pre-Employment Credit Checks," *Review of Economics and Statistics,* 2024, 1–47.

25. Aislinn Bohren, Kareem Haggag, Alex Imas, and Devin G. Pope, "Inaccurate Statistical Discrimination: An Identification Problem," *Review of Economic Studies*, 2023.

26. Dennis J. Aigner and Glen Cain, "Statistical Theories of Discrimination in Labor Markets," *Industrial and Labor Relations Review* 30, no. 2 (1977): 175–187.

27. Joanna N. Lahey and Douglas R. Oxley, "Discrimination at the Intersection of Age, Race, and Gender: Evidence from an Eye-Tracking Experiment," *Journal of Policy Analysis and Management* 40, no. 4 (2021): 1083–1119.

28. Dylan Glover, Amanda Pallais, and William Pariente, "Discrimination as a Self-Fulfilling Prophecy: Evidence from French Grocery Stores," *Quarterly Journal of Economics* 132, no. 3 (2017): 1219–1260.

29. See, for instance, Ester Boserup, *The Conditions of Agricultural Growth: The Economics of Agrarian Change under Population Pressure* (London: Routledge, 1965).

30. Casper Worm Hansen, Peter Sandholt Jensen, and Christian Volmar Skovsgaard, "Modern Gender Roles and Agricultural History: The Neolithic Inheritance," *Journal of Economic Growth* 20 (2015): 365–404.

31. Alberto Alesina, Paola Giuliano, and Nathan Nunn, "On the Origins of Gender Roles: Women and the Plough," *Quarterly Journal of Economics* 128, no. 2 (2013): 469–530.

32. See the Special Eurobarometer 465: "Gender Equality 2017" (database) (European Commission, 2017).

33. See the Special Eurobarometer 465: "Gender Equality 2017" (database) (European Commission, 2017).

34. Anthony G. Greenwald, Debbie E. McGhee, and Jordan L. K. Schwartz, "Measuring Individual Differences in Implicit Cognition: The Implicit Association Test," *Journal of Personality and Social Psychology* 74, no. 6 (1998): 1464–1480. Information on Project Explicit is available at https://implicit.harvard.edu/implicit.

35. See https://www.aauw.org/resource/iat.

36. Marianne Bertrand and Esther Duflo, "Field Experiments on Discrimination," in *Handbook of Field Experiments*, vol. 1, ed. Abhijit V. Banerjee and Esther Duflo (North Holland: Elsevier, 2017), 309–393. On less than expected correlation, see Frederick Oswald, Gregory Mitchell, Hart Blanton, James Jaccard, and Philip E. Tetlock, "Predicting Ethnic and Racial Discrimination: A Meta-Analysis of IAT Criterion Studies," *Journal of Personality and Social Psychology* 105, no. 2 (2013): 171–192.

37. Dan-Olof Rooth, "Automatic Associations and Discrimination in Hiring: Real World Evidence," *Labour Economics* 17, no. 3 (2010): 523–534; Jens Agerström and Dan-Olof Rooth, "The Role of Automatic Obesity Stereotypes in Real Hiring Discrimination," *Journal of Applied Psychology* 96, no. 4 (2011): 790–805.

38. Redzo Mujcic and Paul Frijters, "The Colour of a Free Ride," *Economic Journal* 131, no. 634 (2021): 970–999.

39. Kenneth B. Clark and Mamie P. Clark, "Racial Identification and Racial Preference in Negro Children," in *Readings in Social Psychology*, ed. Theodore M. Newcomb and Eugene L. Hartley (New York: Henry Holt, 1947), 239–252.

40. Steven R. Asher and Vernon L. Allen, "Racial Preference and Social Comparison Processes," *Journal of Social Issues* 25, no. 1 (1969): 157–166.

41. This temptation may, however, be counteracted when discrimination triggers identitarian closure among the minority group. See chapters 2 and 6 on this point.

42. See chapter 9 on this point.

43. More specifically, see the original treaty of 1957 (Treaty Establishing the European Economic Community), which prohibits discrimination on the basis of gender in employment, and Directive 2000/43/EC, which prohibits discrimination on the grounds of race or ethnic origin in employment, the social welfare system, and access to goods and services. Council Directive 2000/78/EC, also known as the Equality Framework Directive, prohibits discrimination on grounds of religion or belief, disability, age, or sexual orientation in employment; Council Directive 2004/113/EC, also known as the Equal Treatment in Goods and Services directive, prohibits any discrimination based on gender with regard to access to goods and services. It should also be noted that Article 21 of the European Union Charter of Fundamental Rights, adopted in 2000, was given binding legal force following the entry into force of the Lisbon Treaty in 2009. Individuals who believe that European legislation or national legislation transposing EU law does not comply with the provisions of the charter are therefore entitled to appeal. The charter prohibits discrimination on the basis of the aforementioned criteria, as well as on the basis of color, social background, genetic characteristics, language, political or any other opinion, membership in a national minority, property ownership, and birthplace.

### Chapter 2

1. Kate Kelly, "The Short Tenure and Abrupt Ouster of Banking's Sole Black C.E.O.," *New York Times*, October 3, 2020.

2. Tidjane Thiam, "La France est une idée, être français une émotion," in *Qu'est-ce qu'être français?*, ed. François Rachline (Paris: Hermann, 2009).

3. Chang-Tai Hsieh, Erik Hurst, Charles I. Jones, and Peter J. Klenow, "The Allocation of Talent and US Economic Growth," *Econometrica* 87, no. 5 (2019): 1439–1474.

4. For more details on her biography, see, for instance, https://supreme.justia.com/justices/ruth-bader-ginsburg.

5. OECD, *The Economic Case for Greater LGBTI+ Equality in the United States* (Paris: OECD Publishing, 2024).

6. M. R. Barlow and J. N. Lahey, "What Race Is Lacey? Intersecting Perceptions of Racial Minority Status and Social Class," *Social Science Quarterly* 99, no. 5 (2018): 1680–1698.

7. Unexplained differences refer to differences that persist when comparing individuals from the two groups under consideration with the same age and educational level. These unexplained differences are interpreted as likely reflecting, at least in part, discrimination on the basis of gender and ethnic origin.

8. France Stratégie, *Le Coût économique des discriminations*, Report to the Minister of Labor, Employment, Vocational Training and Social Dialogue and to the Minister of Housing, Youth and Sports (Paris, 2016).

9. Kilian Huber, Volker Lindenthal, and Fabian Waldinger, "Discrimination, Managers, and Firm Performance: Evidence from "Aryanizations" in Nazi Germany," *Journal of Political Economy* 129, no. 9 (2021).

10. OECD, "Programme Guide of the International Diversity Forum" (Paris: OECD Publishing, 2018). For further information, see also OECD, *All Hands In* (Paris: OECD Publishing, 2020).

11. A. Reynolds and D. Lewis, "Teams Solve Problems Faster When They're More Cognitively Diverse," *Harvard Business Review*, March 30, 2017.

12. See https://www.amsterdamuas.com.

13. On the impact of gender diversity, see Sander Hoogendoorn, Hessel Oosterbeek, and Mirjam van Praag, "The Impact of Gender Diversity on the Performance of Business Teams: Evidence from a Field Experiment," *Management Science* 59, no. 7 (2013): 1514–1528. On the impact of ethnic diversity, see Sander Hoogendoorn, Hessel Oosterbeek, and Mirjam van Praag, "Ethnic Diversity and Team Performance: A Randomized Field Experiment," *Academy of Management Annual Meeting Proceedings* (2018).

14. Elizabeth Lyons, "Team Production in International Labor Markets: Experimental Evidence from the Field," *American Economic Journal: Applied Economics* 9, no. 3 (2017): 70–104.

15. Sophie Calder-Wang, Paul A. Gompers, and Kanyuan Kevin Huang, "Diversity and Performance in Entrepreneurial Teams," NBER Working Paper 28684 (Cambridge, MA: National Bureau of Economic Research, 2021).

16. Sophie Calder-Wang and Paul A. Gompers, "And the Children Shall Lead: Gender Diversity and Performance in Venture Capital," *Journal of Financial Economics* 142, no. 1 (2021): 1–22.

17. Jonas Hjort, "Ethnic Divisions and Production in Firms," *Quarterly Journal of Economics* 129, no. 4 (2014): 1899–1946.

18. For similar results also based on a field experiment in Kenya, see Benjamin Marx, Vincent Pons, and Tavneet Suri, "Diversity and Team Performance in a Kenyan Organization," *Journal of Public Economics* 197 (2021), art. 104332.

19. Mauro Caselli, Paolo Falco, and Gianpiero Mattera, "When the Stadium Goes Silent: How Crowds Affect the Performance of Discriminated Groups," *Journal of Labor Economics* 41, no. 2 (2023).

20. Gordon W. Allport, *The Nature of Prejudice* (New York: Addison-Wesley, 1954). See as well Claude M. Steele, "A Threat in the Air: How Stereotypes Shape Intellectual Identity and Performance," *American Psychologist* 52, no. 6 (1997): 613–629.

21. Jeff Stone, Christian I. Lynch, Mike Sjomeling, and John M. Darley, "Stereotype Threat Effects on Black and White Athletic Performance," *Journal of Personality and Social Psychology* 77, no. 6 (1999): 1213–1227.

22. P. Huguet, S. Brunot, and J. Monteil, "Geometry versus Drawing: Changing the Meaning of the Task as a Means to Change Performance.," *Social Psychology of Education* 4, nos. 3–4 (2001): 219–234. See as well P. Huguet and I. Régner, "Counter-Stereotypic Beliefs in Math Do Not Protect School Girls from Stereotype Threat," *Journal of Experimental Social Psychology* 45, no. 4 (2009): 1024–1027.

23. Karla Hoff and Priyanka Pandey, "Discrimination, Social Identity, and Durable Inequalities," *American Economic Review* 96, no. 2 (2006): 206–211.

24. Reminding an individual not publicly but privately that he or she belongs to a group that is discriminated against is equally destabilizing, as Claude M. Steele and Joshua Aronson have shown in "Stereotype Threat and the Intellectual Test Performance of African Americans," *Journal of Personality and Social Psychology* 69, no.5 (1995): 797–811. See chapter 12 of this book with regard to this point.

25. Farzana Afridi, Sherry Li, and Yufei Ren, "Social Identity and Inequality: The Impact of China's Hukou System," *Journal of Public Economics* 123 (2015): 17–29.

26. Micro-aggressions include being repeatedly followed by a security guard at a store, receiving poorer service than others in restaurants, and experiencing slights, insults, and individually minor conflicts. For further insights, see Mario L. Small and Devah Pager, "Sociological Perspectives on Racial Discrimination," *Journal of Economic Perspectives* 34, no. 2 (2020): 49–67.

27. Marcella Alsan, Owen Garrick, and Grant Graziani, "Does Diversity Matter for Health? Experimental Evidence from Oakland," *American Economic Review* 109, no. 12 (2019): 4071–4111.

28. The authors ran an experiment in Oakland, California, in which they randomly assigned Black men to Black or non-Black male medical doctors. They measured

decisions participants made before (preconsultation) and after (postconsultation) meeting their assigned doctor. The results showed that subjects select a similar number of preventive services in the preconsultation stage but are much more likely to select every preventive service, particularly invasive services (those that require blood sample or an injection), once they meet with a racially concordant doctor.

29. Sujitha Selvarajah, Susanna Corona Maioli, Thilagawathi Abi Deivanayagam, et al., "Racism, Xenophobia, and Discrimination: Mapping Pathways to Health Outcomes," *Lancet* 400 (2022).

30. Marie-Anne Valfort, "LGBTI in OECD Countries: A Review," OECD Social, Employment and Migration Working Paper no. 198 (Paris: OECD Publishing, 2017).

31. Julia Raifman, Ellen Moscoe, S. Bryn Austin, and Margaret McConnell, "Difference-in-Differences Analysis of the Association between State Same-Sex Marriage Policies and Adolescent Suicide Attempts," *JAMA Pediatrics* 171, no. 4 (2017): 350–356.

32. Chad Meyerhoefer, Bingjin Xue, and Anna Poznańska, "Implications of the Decline in LGBT Rights for Population Mental Health: Evidence from Polish 'LGBT-Free Zones,'" NBER Working Paper 31702 (Cambridge, MA: National Bureau of Economic Research, 2023).

33. Jacob Bor, Atheendar S. Venkataramani, David R. Williams, and Alexander C. Tsai, "Police Killings and Their Spillover Effects on the Mental Health of Black Americans: A Population-Based, Quasi-Experimental Study," *Lancet* 392, no. 10144 (2018): 302–310.

34. Patrik Sobocki, Bengt Jönsson, Jules Angst, and Clas Rehnberg, "Cost of Depression in Europe," *Journal of Mental Health Policy and Economics* 9, no. 2 (2006): 87–98.

35. Robert D. Putnam, *Bowling Alone: The Collapse and Revival of American Community* (New York: Simon & Schuster, 2000).

36. Maria Abascal and Delia Baldassarri, "Love Thy Neighbor? Ethnoracial Diversity and Trust Reexamined," *American Journal of Sociology* 121, no. 3 (2015): 722–782.

37. On the school effect of "acting white," see Stuart Buck, *Acting White: The Ironic Legacy of Desegregation* (New Haven, CT: Yale University Press, 2010).

38. Roland G. Fryer, "Acting White," *Education Next* 6, no. 1 (2006): 53–59.

39. Alain Peyrefitte, *La Société de confiance* (Paris: Odile Jacob, 1995).

40. Kenneth J. Arrow, "Gifts and Exchanges," *Philosophy & Public Affairs* 1, no. 4 (1972): 343–362.

41. Yann Algan and Pierre Cahuc, "Inherited Trust and Growth," *American Economic Review* 100, no. 5 (2010): 2060–2092.

## Chapter 3

1. Kevin Lang and Ariella Kahn-Lang Spitzer, "Race Discrimination: An Economic Perspective," *Journal of Economic Perspectives* 34, no. 2 (2020): 68–89.

2. O. P. John and S. Srivastava, "The Big Five Trait Taxonomy: History, Measurement, and Theoretical Perspectives," in *Handbook of Personality: Theory and Research*, vol. 2, ed. L. A. Pervin and O. P. John (New York: Guilford Press, 1999).

3. Erik Plug, Dinand Webbink, and Nick Martin, "Sexual Orientation, Prejudice, and Segregation," *Journal of Labor Economics* 32, no. 1 (2014): 123–159.

4. Derek A. Neal and William R. Johnson, "The Role of Premarket Factors in Black-White Wage Differences," *Journal of Political Economy* 104, no. 5 (1996): 869–895.

5. Kevin Lang and Michael Manove, "Education and Labor Market Discrimination," *American Economic Review* 101, no. 4 (2011): 1467–1496.

6. Ronald L. Oaxaca, "Male-Female Wage Differentials in Urban Labor Markets," *International Economic Review* 14, no. 3 (1973): 693–709; Alan S. Blinder, "Wage Discrimination: Reduced Form and Structural Estimates," *Journal of Human Resources* 8, no. 4 (1973): 436–455.

7. June O'Neill and Dave O'Neill, "What Do Wage Differentials Tell Us about Labor Market Discrimination?," *Research in Labor Economics* 24 (2006): 293–357.

## Chapter 4

1. Ian Ayres and Peter Siegelman, "Race and Gender Discrimination in Bargaining for a New Car," *American Economic Review* 85, no. 3 (1995): 304–321.

2. David Neumark, Roy J. Bank, and Kyle D. Van Nort, "Sex Discrimination in Restaurant Hiring: An Audit Study," *Quarterly Journal of Economics* 111, no. 3 (1996): 915–941.

3. James J. Heckman, "Detecting Discrimination," *Journal of Economic Perspectives* 12, no. 2 (1998): 101–116; James J. Heckman and Peter Siegelman, "The Urban Institute Audit Studies: Their Methods and Findings," in *Clear and Convincing Evidence: Measurement of Discrimination in America*, ed. Michael Fix and Raymond J. Struyk (Washington, DC: Urban Institute Press, 1993), 187–258.

4. Marianne Bertrand and Sendhil Mullainathan, "Are Emily and Greg More Employable Than Lakisha and Jamal? A Field Experiment on Labor Market Discrimination," *American Economic Review* 94, no. 4 (2004): 991–1013.

5. Heckman, "Detecting Discrimination."

6. Magnus Carlsson, Luca Fumarco, and Dan-Olof Rooth, "Does the Design of Correspondence Studies Influence the Measurement of Discrimination?," *IZA Journal of Migration* 3, no. 11 (2014): 1–17.

7. Dan-Olof Rooth, "Correspondence Testing Studies: What Is There to Learn about Discrimination in Hiring?," *IZA World of Labor* 58 (2021): 6–7.

8. David Neumark, "Detecting Discrimination in Audit and Correspondence Studies," *Journal of Human Resources* 47, no. 4 (2012): 1128–1157.

9. Pierre Cahuc, Stéphane Carcillo, Andreea Minea, and Marie-Anne Valfort, "When Correspondence Studies Fail to Detect Discrimination," IZA Discussion Paper no. 12653 (2019).

10. Lincoln Quillian, John J. Lee, Mariana Oliver, "Evidence from Field Experiments in Hiring Shows Substantial Additional Racial Discrimination after the Callback," *Social Forces* 99, no. 2 (December 2020): 732–759.

11. Joanna N. Lahey and Ryan A. Beasley, "Computerizing Audit Studies," *Journal of Economic Behavior & Organization* 70, no. 3 (2009): 508–514.

12. Chaim Fershtman and Uri Gneezy, "Discrimination in a Segmented Society: An Experimental Approach," *Quarterly Journal of Economics* 116, no. 1 (2001): 351–377.

13. Alice H. Eagly, Mona G. Makhijani, and Bruce G. Klonsky, "Gender and the Evaluation of Leaders: A Meta-Analysis," *Psychological Bulletin* 111, no. 1 (1992): 3–22.

## Chapter 5

1. *Weinberger v. Wiesenfeld,* 420 U.S. 636 (1975).

2. *United States v. Virginia,* 518 U.S. 515 (1996).

3. See the OECD Gender Data Portal at https://www.oecd.org/en/topics/policy-issues/gender-equality.html.

4. UNESCO, "Women in Science," Fact Sheet no. 55, June 2019, FS/2019/SCI/55.

5. Pew Research Center, "Wide Partisan Gaps in U.S. over How Far the Country Has Come on Gender Equality" (2017).

6. This means that, on average, a woman working full-time makes around 88 cents for every dollar or euro a full-time working man makes (at median earnings).

7. OECD Employment and Labour Market Statistics database, https://www.oecd-ilibrary.org/employment/data/oecd-employment-and-labour-market-statistics_lfs-data-en.

8. Marianne Bertrand, "Coase Lecture: The Glass Ceiling," *Economica* 85, no. 338 (2018): 205–231.

9. OECD, *Employment Outlook* (Paris: OECD Publishing, 2018), chap. 6.

10. OECD, *The Pursuit of Gender Equality: An Uphill Battle* (Paris: OECD Publishing, 2018).

11. Francine Blau and Lawrence Kahn, "The Gender Wage Gap: Extent, Trends, and Explanations," *Journal of Economic Literature* 55, no. 3 (2017): 789–865a.

12. Alexander Hijzen, "The Gender Wage Gap and the Role of Firms," in *Joining Forces for Gender Equality: What Is Holding Us Back?* (Paris: OECD Publishing, 2023).

13. Francine D. Blau and Lawrence M. Kahn, "The U.S. Gender Pay Gap in the 1990s: Slowing Convergence," *Industrial and Labor Relations Review* 60, no. 1 (2006): 45–66.

14. The unionization rate, which tends to reduce gender wage inequalities, also played a role during this period.

15. Casey B. Mulligan and Yona Rubinstein, "Selection, Investment, and Women's Relative Wages over Time," *Quarterly Journal of Economics* 123, no. 3 (2008): 1061–1110.

16. Nicole M. Fortin, "Gender Role Attitudes and Women's Labor Market Participation: Opting-Out, AIDS, and the Persistent Appeal of Housewifery," *Annals of Economics and Statistics* 117/118 (2015): 379–401.

17. Ipsos survey, "Millennials and Gen Z Less in Favour of Gender Equality Than Older Generations," March 2024, https://www.ipsos.com/en/millennials-and-gen-z-less-favour-gender-equality-older-generations.

18. Susan T. Fiske, "Stereotyping, Prejudice, and Discrimination," in *Handbook of Social Psychology*, ed. Daniel T. Gilbert, Susan T. Fiske, and Gardner Lindzey (Boston: McGraw-Hill, 1998), 357–411.

19. Hannah Van Borm and Stijn Baert, "Diving in the Minds of Recruiters: What Triggers Gender Stereotypes in Hiring?," GLO Discussion Paper no. 1083 (Global Labor Organization, 2022).

20. See Laurie A. Rudman, Corinne A. Moss-Racusin, Julie E. Phelan, Sanne Nauts, "Status Incongruity and Backlash Effects: Defending the Gender Hierarchy Motivates Prejudice Against Female Leaders," *Journal of Experimental Social Psychology* 48, no. 1 (2012); and Anne Koenig, "Comparing Prescriptive and Descriptive Gender Stereotypes about Children, Adults, and the Elderly," *Frontiers in Psychology* 26 (2018).

21. Thomas Breda, Elyès Jouini, Clotilde Napp, and Georgia Thebault, "Gender Stereotypes Can Explain the Gender-Equality Paradox," *Proceedings of the National Academy of Sciences of the United States of America (PNAS)* 117, no. 49 (2020): 31063–31069.

22. Janet K. Swim, "Perceived versus Meta-Analytic Effect Sizes: An Assessment of the Accuracy of Gender Stereotypes," *Journal of Personality and Social Psychology* 66 (1994): 21–36.

23. Marianne Bertrand, "Gender in the Twenty-First Century," *AEA Papers and Proceedings* 110 (2020): 1–24.

24. P. T. Costa, A. Terracciano, and R. R. McCrae, "Gender Differences in Personality Traits across Cultures: Robust and Surprising Findings," *Journal of Personality and Social Psychology* 81 (2001): 322–331, http://dx.doi.org/10.1037/0022-3514.81.2.322.

25. Somewhat moderately higher levels of implicit Neuroticism and higher Agreeableness are observed in women, and moderately higher levels of implicit Openness are observed in men. There is no difference in terms of Conscientiousness. See J. S. Hyde, "Gender Similarities and Differences," *Annual Review of Psychology* 65 (2014): 373–398, https://doi.org/10.1146/annurev-psych-010213-115057; and Michelangelo Vianello, Konrad Schnabel, N. Sriram, and Brian Nosek, "Gender Differences in Implicit and Explicit Personality Traits," *Personality and Individual Differences* 55, no. 8 (2013): 994–999.

26. Hyde, "Gender Similarities and Differences."

27. OECD, *PISA 2018 Results (Volume II): Where All Students Can Succeed* (Paris: OECD Publishing, 2019).

28. Gaia Dossi et al., "Born in the Family: Preferences for Boys and the Gender Gap in Math," *Journal of Economic Behavior & Organization* 183 (2021): 175–188.

29. Rachel Croson and Uri Gneezy, "Gender Differences in Preferences," *Journal of Economic Literature* 47, no. 2 (2009): 448–474.

30. Muriel Niederle and Lise Vesterlund, "Do Women Shy Away from Competition? Do Men Compete Too Much?," *Quarterly Journal of Economics* 122, no. 3 (2007): 1067–1101.

31. Uri Gneezy, Muriel Niederle, and Aldo Rustichini, "Performance in Competitive Environments: Gender Differences," *Quarterly Journal of Economics* 118, no. 3 (2003): 1049–1074.

32. Uri Gneezy, Kenneth L. Leonard, and John A. List, "Gender Differences in Competition: Evidence from a Matrilineal and a Patriarchal Society," *Econometrica* 77, no. 5 (2009): 1637–1664.

33. Thomas Buser, Muriel Niederle, and Hessel Oosterbeek, "Gender, Competitiveness, and Career Choices," *Quarterly Journal of Economics* 129, no. 3 (2014): 1409–1447.

34. Jeffrey A. Flory, Andreas Leibbrandt, and John A. List, "Do Competitive Workplaces Deter Female Workers? A Large-Scale Natural Field Experiment on Job Entry Decisions," *Review of Economic Studies* 82, no. 1 (January 2015): 122–155.

35. Blau and Kahn, "The Gender Wage Gap."

36. Gerrit Mueller and Erik Plug, "Estimating the Effect of Male and Female Personality Traits on Earnings," *Industrial and Labor Relations Review* 60, no. 1 (2006).

37. Ernesto Reuben, Paola Sapienza, and Luigi Zingales, "Overconfidence and Preferences for Competition," *Journal of Finance* (2024).

38. Based on studies conducted since 2000 in several countries, Judith Rich shows that discrimination against women in predominantly male professions is, however, lower than discrimination suffered by men when they apply for predominantly female jobs. See Judith Rich, "What Do Field Experiments of Discrimination in Markets Tell Us? A Meta-Analysis of Studies Conducted since 2000," IZA Discussion Paper no. 8584 (2014).

39. For Australia, see Alison Booth and Andrew Leigh, "Do Employers Discriminate by Gender? A Field Experiment in Female-Dominated Occupations," *Economics Letters* 107, no. 2 (2010): 236–238. For Europe, see Doris Weichselbaumer, "Is It Sex or Personality? The Impact of Sex Stereotypes on Discrimination in Applicant Selection," *Eastern Economic Journal* 30, no. 2 (2004): 159–186. For the United States, see Peter A. Riach and Judith Rich, "Field Experiments of Discrimination in the Market Place," *Economic Journal* 112, no. 483 (2002): F480–F518.

40. Gunn Elisabeth Birkelund, Bram Lancee, Edvard Nergård Larsen, Javier G Polavieja, Jonas Radl, and Ruta Yemane, "Gender Discrimination in Hiring: Evidence from a Cross-National Harmonized Field Experiment. *European Sociological Review* 38, no. 3 (2022): 337–354. For a similar result, see Magnus Carlsson, "Does Hiring Discrimination Cause Gender Segregation in the Swedish Labor Market?," *Feminist Economics* 17, no. 3 (2011): 71–102.

41. Pascale Petit, "The Effects of Age and Family Constraints on Gender Hiring Discrimination: A Field Experiment in the French Financial Sector," *Labour Economics* 14, no. 3 (2007): 371–391.

42. In 2019, women do nearly two-thirds of domestic work (household, kitchen, laundry) and family work (taking care of children) in OECD countries; gender inequality in unpaid work is not fully compensated by gender inequality in paid work: women do carry out a significant share (more than 40 percent) of paid work. Source: OECD Gender Data Portal, "OECD Dashboard on Gender Gaps" (database), https://www.oecd.org/en/data/dashboards/gender-dashboard.html.

43. Stijn Baert, Ann-Sophie De Pauw, and Nick Deschacht, "Do Employer Preferences Contribute to Sticky Floors?," *Industrial and Labor Relations Review* 69, no. 3 (2016): 714–736.

44. Institut des Politiques Publiques, "Discrimination à l'embauche selon le sexe: Les enseignements d'un testing de grande ampleur," Note IPP no. 67 (2021).

45. For evidence of this nonlinear relationship between hourly wage and working hours, see C. Goldin, "A Grand Gender Convergence: Its Last Chapter," *American Economic Review* 104, no. 4 (2014): 1091–1119.

46. See the following two seminal papers: C. Goldin, S. P. Kerr, C. Olivetti, and E. Barth, "The Expanding Gender Earnings Gap: Evidence from the LEHD-2000 Census," *American Economic Review: Papers and Proceedings*. 107, no. 5 (2017): 110–114; and

D. Card, A. Cardoso, and P. Kline, "Bargaining, Sorting, and the Gender Wage Gap: Quantifying the Impact of Firms on the Relative Pay of Women," *Quarterly Journal of Economics* 131, no. 2 (2016): 633–686.

47. The sixteen OECD countries studied were Austria, Costa Rica, Denmark, Estonia, Finland, France, Germany, Hungary, Italy, Japan, Netherlands, Portugal, the Slovak Republic, Spain, Sweden, and the UK. Antoine Bertheau, Gabriele Ciminelli, Chiara Criscuolo, Katarzyna Grabska-Romagosa, Ryo Kambayashi, Michael Koelle, Balazs Murakőzy, Vladimir, Andrei Gorshkov, Oskar Nordström Skans, Satu Nurmi, Catalina Sandoval, Jonathan Garita, Nathalie Scholl, Cyrille Schwellnus, and Richard Upward, "Is It Where You Work, What You Do, or What You Get? Unpacking the Gender Wage Gap and Its Evolution over the Life-Course," in *The Role of Firms in Wage Inequality: Policy Lessons from a Large Scale Cross-Country Study* (Paris: OECD Publishing, 2021), chap. 5.

48. The fact that employers have scope for exploiting their wage-setting power over women is referred to as "monopsonic wage discrimination." See B. Hirsch, "Gender Wage Discrimination," *IZA World of Labor* 310 (2016).

49. See T. Le Barbanchon, R. Rathelot, and A. Roulet, "Gender Differences in Job Search: Trading Off Commute Against Wage," *Quarterly Journal of Economics* 136, no. 1 (2020): 381–426; Jonas Fluchtmann, Anita Marie Glenny, Nikolaj Harmon, and Jonas Maibom, "The Gender Application Gap: Do Men and Women Apply for the Same Jobs?," *American Economic Journal* 16, no. 2 (2024): 182–219.

50. Nina Roussille, "The Role of the Ask Gap in Gender Pay Inequality," *Quarterly Journal of Economics* (forthcoming).

51. Alan Benson, Danielle Li, and Kelly Shue, "'Potential' and the Gender Promotion Gap," *Academy of Management Proceedings* 2023, no. 1 (2023).

52. Laurent Gobillon, Dominique Meurs, and Sébastien Roux, "Estimating Gender Differences in Access to Jobs," *Journal of Labor Economics* 33, no. 2 (2015): 317–363.

53. George-Levi Gayle, Limor Golan, and Robert A. Miller, "Gender Differences in Executive Compensation and Job Mobility," *Journal of Labor Economics* 30, no. 4 (2012): 829–872.

54. Consistent with this interpretation, Bertheau et al., "Is It Where You Work, What You Do, or What You Get?," find that women aged twenty-five to thirty-four years are much more likely than men to experience a nonemployment spell of one or more years, while there is only small difference between women and men aged thirty-five to fifty-four This finding echoes a result from the 2018 edition of the OECD *Employment Outlook* according to which the gap in the cumulative length of career breaks between women and men is on average twice as high among individuals with children as among childless individuals. It is worth noting that career breaks following childbirth are not all voluntary. Some are due to a lack of adequate

provision of affordable childcare when children are younger than school age, to poor supply of out-of-school-hours services when children attend primary education and beyond, and to low access to flexible working time arrangements, that is, the possibility of accumulating hours for days off (full or half days) or of varying the start and end of daily work.

55. Shelley Correll, Stephen Benard, and In Paik, "Getting a Job: Is There a Motherhood Penalty?," *American Journal of Sociology* 112, no. 5 (2007): 1297–1338.

56. Petter Lundborg, Erik Plug, and Astrid Würtz Rasmussen, "Can Women Have Children and a Career? IV Evidence from IVF Treatments," *American Economic Review* 107, no. 6 (2017): 1611–1637.

57. Henrik Kleven, Camille Landais, and Jakob Egholt Søgaard, "Children and Gender Inequality: Evidence from Denmark," *American Economic Journal: Applied Economics* 11, no. 4 (2019)): 181–209.

58. This hypothesis is nonetheless open to criticism. For example, the date of birth of the first child may depend on the stability or, more broadly, on the quality of the parents' employment. In this case, parents with less favorable labor market prospects would tend to delay births. This bias would underestimate the child penalty as defined by the authors.

59. Henrik Kleven, Camille Landais and Gabriel Leite-Mariante, "The Child Penalty Atlas." *Review of Economic Studies* (forthcoming).

## Chapter 6

1. Pew Research Center, "Most Americans Say the Legacy of Slavery Still Affects Black People in the U.S. Today" (2019). See https://www.pewresearch.org/fact-tank/2019/06/17/most-americans-say-the-legacy-of-slavery-still-affects-black-people-in-the-u-s-today.

2. Pew Research Center, "Race, Immigration and Discrimination" (2017). See https://www.pewresearch.org/politics/2017/10/05/4-race-immigration-and-discrimination.

3. OECD, *Catching Up? Intergenerational Mobility and Children of Immigrants* (Paris: OECD Publishing, 2017).

4. The TeO survey aims to analyze the trajectories of individuals according to their social origins and their link to migration. It was conducted by the French Institute for Demographic Studies (INED) and by the French National Statistics Bureau (INSEE) in 2008–2009 and in 2019–2020.

5. Cris Beauchemin, Christelle Hamel, Maud Lesné, Patrick Simon, and TeO Survey, "Les discriminations: Une question de minorités visibles," *Population & Sociétés* 466 (2010). This finding stemming from the 2009–2009 wave of the TeO survey is

also confirmed in the 2019–2020 wave (see https://www.francetvinfo.fr/societe/infographies-racisme-sexisme-islamophobie-le-sentiment-de-discrimination-augmente-en-france-surtout-chez-les-femmes_5237356.html).

6. OECD, *Catching Up?*

7. Ran Abramitzky and Leah Boustan, *Streets of Gold: America's Untold Story of Immigrant Success* (New York: PublicAffairs, 2022).

8. OECD, *Catching Up?*

9. See the analyses by Derek Neal and William Johnson and by Kevin Lang and Michael Manove discussed in chapter 3. See also Raj Chetty, Nathaniel Hendren, Maggie R. Jones, and Sonya R. Porter, "Race and Economic Opportunity in the United States: An Intergenerational Perspective," *Quarterly Journal of Economics* 135, no. 2 (2020): 711–783.

10. For the United States and Canada, see respectively Raj Chetty et al., "Race and Economic Opportunity in the United States," and Daniel Wilson and David Macdonald, "The Income Gap between Aboriginal Peoples and the Rest of Canada (Ottawa: Canadian Centre for Policy Alternatives, 2010). The situation of Indigenous peoples is also worrying in other parts of the world, such as Latin America and Australia. For each of these two countries, see respectively World Bank, *Indigenous Latin America in the Twenty-First Century* (Washington, DC: World Bank, 2015), and Commonwealth of Australia, *Closing the Gap: Prime Minister's Report* (Canberra, 2018).

11. Alexander Bryson, John Forth, and Nikos Theodoropoulos, "The Role of the Workplace in Ethnic Wage Differentials," *British Journal of Industrial Relations* 61, no. 2 (2023): 259–290.

12. W. Carrington and K. Troske, "Interfirm Segregation and the Black/White Wage Gap," *Journal of Labor Economics* 16, no. 2 (1998): 231–260.

13. Elizabeth Linos, Sanaz Mobasseri, and Nina Roussille. "Intersectional Peer Effects at Work: The Effect of White Coworkers on Black Women's Careers," *Management Science* (forthcoming).

14. Rim, Nayoung, Roman Rivera, Andrea Kiss, and Bocar Ba, "The Black-White Recognition Gap in Award Nominations," *Journal of Labor Economics* 42, no. 1 (2024).

15. Morela Hernandez, Derek R. Avery, Sabrina D. Volpone, and Cheryl R. Kaiser, "Bargaining while Black: The Role of Race in Salary Negotiations," *Journal of Applied Psychology* 104, no. 4 (2019): 581–592.

16. Roger Jowell and Patricia Prescott-Clarke, "Racial Discrimination and White-Collar Workers in Britain," *Race & Class* 11, no. 4 (1970): 397–417. This question is also the one that motivated the first correspondence study that was carried out in France in 1979 by the Centre de recherche et d'études des dysfonctions de l'adaptation (CREDA) of the École des Hautes Études en Sciences Sociales (EHESS).

This correspondence study tested the existence of discrimination against racial/ethnic minorities by comparing the interview rates for French people originating in the French West Indies and metropolitan France respectively.

17. Seven main literature reviews have been published on this subject since the early 2000s: Peter A. Riach and Judith Rich, "Field Experiments of Discrimination in the Market Place," *Economic Journal* 112, no. 483 (2002): F480–F518; Judith Rich, "What Do Field Experiments of Discrimination in Markets Tell Us? A Meta-Analysis of Studies Conducted since 2000," IZA Discussion Paper no. 8584 (2014); Eva Zschirnt and Didier Ruedin, "Ethnic Discrimination in Hiring Decisions: A Meta-Analysis of Correspondence Tests 1990–2015," *Journal of Ethnic and Migration Studies* 42, no. 7 (2016): 1115–1134; Marianne Bertrand and Esther Duflo, "Field Experiments on Discrimination," in *Handbook of Field Experiments,* vol. 1, ed. Abhijit V. Banerjee and Esther Duflo (North Holland: Elsevier, 2017), 309–393; Stijn Baert, "Hiring Discrimination: An Overview of (Almost) All Correspondence Experiments since 2005," in *Audit Studies: Behind the Scenes with Theory, Method, and Nuance,* ed. S. Michael Gaddis (New York: Springer, 2018), 63–77; David Neumark, "Experimental Research on Labor Market Discrimination," *Journal of Economic Literature* 56, no. 3 (2018): 799–866; and Louis Lippens, Siel Vermeiren, and Stijn Baert, "The State of Hiring Discrimination: A Meta-Analysis of (Almost) All Recent Correspondence Experiments," *European Economic Review* 151 (2023).

18. The meta-analysis was conducted by Lincoln Quillian, Anthony Heath, Devah Pager, Arnfinn H. Midtbøen, Fenella Fleischmann, and Ole Hexel, "Do Some Countries Discriminate More than Others? Evidence from 97 Field Experiments of Racial Discrimination in Hiring," *Sociological Science* 6 (2019): 467–496. The nine OECD countries were Belgium, Canada, France, Germany, Great Britain, the Netherlands, Norway, Sweden, and the United States.

19. On Aboriginals in Australia, see Alison L. Booth, Andrew Leigh, and Elena Varganova, "Does Ethnic Discrimination Vary Across Minority Groups? Evidence from a Field Experiment," *Oxford Bulletin of Economics and Statistics* 74, no. 4 (2012): 547–573. On Quechua in Peru, see Francisco B. Galarza and Gustavo Yamada, "Labor Market Discrimination in Lima, Peru: Evidence from a Field Experiment," *World Development* 58 (2014): 83–94. On Mongols, Uighurs, and Tibetans in China, see Margaret Maurer-Fazio, "Ethnic Discrimination in China's Internet Job Board Labor Market," *IZA Journal of Migration* 1, no. 12 (2012): 1–24.

20. Nick Drydakis, Peter MacDonald, Vangelis Chiotis, and Laurence Somers, "Age Discrimination in the UK Labour Market: Does Race Moderate Ageism? An Experimental Investigation," *Applied Economics Letters* 25, no. 1 (2018), https://www.tandfonline.com/doi/full/10.1080/13504851.2017.1290763; Nick Drydakis, Anna Paraskevopoulou, and Vasiliki Bozani, "A Field Study of Age Discrimination in the Workplace: The Importance of Gender and Race—Pay the Gap," *Employee Relations* 45, no. 2 (2022), https://www.emerald.com/insight/content/doi/10.1108/ER-06-2021-0277/full/html.

21. Carlos Gomez-Gonzalez, Cornel Nesseler, and Helmut M. Dietl, "Mapping Discrimination in Europe through a Field Experiment in Amateur Sport," *Humanities and Social Sciences Communications* 95 (2021).

22. Anders R. Villadsen and Jesper N. Wulff, "Is the Public Sector a Fairer Employer? Ethnic Employment Discrimination in the Public and Private Sectors," *Academy of Management Discoveries* 4, no. 4 (2018).

23. Mladen Adamovic and Andreas Leibbrandt, "Is There a Glass Ceiling for Ethnic Minorities to Enter Leadership Positions? Evidence from a Field Experiment with over 12,000 Job Applications," *Leadership Quarterly* 34, no. 2 (2023).

24. Stijn Baert, Ann-Sofie De Meyer, Yentl Moerman, and Eddy Omey, "Does Size Matter? Hiring Discrimination and Firm Size," *International Journal of Manpower* 39, no. 4 (2018): 550–566.

25. S. Michael Gaddis, "How Black Are Lakisha and Jamal? Racial Perceptions from Names Used in Correspondence Audit Studies," *Sociological Science* 4 (2017): 469–489. See also Stijn Baert, Louis Lippens, and Hannah Van Borm, "Selecting Names for Experiments on Ethnic Discrimination," IZA Discussion Paper no. 15524 (2022).

26. Javier G. Polavieja, Bram Lancee, María Ramos, Susanne Veit, and Ruta Yemane, "In Your Face: A Comparative Field Experiment on Racial Discrimination in Europe. *Socio-Economic Review* 21, no. 3 (2023): 1551–1578.

27. Louis Lippens, Stijn Baert, Abel Ghekiere, Pieter-Paul Verhaeghe, and Eva Derous, "Is Labour Market Discrimination Against Ethnic Minorities Better Explained by Taste or Statistics? A Systematic Review of the Empirical Evidence," *Journal of Ethnic and Migration Studies* 48, no. 17 (2022): 4243–4276.

28. Philip Oreopoulos, "Why Do Skilled Immigrants Struggle in the Labor Market? A Field Experiment with Thirteen Thousand Resumes," *American Economic Journal: Economic Policy*, 3, no. 4 (2011): 148–171.

29. See Zschirnt and Ruedin, "Ethnic Discrimination in Hiring Decisions."

30. See OECD, *Settling In: Indicators of Immigrant Integration* (Paris: OECD Publishing, 2023). See also OECD, *Making Integration Work: Young People with Migrant Parents* (Paris: OECD Publishing, 2021).

31. Marcus Eyting, "Why Do We Discriminate? The Role of Motivated Reasoning," working paper (2024).

32. Alan Benson and Louis-Pierre Lepage, "Learning to Discriminate on the Job," working paper (2024).

33. See Lincoln Quillian, Devah Pager, Ole Hexel, and Arnfinn H. Midtbøen, "Meta-Analysis of Field Experiments Shows No Change in Racial Discrimination in Hiring

over Time," *Proceedings of the National Academy of Sciences of the United States of America (PNAS)* 114, no. 41 (2017): 10870–10875.

34. Lincoln Quillian and John J. Lee. 2023. "Trends in Racial and Ethnic Discrimination in Hiring in Six Western Countries," *Proceedings of the National Academy of Sciences of the United States of America (PNAS)* 120, no. 6 (2023).

35. Louis Lippens, Siel Vermeiren, and Stijn Baert. 2023. "The State of Hiring Discrimination: A Meta-Analysis of (Almost) All Recent Correspondence Experiments," *European Economic Review* 151 (2023).

36. See, for example, Stijn Baert, Bart Cockx, Niels Gheyle and Cora Vandamme "Is There Less Discrimination in Occupations Where Recruitment Is Difficult?," *Industrial and Labor Relations Review*, 68, no. 3 (2015):. 467–500.

37. For evidence of this mechanism regarding racial/ethnic discrimination, see Karl David Boulware and Kenneth N. Kuttner, "Labor Market Conditions and Discrimination: Is There a Link?," *AEA Papers and Proceedings* 109 (2019): 166–170. Concerning age-based discrimination, see Gordon B. Dahl and Matthew Knepper, "Age Discrimination across the Business Cycle," *American Economic Journal: Economic Policy* 15, no. 4 (2023): 75–112.

38. Laetitia Challe, Yannick L'Horty, Pascale Petit, and François-Charles Wolff, "Cyclical Behavior of Hiring Discrimination: Evidence from Repeated Experiments in France," *The Annals of Regional Science* 72 (2024): 711–733.

39. For the United States, Nicolas Jacquemet and Constantine Yannelis, "Indiscriminate Discrimination: A Correspondence Test for Ethnic Homophily in the Chicago Labor Market," *Labour Economics* 19, no. 6 (2012): 824–832. For France, see Anthony Edo and Nicolas Jacquemet, "Discrimination à l'embauche selon l'origine et le genre: Défiance indifférenciée ou ciblée sur certains groupes?," *Économie et Statistique* 464–465–466 (2013).

40. Anthony Edo and Nicolas Jacquemet, *La Discrimination à l'embauche sur le marché du travail français* (Paris: Éditions rue d'Ulm, 2013).

41. Zschirnt and Ruedin, "Ethnic Discrimination in Hiring Decisions."

42. See Siri Thanasombat and John Trasviña, "Screening Names Instead of Qualifications: Testing with Emailed Resumes Reveals Racial Preferences," *AAPI Nexus Journal: Policy, Practice, and Community* 3, no. 2 (2005): 105–115.

43. Fabrice Foroni, "Résultats du testing sollicité par le groupe Casino" (ISM-CORUM, 2008).

44. Emmanuel Duguet, Noam Leandri, Yannick L'Horty, and Pascale Petit, "Are Young French Jobseekers of Ethnic Immigrant Origin Discriminated Against? A Controlled Experiment in the Paris Area," *Annals of Economics and Statistics* 99–100 (2010): 187–215.

45. Several correspondence studies have revealed the marked hiring discrimination experienced by candidates from Muslim-majority countries in Europe and in countries predominantly inhabited by people of European origin. For a review of this literature, see appendix 2 in Marie-Anne Valfort, "Religious Discrimination in Access to Employment: A Reality" (Paris: Institut Montaigne, 2015).

46. Steven Fish, *Are Muslims Distinctive? A Look at the Evidence* (Oxford: Oxford University Press, 2011).

47. Sylvain Brouard and Vincent Tiberj, *As French as Everyone Else? A Survey of French Citizens of Maghrebin, African, and Turkish Origin* (Philadelphia: Temple University Press, 2011). See also the French version of this study: Sylvain Brouard and Vincent Tiberj, *Français comme les autres? Enquête sur les citoyens d'origine maghrébine, africaine et turque* (Paris: Presses de Sciences Po, 2005).

48. Marie-Anne Valfort, "Anti-Muslim Discrimination in France: Evidence from a Field Experiment," *World Development* 135 (2020).

49. These first names were determined from INSEE's "Surname File," which lists all given names found in France since 1946 and their frequency. The names Michel/Nathalie and Mohammed (or Mohamed)/Samira are among the five most common Christian and Muslim first names in France during the postwar period.

50. Previous correspondence studies that have attempted to identify religious discrimination have failed to remove all of the confounding factors discussed here. Notably, none managed to isolate the effect of the candidates' religious tradition from their degree of religious practice as adults. There are five such CV test studies: Claire L. Adida, David D. Laitin, and Marie-Anne Valfort, "Identifying Barriers to Muslim Integration in France," *Proceedings of the National Academy of Sciences of the United States of America (PNAS)* 107, no. 52 (2010): 384–390; Guillaume Pierné, "Hiring Discrimination Based on National Origin and Religious Closeness: Results from a Field Experiment in the Paris Area," *IZA Journal of Labor Economics* 2, no. 4 (2013): 1–15; Bradley R. E. Wright, Michael Wallace, John Bailey, and Allen Hyde, "Religious Affiliation and Hiring Discrimination in New England: A Field Experiment," *Research in Social Stratification and Mobility* 34 (2013): 111–126; Michael Wallace, Bradley R. E. Wright, and Allen Hyde, "Religious Affiliation and Hiring Discrimination in the American South: A Field Experiment," *Social Currents* 1, no. 2 (2014): 189–207; and Alessandro Acquisti and Christina M. Fong, "An Experiment in Hiring Discrimination via Online Social Networks," *Management Science* 66, no. 3 (2020): 1005–1024.

51. For a discussion of these problematic behaviors, see Claire L. Adida, David D. Laitin, and Marie-Anne Valfort, "Women, Muslim Immigrants, and Economic Integration in France," *Economics and Politics* 26, no. 1 (2014): 79–95, and Claire L. Adida, David D. Laitin, and Marie-Anne Valfort, *Why Muslim Integration Fails in Christian-Heritage Societies* (Cambridge, MA: Harvard University Press, 2016).

52. This finding matches that of Claire L. Adida, David D. Laitin, and Marie-Anne Valfort, "Muslims in France: Identifying a Discriminatory Equilibrium," *Journal of Population Economics* 27, no. 4 (2014): 1039–1086.

53. Valfort, "Anti-Muslim Discrimination in France."

54. See Claire L. Adida, David D. Laitin, and Marie-Anne Valfort, "How Do Muslims qua Muslims Integrate in the US?," *Economics Bulletin* 35, no. 4 (2015): 1–17; and Adida et al., *Why Muslim Integration Fails in Christian-Heritage Societies.*

55. Valentina Di Stasio, Bram Lancee, Susanne Veit, and Ruta Yemane, "Muslim by Default or Religious Discrimination? Results from a Cross-National Field Experiment on Hiring Discrimination," *Journal of Ethnic and Migration Studies* 47, no. 6 (2021): 1305–1326.

56. On the headscarf as barrier, see Mariña Fernández-Reino, Valentina Di Stasio, and Susanne Veit, "Discrimination Unveiled: A Field Experiment on the Barriers Faced by Muslim Women in Germany, the Netherlands, and Spain," *European Sociological Review* 39, no. 3 (2023): 479–497. For results specifically for Germany, see Doris Weichselbaumer, "Multiple Discrimination Against Female Immigrants Wearing Headscarves," *Industrial and Labor Relations Review* 73, no. 3 (2020): 600–627.

57. On this topic, see IMS-Entreprendre pour la Cité, "Les stéréotypes sur les origins: Comprendre et agir dans l'entreprise" (2014).

58. Eric D. Gould and Esteban F. Klor, "The Long-Run Effect of 9/11: Terrorism, Backlash, and the Assimilation of Muslim Immigrants in the West," *Economic Journal* 126, no. 597 (2016): F2064–F2114.

59. Efraim Benmelech and Esteban F. Klor, "What Explains the Flow of Foreign Fighters to ISIS?," *Terrorism and Political Violence* 32, no. 7 (2020).

60. Philip Verwimp, "Foreign Fighters in Syria and Iraq and the Socio-Economic Environment They Faced at Home: A Comparison of European Countries," *Perspectives on Terrorism* 10, no. 6 (2016): 68–81.

61. Adida et al., *Why Muslim Integration Fails in Christian-Heritage Societies.*

62. Consistent with this finding, the sociologists Anne Muxel and Olivier Galland show, based on a survey of seven thousand French secondary school students stemming mostly from deprived areas (the so-called "Quartiers de la Politique de la Ville"), that attraction for radicalism is much stronger among young Muslims than among young Christians. See Olivier Galland and Anne Muxel, *La Tentation radicale: Enquête auprès des lycéens* (Paris: Presses Universitaires de France, 2018).

63. Vasiliki Fouka, "How do Immigrants Respond to Discrimination? The Case of Germans in the US during World War I," *American Political Science Review* 113, no. 2 (2019): 405–422.

64. Vasiliki Fouka, "Backlash: The Unintended Effects of Language Prohibition in US Schools after World War I," *Review of Economic Studies* 87, no. 1 (2020): 204–239.

65. See, for example, Pew Research Center, "The Future of the Global Muslim Population: Projections for 2010–2030" (2011).

66. Gordon W. Allport, *The Nature of Prejudice* (New York: Addison-Wesley, 1954).

67. Hubert M. Blalock, *Toward a Theory of Minority-Group Relations* (New York: Capricorn Books, 1967).

68. Claire L. Adida, David D. Laitin, and Marie-Anne Valfort, "'One Muslim Is Enough!' Evidence from a Field Experiment in France," *Annals of Economics and Statistics* 121–122 (2016): 121–160.

69. This remark was uttered in French during a photo-op at the UMP (Union for a Popular Movement, the center-right political party in France led at the time by Nicolas Sarkozy and now called Les Républicains) Summer School, in which the minister was interacting with a young militant, Hamid. Brice Hortefeux joked that this militant, who was known to be Muslim, "does not correspond at all to the prototype" after having been told that the militant eats pork and drinks beer. He then added, "You always have to have one; when there's one, that's OK; it's when there's a lot of them that there are problems."

70. As explained in chapter 4, the dictator game is an economic game designed to test the self-interest versus the altruism of individuals.

71. Valfort, "Anti-Muslim Discrimination in France."

72. Linos, Mobasseri, and Roussille, "Intersectional Peer Effects at Work."

## Chapter 7

1. How productivity develops from prime working age to retirement is still being debated, but a majority of studies in Europe and the United States that are based on linked employer-employee data sets tend to find that productivity does not decline substantially with age but instead stabilizes, at least until age fifty-five to sixty years. Older workers appear to be, on average, as productive as prime-age workers. See OECD, *Promoting an Age-Inclusive Workforce* (Paris: OECD Publishing, 2020), chapter 2, for a synthesis.

2. The employment rate by age group is defined as the ratio of the number of people employed in the age group considered to the total number of people in this age group.

3. OECD, *Skills Matter: Further Results from the Survey of Adult Skills (PIAAC)* (Paris: OECD Publishing, 2019).

4. Rebecca Perron, "The Value of Experience: Age Discrimination Against Older Workers Persists," AARP Research (2018).

5. TNS Sofres, "Baromètre de perception de l'égalité des chances en entreprise" (survey), fifth wave, carried out for MEDEF (2016).

6. See, for example, Richard Johnson and David Neumark, "Age Discrimination, Job Separations, and Employment Status of Older Workers: Evidence from Self-Reports," *Journal of Human Resources* 32, no. 4 (1997): 779–811.

7. In the French case, see DARES, "L'opinion des employeurs sur les seniors: Les craintes liées au vieillissement s'atténuent," DARES Analyses no. 55 (2010).

8. For a survey, see R. A. Posthuma and M. A. Campion, "Age Stereotypes in the Workplace: Common Stereotypes, Moderators, and Future Research Directions," *Journal of Management* 35, no. 1 (2009): 158–188. See also E. Toomey and C. Rudolph, "Age Stereotypes in the Workplace," in *Encyclopedia of Geropsychology*. ed. N. A. Pachana (Singapore: Springer, 2017).

9. Victoria Büsch, Svenn-Åge Dahl, and Dennis A. V. Dittrich, "An Empirical Study of Age Discrimination in Norway and Germany," *Applied Economics* 41, no. 5 (2009): 633–651.

10. B. Richardson, J. Webb, L. Webber, and K. Smith, "Age Discrimination in the Evaluation of Job Applicants," *Journal of Applied Social Psychology* 43 (2013): 35–44.

11. T. W. H. Ng and D. C. Feldman, "Evaluating Six Common Stereotypes about Older Workers with Meta- Analytical Data," *Personnel Psychology* 65 (2012): 821–858.

12. Stijn Baert, Jennifer Norga, Yannick Thuy, and Marieke Van Hecke, "Getting Grey Hairs in the Labour Market: An Alternative Experiment on Age Discrimination," *Journal of Economic Psychology* 57 (2016): 86–101.

13. Marc Bendick Jr., Charles W. Jackson, and J. Horacio Romero, "Employment Discrimination Against Older Workers: An Experimental Study of Hiring Practices," *Journal of Aging & Social Policy* 8, no. 4 (1997): 25–46.

14. Marc Bendick Jr., Lauren E. Brown, and Kennington Wall, "No Foot in the Door: An Experimental Study of Employment Discrimination Against Older Workers," *Journal of Aging & Social Policy* 10, no. 4 (1999): 5–23.

15. Henry S. Farber, Dan Silverman, and Till M. von Wachter, "Factors Determining Callbacks to Job Applications by the Unemployed: An Audit Study," *RSF: The Russell Sage Foundation Journal of the Social Sciences* 3, no. 3 (2017): 168–201. See also Henry S. Farber, Dan Silverman, and Till M. von Wachter, "Determinants of Callbacks to Job Applications: An Audit Study," *American Economic Review* 106, no. 5 (2016): 314–318.

16. In a more recent study, the same authors obtained lower callback rates for people who had been unemployed for more than a year, a finding that is consistent with other studies on the subject. See Liam D'hert, Stijn Baert, and Louis Lippens. "Unemployment, Inactivity, and Hiring Chances: A Systematic Review and Meta-Analysis." IZA Discussion Paper no. 17141 (2024); Henry S. Farber, Chris M. Herbst,

Dan Silverman, and Till M. von Wachter, "Whom Do Employers Want? The Role of Recent Employment History and Age," *Journal of Labor Economics* 37, no. 2 (2019); Florent Fremigacci, Rémi Le Gall, Yannick L'Horty, and Pascale Petit, "Le conformisme des recruteurs: Projet SPECTRE," file "Pratiques et impact des activités réduites: Les résultats issus de 5 recherches soutenues par Pôle employ," *Études et Recherches Pôle emploi* (August 8, 2016), 271–297; Kory Kroft, Fabian Lange, and Matthew J. Notowidigdo, "Duration Dependence and Labor Market Conditions: Evidence from a Field Experiment," *Quarterly Journal of Economics* 128, no. 3 (2013): 1123–1167.

17. Peter A. Riach, "A Field Experiment Investigating Age Discrimination in Four European Labour Markets," *International Review of Applied Economics* 29, no. 5 (2015): 1–12.

18. Ali M. Ahmed, Lina Andersson, and Mats Hammarstedt, "Does Age Matter for Employability? A Field Experiment on Ageism in the Swedish Labour Market," *Applied Economics Letters* 19 (2012): 403–406.

19. David Neumark, Ian Burn, and Patrick Button, "Is It Harder for Older Workers to Find Jobs? New and Improved Evidence from a Field Experiment," *Journal of Political Economy* 127 (2019): 915–41.

20. Peter A. Riach and Judith Rich, "An Experimental Investigation of Age Discrimination in the French Labour Market," IZA Discussion Paper no. 2522 (2006).

21. Peter A. Riach and Judith Rich, "An Experimental Investigation of Age Discrimination in the English Labor Market," *Annals of Economics and Statistics* 99/100 (2010): 169–185.

22. Joanna N. Lahey, "Age, Women, and Hiring: An Experimental Study," *Journal of Human Resources* 43, no. 1 (2008): 30–56.

23. Matthew Tinsley, *Too Much to Lose: Understanding and Supporting Britain's Older Workers* (London: Policy Exchange, 2012).

24. Neumark, Burn, and Button, "Is It Harder for Older Workers to Find Jobs?"

25. Baert, Norga, Thuy, and Van Hecke, "Getting Grey Hairs in the Labour Market."

26. Nick Drydakis, Peter MacDonald, Vangelis Chiotis, and Laurence Somers, "Age Discrimination in the UK Labour Market: Does Race Moderate Ageism? An Experimental Investigation," *Applied Economics Letters* 25, no. 1 (2018), https://www.tandfonline.com/doi/full/10.1080/13504851.2017.1290763; Nick Drydakis, Anna Paraskevopoulou, and Vasiliki Bozani, "A Field Study of Age Discrimination in the Workplace: The Importance of Gender and Race—Pay the Gap," *Employee Relations* 45, no. 2 (2022), https://www.emerald.com/insight/content/doi/10.1108/ER-06-2021-0277/full/html.

27. David Neumark, "Detecting Discrimination in Audit and Correspondence Studies," *Journal of Human Resources* 47, no. 4 (2012): 1128–1157.

28. Neumark, Burn, and Button, "Is It Harder for Older Workers to Find Jobs?"

29. David Neumark, "Age Discrimination in Hiring: Evidence from Age-Blind vs. Non-Age-Blind Hiring Procedures," *Journal of Human Resources* 57, no. 4 (2022).

## Chapter 8

1. Judith Duportail, "Le patron refuse de m'embaucher parce qu'il me trouve moche," *Le Monde,* August 18, 2010.

2. Catherine Valenti, "Victims of 'Lookism' Face Uphill Battle," *ABC News,* January 6, 2006.

3. Jean-François Amadieu, *Le Poids des apparences* (Paris, Odile Jacob, 2002).

4. Angela M. Griffin and Judith H. Langlois "Stereotype Directionality and Attractiveness Stereotyping: Is Beauty Good or Is Ugly Bad?," *Social Cognition* 24, no. 2 (2006): 187–206.

5. Judith H. Langlois, Lisa Kalakanis, Adam J. Rubenstein, Andrea Larson, Monica Hallam, and Monica Smoot, "Maxims or Myths of Beauty? A Meta-Analytic and Theoretical Review," *Psychological Bulletin* 126, no. 3 (2000): 390–423.

6. For a meta-analysis, see Langlois et al., "Maxims or Myths of Beauty?"

7. Gillian Rhodes, "The Evolutionary Psychology of Facial Beauty," *Annual Review of Psychology* 57 (2006): 199–226.

8. The Canadian Quality of Life Study, analyzed by Daniel Hamermesh and Jeff Biddle, "Beauty and the Labor Market," *American Economic Review* 84, no. 5 (1994): 1174–1194.

9. Jeff Biddle and Daniel Hamermesh, "Beauty, Productivity, and Discrimination: Lawyers' Looks and Lucre," *Journal of Labor Economics* 16, no. 1 (1998): 172–201.

10. The Quality of Employment Survey (QES) conducted in 1971 on 2,000 individuals, and the Quality of Employment Survey (QES) conducted in 1977 on 1,500 individuals.

11. Daniel Hamermesh, *Beauty Pays* (Princeton, NJ: Princeton University Press, 2011).

12. Samuel Bruton, "Looks-Based Hiring and Wrongful Discrimination," *Business and Society Review* 120, no. 4 (2015): 607–635.

13. Daniel Hamermesh and Jeff Biddle, "Beauty and the Labor Market," *American Economic Review* 84, no. 5 (1994): 1174–1194.

14. Based on an average hourly wage of $20, two thousand hours of work a year for forty years.

15. These calculations apply to the United States and were taken from Hamermesh, *Beauty Pays.*

16. Jason M. Fletcher, "Beauty vs. Brains: Early Labor Market Outcomes of High School Graduates," *Economics Letters* 105, no. 3 (2009): 321–325.

17. For premiums on beauty across countries and occupations, see, for example, for the UK, Barry Harper, "Beauty, Stature and the Labour Market: A British Cohort Study," *Oxford Bulletin of Economics and Statistics* 62 (2000): 771–800; for Germany, Karina Doorley and Eva Sierminska, "Myth or Fact? The Beauty Premium across the Wage Distribution in Germany," *Economic Letters* 129 (2015): 29–34; for Australia, Jeff Borland and Andrew Leigh, "Unpacking the Beauty Premium: What Channels Does It Operate Through, and Has It Changed over Time?," *Economic Records* 90, no. 288 ( 2014): 17–32; for China, Daniel S Hamermesh, Xin Meng, and Junsen Zhang, "Dress for Success: Does Primping Pay?," *Labour Economics* 9, no. (2002): 361–373.

18. John Karl Scholz and Kamil Sicinski, "Facial Attractiveness and Lifetime Earnings: Evidence from a Cohort Study," *Review of Economics and Statistics* 97, no. 1 (2015): 14–28.

19. In this panel, beauty does not come positively and significantly correlated with IQ once family background is accounted for, or with class rank, total years of educational attainment, or mortality. Hence the observed beauty premium does not stem from attractiveness capturing the effects of cognitive skills or health. However, other research based on the National Longitudinal Study of Adolescent Health (Add Health) has found that being unattractive is associated with deteriorated high school outcomes, such as grade point averages, problems with teachers, or school suspensions, leading later in life to higher chances of being involved in criminal activities. See Naci Mocan and Erdal Tekin, "Ugly Criminals," *Review of Economics and Statistics* 92, no. 1 (2010): 15–30. This is not surprising to the extent that educational choices are influenced by labor market rewards later in life (see chapter 12).

20. Daniel Hamermesh and Jeff Biddle confirm the importance of beauty in such occupations. More precisely, focusing on the legal sector, where contacts between lawyers and clients are frequent and thus have the potential to greatly affect income, these authors followed more than two thousand individuals who graduated from a major U.S. law school in the 1970s, for at least five years. The physical appearance of these individuals was assessed by asking a panel of observers to rate their photographs. As expected, lawyers considered the best-looking were earning more than others after five years of practice in the legal sector, and the gap widened with the number of years of professional experience. This advantage was found in all areas of legal expertise, including among independent lawyers. One plausible explanation is clients' preference for the best-looking lawyers, which would provide them both with more cases and with the capacity to charge higher fees per case. See Biddle and Hamermesh, "Beauty, Productivity, and Discrimination."

21. Langlois et al., "Maxims or Myths of Beauty?"

22. Markus M. Mobius and Tanya S. Rosenblat, "Why Beauty Matters," *American Economic Review* 96, no. 1 (2006): 222–235.

23. Ralph Stinebrickner, Todd Stinebrickner, and Paul Sullivan, "Beauty, Job Tasks, and Wages: A New Conclusion about Employer Taste-Based Discrimination," *Review of Economics and Statistics* 101, no. 4 (2019): 602–615.

24. Consistent with this finding, a group of economists have shown that having good-looking managers increases the turnover of advertising companies in the Netherlands to an extent that is greater than the impact of these managers' beauty on their own salaries. See Gerard A. Pfann, Jeff E. Biddle, Daniel S. Hamermesh, and Ciska M. Bosman, "Business Success and Businesses' Beauty Capital," *Economics Letters* 67, no. 2 (2000): 201–207.

25. Michèle Belot, Venkataraman Bhaskar, and Jeroen van de Ven, "Beauty and the Sources of Discrimination," *Journal of Human Resources* 47, no. 3 (2012): 851–872.

26. Florencia López Bóo, Martín A. Rossi, and Sergio S. Urzúa, "The Labor Market Return to an Attractive Face: Evidence from a Field Experiment," *Economics Letters* 118, no. 1 (2013): 170–172.

27. Eleonora Patacchini, Giuseppe Ragusa, and Yves Zenou, "Unexplored Dimensions of Discrimination in Europe: Homosexuality and Physical Appearance," *Journal of Population Economics* 28, no. 4 (2015): 1045–1073.

28. Bradley Ruffle and Ze'ev Shtudiner, "Are Good-Looking People More Employable?," *Management Science* 61, no. 8 (2015): 1760–1776.

29. Stijn Baert, "Facebook Profile Picture Appearance Affects Recruiters' First Hiring Decisions," *New Media & Society* 20, no. 3 (2018): 1220–1239.

30. For additional and somewhat contrasting evidence on the interaction between the beauty premium and educational attainment, see also Weiguang Deng, Dayang Li, and Dong Zhou," "Beauty and Job Accessibility: New Evidence from a Field Experiment," *Journal of Population Economics* 33 (2020): 1303–1341, which finds in China that better educational credentials reduce the beauty premium among men but not among women.

31. Dan-Olof Rooth, "Obesity, Attractiveness, and Differential Treatment in Hiring: A Field Experiment," *Journal of Human Resources* 44, no. 3 (2009): 710–735.

32. John Cawley, "The Impact of Obesity on Wages," *Journal of Human Resources* 39, no. 2 (2004):. 451–474.

33. Petter Lundborg, Kristian Bolin, Sören Höjgård, and Björn Lindgren, "Obesity and Occupational Attainment among the 50+ of Europe," in *Advances in Health*

*Economics and Health Services Research*, vol. 17, *The Economics of Obesity*, ed. Kristian Bolin and John Cawley (Amsterdam: Elsevier, 2006).

34. Petter Lundborg, Paul Nystedt, and Dan-Olof Rooth, "Body Size, Skills, and Income: Evidence from 150,000 Teenage Siblings," *Demography* 51, no. 5 (2014): 1573–1596.

35. Euna Han, Edward C. Norton, and Lisa M. Powell, "Direct and Indirect Effects of Body Weight on Adult Wages," *Economics & Human Biology* 9, no. 4 (2011): 381–392.

36. Nicola Persico, Andrew Postlewaite, and Dan Silverman, "The Effect of Adolescent Experience on Labor Market Outcomes: The Case of Height," *Journal of Political Economy* 112, no. 5 (2004): 1019–1053.

37. Nicolas Herpin, "La taille des hommes: Son incidence sur la vie en couple et la carrière professionnelle," *Économie et Statistique* 361 (2003): 71–90.

38. Anne Case and Christina Paxson, "Stature and Status: Height, Ability, and Labor Market Outcomes," *Journal of Political Economy* 116, no. 3 (2008): 499–532.

39. Case and Paxson, "Stature and Status."

40. Persico, Postlewaite, and Silverman, "The Effect of Adolescent Experience on Labor Market Outcomes."

41. Lundborg, Nystedt, and Rooth, "Body Size, Skills, and Income."

## Chapter 9

1. Among a convenience (i.e., nonrepresentative) sample of 272 intersex individuals in Australia, 52 percent self-identified as lesbians, gay men, or bisexuals and 8 percent self-identified as transgender. See T. Jones et al., *Intersex: Stories and Statistics from Australia* (Open Book Publishers, 2016).

2. European Union Agency for Fundamental Rights, *The Fundamental Rights Situation of Intersex People* (Vienna, 2015).

3. Timothy W. Jones, "Reviled, Reclaimed and Respected: The History of the Word 'Queer,'" The Conversation, January 18, 2023.

4. OECD, "The LGBT Challenge: How to Better Include Sexual and Gender Minorities?," in *Society at Glance: OECD Social Indicators* (Paris: OECD Publishing, 2019).

5. Ipsos, *LGBT+ Pride 2021 Global Survey* (2021).

6. United Nations Department of Economic and Social Affairs, Population Division, *World Population Prospects 2024: Summary of Results,* UN DESA/POP/2024/TR/NO. 9 (2024).

7. OECD, "The LGBT Challenge."

8. Katherine Baldiga Coffman, Lucas C. Coffman, and Keith M. Marzilli Ericson, "The Size of the LGBT Population and the Magnitude of Anti-Gay Sentiment Are Substantially Underestimated," *Management Science* 63, no. 10 (2017): 3168–3186. The item count technique was devised in the early 1980s to ensure the anonymity of those surveyed, and thus to better estimate the proportion of individuals for whom assertions of a sensitive nature—such as being homosexual or bisexual—are true. It involves asking respondents to select, from a list of descriptive items, how many apply to them. More specifically, the item count technique involves dividing respondents into two groups by means of a random draw. A list of four nonsensitive assertions is given to the first group, such as "I remember where I was on the day of the *Challenger* space shuttle disaster" or "I spent a lot of time playing video games when I was a child." The same list is given to the second group, supplemented by a sensitive assertion regarding the person's sexual orientation: "I consider myself to be homosexual or bisexual" or "I happen to have sexual relationships with people of the same sex" or "I happen to be physically attracted to people of the same sex." As a result of the random distribution of respondents between group 1 and group 2, the number of nonsensitive assertions that, according to the respondents, apply to them, is the same on average in each group. Therefore, since the assertion on sexual orientation is present only in group 2, the proportion of LGB persons is calculated from the difference between the average number of assertions selected by individuals in group 2 and those in group 1. For example, suppose that group 1 and group 2 each consist of one hundred people, of whom five are homosexual or bisexual. The item count technique should reveal this 5 percent proportion. In group 1, let's say two items are selected by each participant, that is, the average number of items confirmed is two. In group 2, the ninety-five heterosexual individuals will also select two items, but the five homosexual/bisexual individuals will select three, since the item on sexual orientation applies to them. In other words, the average number of items confirmed in group 2 is 2.05 (95 percent*2+5 percent*3). The difference between this number and its equivalent in group 1 yields the proportion of 5 percent. For more information on this technique, see Judith D. Miller, "A New Survey Technique for Studying Deviant Behavior" (PhD thesis, George Washington University, 1984).

9. For the Gallup study, see https://news.gallup.com/poll/389792/lgbt-identification-ticks-up.aspx.

10. Maria Laura Bettinsoli, Alexandra Suppes, and Jaime L. Napier, "Predictors of Attitudes toward Gay Men and Lesbian Women in 23 Countries," *Social Psychological and Personality Science* 11, no. 5 (2020): 697–708.

11. Bettinsoli, Suppes, and Napier, "Predictors of Attitudes toward Gay Men and Lesbian Women in 23 Countries." Endorsement of traditional gender norms was measured by asking respondents to rate the importance for them of adhering to the following ten norms: "men should not be too emotional," "men should not be

too affectionate," "a man should never admit when others hurt his feelings," "men should be able to fix most things around the house," "boys should play with trucks rather than dolls," "men should be physically tough," "men should act masculine," "women should act feminine," "women should be caring and nurturing," and "women should not be too dominant." The twenty-three countries were Argentina, Australia, Belgium, Brazil, Canada, China, France, Germany, Great Britain, Hungary, Italy, India, Japan, Mexico, Peru, Poland, Russia, South Africa, South Korea, Spain, Sweden, Turkey, and the United States.

The authors failed to identify a positive association between endorsement of traditional gender norms and negative attitudes toward gay men and lesbians in only three countries. In South Korea, endorsement of gender norms was unrelated to attitudes, while in China and India, endorsement of gender norms was *positively* associated with openness toward gay men and lesbians. This last result is counterintuitive and calls for further research. It is worthwhile noting, however, that this finding is not robust to the use of alternative data sets. Relying on the six waves of the China General Social Survey conducted in the 2010s, Yun Zhou does find that greater endorsement of traditional gender norms is related to lower acceptance of same-sex sexual behavior. See Yun Zhou, "Visualizing Gendered Attitudes toward Same-Sex Sexual Behavior in China over a Decade," *Socius: Sociological Research for a Dynamic World* 8 (2022).

12. In the eleventh revision of the *International Classification of Diseases* (ICD-11), which constitutes the current global standard for recording health information and causes of death, intersex variations are pathologized—that is, they are codified as pathologies—and described as "disorders of sex development."

13. The ICD-11 classifications went into effect in all member states of the World Health Organization on January 1, 2022. The ICD-11 has redefined gender identity–related health, replacing outdated diagnostic categories such as the ICD-10's "transsexualism" and "gender identity disorder of children" with "gender incongruence of adolescence and adulthood" and "gender incongruence of childhood," respectively, moving them out of the "Mental and Behavioral Disorders" category. However, this important move toward depathologizing being transgender may not be followed by significant shifts at the national level. The implementation date is indicative, not mandatory, meaning that member states are free to adjust to ICD-11 at their own pace.

14. OECD, *Over the Rainbow? The Road to LGBTI Inclusion* (Paris: OECD Publishing, 2020).

15. OECD, *Man Enough? Measuring Masculine Norms to Promote Women's Empowerment* (Paris: OECD Publishing, 2021).

16. Lucas Ramon Mendos and Dhia Rezki Rohaizad, *Laws on Us: A Global Overview of Legal Progress and Backtracking on Sexual Orientation, Gender Identity, Gender Expression, and Sex Characteristics* (Geneva: ILGA World, 2024).

17. The death penalty provision is accompanied by several other harsh sanctions. Notably, individuals convicted of "*attempted* aggravated homosexuality" can face imprisonment for up to fourteen years. Additionally, a twenty-year prison sentence is imposed for those found guilty of "promoting" homosexuality, a broadly defined offense that can affect a wide range of people, including journalists, human rights activists, and campaigners.

18. Declarations regarding the moral duty to fight against other types of discrimination have also been made by the United Nations General Assembly, for instance the Declaration on the Elimination of All Forms of Intolerance and Discrimination Based on Religion or Belief.

19. Archbishop Celestino Migliore quoted in "Vatican Opines on UN Sexuality Initiative," *Spero News*, December 20, 2008.

20. OECD, *Over the Rainbow?*

21. According to EU case law, transgender individuals are also granted some protection against discrimination. More precisely, in the case of *P. v. S. and Cornwall County Council* (Case C-13/94, [1996] IRLR 347), the Court of Justice of the European Union ruled in 1996 that the category of sex protects gender identity, although in a narrow sense. It held that the right to equal treatment and prohibition of discrimination is not confined solely on the fact that an individual is of one sex or the other. Rather, "it must extend to discrimination arising from gender reassignment . . . since to dismiss a person on the ground that he or she intends to undergo, or has undergone, gender reassignment is to treat him or her unfavorably by comparison with persons of the sex to which he or she was deemed to belong to before that operation."

22. See Justin McCarthy, "Same-Sex Marriage Support Inches Up to New High of 71%" (Gallup, June 1, 2022). On the LGBT-GAI, see Andrew Flores, *Social Acceptance of LGBT People in 174 Countries, 1981 to 2017* (Los Angeles: Williams Institute, 2019).

23. Billur Aksoy, Christopher S. Carpenter, and Dario Sansone, "Understanding Labor Market Discrimination Against Transgender People: Evidence from a Double List Experiment and a Survey," *Management Science* (2024).

24. In the internal guide issued by Accenture to help managers foster LGBTIQ+ inclusion, this view is described as the most widespread misconception that prevails in the workplace.

25. K.-B. Bryant-Lees and M. E. Kite, "Evaluations of LGBT Job Applicants: Consequences of Applying 'Out,'" *Equality, Diversity and Inclusion* 40 no. 7 (2021): 874–891.

26. For a comprehensive overview of this literature, see Marie-Anne Valfort. "LGBTI in OECD Countries: A Review," OECD Social, Employment and Migration Working Papers n°198 (2017), and OECD, "The LGBT Challenge." Recent literature reviews

include- M. V. Lee Badgett, Christopher S. Carpenter, and Dario Sansone, "LGBTQ Economics," *Journal of Economic Perspectives* 35, no. 2 (2021): 141–170; Nick Drydakis, "Sexual Orientation and Earnings: A Meta-Analysis 2012–2020," *Journal of Population Economics* 35 (2022): 409–440; M. V. Lee Badgett, Christopher S. Carpenter, Maxine J. Lee, and Dario Sansone, "A Review of the Economics of Sexual Orientation and Gender Identity," *Journal of Economic Literature* 62, no. 3 (2024): 948–994.

27. Drydakis, "Sexual Orientation and Earnings."

28. Christopher S. Carpenter, Samuel T. Eppink, and Gilbert Gonzales, "Transgender Status, Gender Identity, and Economic Outcomes in the United States," *Industrial and Labor Relations Review* 73, no. 3 (2020): 573–399.

29. Lydia Geijtenbeek and Erik Plug, "Is There a Penalty for Registered Women? Is There a Premium for Registered Men? Evidence from a Sample of Transsexual Workers," *European Economic Review* 109 (2018): 334–347. For similar findings, see Kristen Schilt and Matthew Wiswall, "Before and After: Gender Transitions, Human Capital, and Workplace Experiences," *BE Journal of Economic Analysis & Policy* 8, no. 1 (2008), art. 39. These authors investigate the labor earnings of transgender individuals before and after their gender transitions, based on a convenience sample in the United States. They find that individuals who transition from male to female experience a large earnings decline (of the order of 30 percent), while individuals who transition from female to male experience a nonsignificant earnings increase.

30. See, in particular, for evidence in the Netherlands, Eva Jaspers and Ellen Verbakel, "The Division of Paid Labor in Same-Sex Couples in the Netherlands," *Sex Roles* 68, no. 5 (2013): 335–348; for evidence in the United States, Lisa K. Jepsen and Christopher A. Jepsen, "An Empirical Analysis of the Matching Patterns of Same-Sex and Opposite-Sex Couples," *Demography* 39, no. 3, (2002):. 435–453; and Christopher A. Jepsen and Lisa K. Jepsen, "Labor-Market Specialization within Same-Sex and Different-Sex Couples," *Industrial Relations: A Journal of Economy and Society* 54, no. 1 (2015): 109–130; for evidence in Australia, Austria, Belgium, France, the Netherlands, Norway, and Sweden, Gerrit Bauer, "Gender Roles, Comparative Advantages and the Life Course: The Division of Domestic Labor in Same-Sex and Different-Sex Couples, *European Journal of Population* 32, no. 1 (2016): 99–128; for evidence in Denmark, Finland, Norway, and Sweden, Maaike van der Vleuten, Marie Evertsson, and Ylva Moberg, "Joint Utility or Sub-optimal Outcomes? Household Income Development of Same-Sex and Different-Sex Couples Transitioning to Parenthood in Denmark, Finland, Norway, and Sweden," *Journal of Family Issues* (2024).

31. See, for instance, Cevat G. Aksoy, Christopher S. Carpenter, and Jeff Frank, "Sexual Orientation and Earnings: New Evidence from the United Kingdom," *ILR Review* 71, no. 1 (2018): 242–272.

32. Valfort, "LGBTI in OECD Countries."

33. Billur Aksov, Ian Chadd, and Boon Han Koh, "Sexual Identity, Gender, and Anticipated Discrimination in Prosocial Behavior," *European Economic Review* 154 (2023).

34. Marc Folch, "The LGBTQ+ Gap: Recent Estimates for Young Adults in the United States," Working paper (2022).

35. Comparing the career choices of monozygotic twins using the Australian Twin Registry database, Erik Plug, Dinand Webbink and Nick Martin show similar results: with the same family background, personality traits, and even academic results, a gay man or lesbian is much more likely than his or her heterosexual twin to have chosen a sector and an occupation where employers and employees are less hostile to homosexuals. Focusing on monozygotic twins has the great advantage of ensuring that the family antecedents as well as a whole set of innate characteristics influencing the trajectories of individuals in the labor market are the same for a given pair of same-sex siblings. See Erik Plug, Dinand Webbink, and Nick Martin, "Sexual Orientation, Prejudice, and Segregation," *Journal of Labor Economics* 32, no. 1, (2014): 123–159.

36. Cevat Giray Aksov, Christopher S. Carpenter, Jefferson Frank, and Matt L. Huffman, "Gay Glass Ceilings: Sexual Orientation and Workplace Authority in the UK," *Journal of Economic Behavior & Organization* 159 (2019): 167–180.

37. For evidence that acceptance of LGBTIQ+ individuals increases with income, see OECD, "The LGBT Challenge."

38. See Donald C. Barrett and Lance M. Pollack, "Whose Gay Community? Social Class, Sexual Self-Expression, and Gay Community Involvement," *Sociological Quarterly* 46, no. 3 (2005): 437–456; and Preeti Pathela, Anjum Hajat, Julia Schillinger, Susan Blank, Randall Sell, and Farzad Mostashari, "Discordance between Sexual Behavior and Self-Reported Sexual Identity: A Population-Based Survey of New York City Men," *Annals of Internal Medicine* 145, no. 6 (2006): 416–425.

39. Alternative explanations include the fact that some (highly educated) individuals may start to identify as LGB only in adulthood and that, despite the initial low academic performance in high school, LGB students quickly catch up once they live in a more welcoming environment such as a college campus.

40. On this issue, see the five following US-based studies: Stephen T. Russell, Hinda Seif and Nhan L. Truong, "School Outcomes of Sexual Minority Youth in the United States: Evidence from a National Study," *Journal of Adolescence* 24, no. 1 (2001): 111–127; Jennifer Pearson, Chandra Muller, and Lindsey Wilkinson, "Adolescent Same-Sex Attraction and Academic Outcomes: The Role of School Attachment and Engagement," *Social Problems* 54, no. 4 (2007): 524–542; Katrina M. Walsemann, Lisa L. Lindley, Danielle Gentile, and Shehan V. Welihindha, "Educational Attainment by Life Course Sexual Attraction: Prevalence and Correlates in a Nationally Representative Sample of Young Adults," *Population Research and Policy Review* 33, no.

4 (2014): 579–602; Jennifer Pearson and Lindsey Wilkinson, "Same-Sex Sexuality and Educational Attainment: The Pathway to College," *Journal of Homosexuality* 64, no. 4 (2017): 538–576; Dario Sansone, "LGBT Students: New Evidence on Demographics and Educational Outcomes," *Economics of Education Review* 73 (2019): 101933.

41. Valfort, "LGBTI in OECD Countries."

42. On violence at school, see UNESCO, Out in the Open, 2016. On educational attainment in adulthood, see Carpenter, Eppink, and Gonzales, "Transgender Status, Gender Identity, and Economic Outcomes in the United States."

43. To the best of our knowledge, only one correspondence study was conducted outside the OECD, in Cyprus. The results reveal much stronger hiring discrimination against fictitious male and female homosexual applicants than that computed in OECD countries: heterosexual men and women are 3.7 and 4.5 times more likely respectively than their homosexual counterparts to be invited to a job interview. See Nick Drydakis, "Sexual Orientation Discrimination in the Cypriot Labour Market: Distastes or Uncertainty?," *International Journal of Manpower* 35, no. 5 (2014): 720–744.

44. The nine studies are (1) Barry D. Adam, "Stigma and Employability: Discrimination by Sex and Sexual Orientation in the Ontario Legal Profession," *Canadian Review of Sociology and Anthropology* 18, no. 2 (1981): 216–221; (2) Doris Weichselbaumer, "Sexual Orientation Discrimination in Hiring," *Labour Economics* 10, no. 6 (2003): 629–642; (3) Nick Drydakis, "Sexual Orientation Discrimination in the Labour Market," *Labour Economics* 16, no. 4 (2009): 364–372; (4) Nick Drydakis, "Women's Sexual Orientation and Labor Market Outcomes in Greece," *Feminist Economics* 17, no. 1 (2011): 89–117; (5) A. Tilcsik, "Pride and Prejudice: Employment Discrimination Against Openly Gay Men in the United States," *American Journal of Sociology* 117, no. 2 (2011): 586–626; (6) John Bailey, Michael Wallace, and Bradley Wright, "Are Gay Men and Lesbians Discriminated Against When Applying for Jobs? A Four-City, Internet-Based Field Experiment," *Journal of Homosexuality* 60, no. 6 (2013)): 873–894; (7) Eleonora Patacchini, Giuseppe Ragusa, and Yves Zenou, "Unexplored Dimensions of Discrimination in Europe: Homosexuality and Physical Appearance," *Journal of Population Economics* 28, no. 4 (2015): 1045–1073; (8) Doris Weichselbaumer, "Testing for Discrimination Against Lesbians of Different Marital Status: A Field Experiment," *Industrial Relations: A Journal of Economy and Society* 54, no. 1 (2015): 131–161; (9) Nick Drydakis, "Sexual Orientation Discrimination in the United Kingdom's Labour Market: A Field Experiment," *Human Relations* 68, no. 11 (2015). On employers valuing volunteering, see Stijn Baert and Sunčica Vujić, "Does It Pay to Care? Volunteering and Employment Opportunities," *Journal of Population Economics* 31, no. 3 (2018): 819–836.

45. The two studies are Stijn Baert, "Career Lesbians: Getting Hired for Not Having Kids?," *Industrial Relations Journal* 45, no. 6 (2014): 543–561; and Weichselbaumer, "Testing for Discrimination Against Lesbians of Different Marital Status."

46. The three studies are (1) Ali M. Ahmed, Lina Andersson, and Mats Hammarstedt, "Are Gay Men and Lesbians Discriminated Against in the Hiring Process?," *Southern Economic Journal* 79. no 3 (2013): 565–585; (2) Laetitia Challe, Yannick L'Horty, Pascale Petit, and François-Charles Wolff, "Les discriminations dans l'accès à l'emploi privé et public: Les effets de l'origine, de l'adresse, du sexe et de l'orientation sexuelle," Working Papers HAL-SHS-01878469 (2018); and (3) Alessandro Acquisti and Christina M. Fong, "An Experiment in Hiring Discrimination via Online Social Networks," *Management Science* 66, no. 3 (2020): 1005–1024.

47. Alexandre Flage, "Discrimination Against Gays and Lesbians in Hiring Decisions: A Meta-Analysis." *International Journal of Manpower* 41, no. 6 (2019): 671–691. https://www.emerald.com/insight/content/doi/10.1108/IJM-08-2018-0239/full/html.

48. See Drydakis, "Sexual Orientation Discrimination in the Labour Market," and Drydakis, "Women's Sexual Orientation and Labor Market Outcomes in Greece."

49. Nick Drydakis also provides evidence of wage discrimination in the UK: the wage penalty for gay men and for lesbians is equal to 2 percent and 1.4 percent, respectively. These findings must be taken with caution, however. Drydakis relies on real applicants, young men and women who have just graduated from university. Therefore, although the difference in callback rates is measured between homosexual and heterosexual job seekers who sent similar applications, these subjects were not trained to act alike at the job interview, since their objective as real job seekers is to get hired, not to have an audit study succeed. It is therefore possible that the wage difference between the homosexual and heterosexual applicants reflects differences in unobservable characteristics detected by the recruiter during the job interview rather than discrimination. See Drydakis, "Sexual Orientation Discrimination in the United Kingdom's Labour Market."

50. Flage, "Discrimination Against Gays and Lesbians in Hiring Decisions."

51. In all twenty-three countries they surveyed, Maria Laura Bettinsoli and her coauthors confirmed this result. See Bettinsoli, Suppes, and Napier, "Predictors of Attitudes toward Gay Men and Lesbian Women in 23 Countries."

52. For people at the intersection of several minority groups, stereotypes can reinforce each other, but may also sometimes neutralize each other. David Pedulla, for instance, has used an internet survey experiment to test how being gay and Black affects the ratings of manipulated CVs by randomly selected respondents who are asked to recommend starting salaries. He finds that stereotypes of Black men—seen, for example, as threatening, violent. and criminal—somewhat counteract stereotypes of gay men—seen, for example, as feminine, weak, and sensitive. While Black applicants receive on average lower starting salaries than white applicants, gay Black applicants receive higher salary recommendations than straight Black applicants, which is the opposite of what is observed for white applicants. David S. Pedulla, "The Positive Consequences of Negative Stereotypes: Race, Sexual

Orientation, and the Job Application," *Process. Social Psychology Quarterly* 77, no. 1 (2014): 75–94.

53. Tilcsik, "Pride and Prejudice."

54. Weichselbaumer, "Testing for Discrimination Against Lesbians of Different Marital Status."

55. Drydakis, "Sexual Orientation Discrimination in the Labour Market."

56. Ian Burn, "The Relationship between Prejudice and Wage Penalties for Gay Men in the United States," *Industrial and Labor Relations Review* 73, no. 3 (2020).

57. Ahmed, Andersson, and Hammarstedt, "Are Gay Men and Lesbians Discriminated Against in the Hiring Process?"

58. Drydakis, "Sexual Orientation Discrimination in the United Kingdom's Labour Market."

59. Rebecca F. Baggaley, Richard G. White, and Marie-Claude Boily, "HIV Transmission Risk through Anal Intercourse: Systematic Review, Meta-Analysis and Implications for HIV Prevention," *International Journal of Epidemiology* 39, no. 4 (2010): 1048–1063.

60. OECD. "The LGBT Challenge."

61. David Kasprowski, Mirjam Fischer, Lisa de Vries, et al. "LGBTQI* People in Germany Face Staggering Health Disparities," *DIW Weekly Report* 5–6 (2021): 42–50.

62. Drydakis, "Sexual Orientation Discrimination in the Cypriot Labour Market."

63. Eleonora Patacchini, Giuseppe Ragusa and Yves Zenou, "Unexplored Dimensions of Discrimination in Europe: Homosexuality and Physical Appearance," *Journal of Population Economics*, 28, no. 4 (2015): 1045–1073.

64. Nick Drydakis, "Sexual Orientation Discrimination in the Labor Market Against Gay Men," *Review of Economics of the Household* 20 (2022): 1027–1058.

65. In the same vein, positive attitudinal change may take time to translate into behavioral change, as shown by economists Christopher Jepsen and Lisa Jepsen in the United States. Using data from the American Community Survey on individuals in couples from 2000 to 2019, the authors find no evidence that labor earnings of men in same-sex couples are improving relative to those of married men in different-sex couples. In other words, by 2019 and among full-time workers, men in same-sex couples still had lower wages of approximately 10 percent compared to married men in different-sex couples. See Christopher Jepsen and Lisa Jepsen, "Convergence over Time or Not? U.S. Wages by Sexual Orientation, 2000–2019," *Labour Economics* 74 (2022): 102086.

66. Flage, "Discrimination Against Gays and Lesbians in Hiring Decisions."

67. M. Granberg, P. Andersson, and A. Ahmed, "Hiring Discrimination Against Transgender People: Evidence from a Field Experiment," *Labour Economics* 65 (2020): 101860.

68. J. Gerhards, T. Sawert, and J. Tuppat, "Reversing the Symbolic Order of Discrimination: Results from a Field Experiment on the Discrimination of Migrants and Transgender People in Theatre," *Journal of Ethnic and Migration Studies* 47/15 (2021): 3622–3640.

69. Nujavi Bardales, "Finding a Job 'in a Beard and a Dress': Evaluating the Effectiveness of Transgender Anti- Discrimination Laws," manuscript, 2013.

70. Make the Road New York, *Transgender Need Not Apply: A Report on Gender Identity Job Discrimination* (New York, 2010).

71. Kasprowski et al., "LGBTQI* People in Germany Face Staggering Health Disparities."

72. In line with this claim, Samuel Mann and his coauthors demonstrate that Medicaid coverage of gender-affirming care significantly improves the mental health of transgender people, a result driven by increased uptake of gender-affirming care. See Samuel Mann, Travis Campbell, and Nguyen Duc Hien, "Access to Gender-Affirming Care and Transgender Mental Health: Evidence from Medicaid Coverage," *American Journal of Health Economics* 10, no. 2 (2024).

73. For instance, Carlo D'Ippoliti and Fabrizio Botti find that past experiences of discrimination are strongly correlated with transgender people's decision to become sex workers. See C. D'Ippoliti and F. Botti, "Sex Work among Trans People: Evidence from Southern Italy," *Feminist Economics* 23, no. 3 (2017): 77–109.

74. That noncisgender individuals face discrimination in access to health care is the preliminary result of an ongoing audit study on the extent to which cisgender women, transgender women, transgender men, nonbinary people, and racial and ethnic minorities (African American and Hispanic individuals) face discrimination in access to mental health service. See Luca Fumarco, Benjamin J. Harrell, Patrick Button, David J. Schwegman, and E. Dils, "Gender Identity, Race, and Ethnicity-Based Discrimination in Access to Mental Health Care: Evidence from anAudit Correspondence Field Experiment," *American Journal of Health Economics* 10, no. 2 (2024).

75. Such discrimination would also diminish with the amount of experience reported on fictitious applicants' CVs, a pattern that Mark Granberg, Per A. Andersson, and Ali Ahmed tested but could not empirically support in the correspondence study they conducted in the Swedish labor market.

76. Hannah Van Borm and Stijn Baert, "What Drives Hiring Discrimination Against Transgenders?," *International Journal of Manpower* 39, no. 4 (2018): 581–599.

77. See, for example, N. Rule. and N. Ambady, "Brief Exposures: Male Sexual Orientation Is Accurately Perceived at 50ms," *Journal of Experimental Social Psychology* 44, no. 4 (2008): 1100–1105.

## Chapter 10

1. See LBJ's remarks at https://www.presidency.ucsb.edu/documents/radio-and-television-remarks-upon-signing-the-civil-rights-bill.

2. In France, for instance, research confirmed that the threat of legal sanction does discourage discriminators from discriminating when this threat is credible. More precisely, the group of economists in charge of this study proceeded in two steps. In a first step, based on a correspondence study, they identified a set of real estate agencies that discriminated against French people of North African origin (relative to French people with no recent immigrant background). In a second step, the researchers randomly drew half of these agencies. These agencies were sent a letter from the Defender of Rights (the French Ombudsman) indicating that the way they were selecting housing applicants was being scrutinized through a correspondence study and that discrimination in access to housing was subject to significant fines and penalties. The results show that this letter put an end to the discriminatory behavior of agencies to which it was sent up to nine months following receipt of the letter, while the behavior of agencies that did not receive the letter remained unchanged. See S. Chareyron, Y. L'Horty, S. Mbaye, and P. Petit, "Reducing Ethnic Discrimination through Formal Warning: Evidence from Two Combined Field Experiments," *Regional Science and Urban Economics* 98 (2023).

3. J. Menasce Horowitz, A. Brown, and K. Cox, *Race in America, 2019* (Pew Research Center); European Commission, Special Eurobarometer 493, "Discrimination in the EU in 2019 (Including LGBTI)" (data set) (2019).

4. Article 23 adumbrates the rights this way:

   1. Everyone has the right to work, to free choice of employment, to just and favourable conditions of work and to protection against unemployment.
   2. Everyone, without any discrimination, has the right to equal pay for equal work.
   3. Everyone who works has the right to just and favourable remuneration ensuring for himself and his family an existence worthy of human dignity, and supplemented, if necessary, by other means of social protection.
   4. Everyone has the right to form and to join trade unions for the protection of his interests.

5. Jody Heymann, Bijetri Bose, Willetta Waisath, Amy Raub, and Michael McCormack, "Legislative Approaches to Nondiscrimination at Work: A Comparative Analysis across 13 Groups in 193 Countries," *Equality, Diversity and Inclusion: An International Journal* 40, no. 3 (2021): 225–241.

6. OECD, *Over the Rainbow? The Road to LGBTI Inclusion* (Paris: OECD Publishing, 2020).

7. Margaret E. Tankard and Elizabeth Levy Paluck, "The Effect of a Supreme Court Decision Regarding Gay Marriage on Social Norms and Personal Attitudes," *Psychological Science* 28, no. 9 (2017): 1334–1344.

8. Cevat G. Aksoy, Christopher S. Carpenter, Ralph De Haas, and Kevin Tran, "Do Laws Shape Attitudes? Evidence from Same-Sex Relationship Recognition Policies in Europe," *European Economic Review* 24 (2020): 1–18.

9. Dario Sansone, "Pink Work: Same-Sex Marriage, Employment and Discrimination," *Journal of Public Economics* (2019): 180.

10. Samuel Mann, "Anti-Discrimination Laws and Mental Health: Evidence from Sexual Minorities," revised and resubmitted to the *Journal of Human Resources* (2023).

11. Julie Ringelheim, "The Burden of Proof in Antidiscrimination Proceedings. A Focus on Belgium, France, and Ireland," *European Equality Law Review* 2 (2019). The two cases mentioned are C-109/88, *Handels- og Kontorfunktionærernes Forbund I Danmark v Dansk Arbejdsgiverforening,* acting on behalf of Danfoss [1989] ECR 3199, and C-127/92, *Dr. Pamela Mary Enderby v Frenchay Health Authority and Secretary of State for Health* [1993] ECR I-5535.

12. See https://www.americanbar.org/groups/young_lawyers/projects/no-limits/proving-title-vii-discrimination-in-2019. Title VII of the Civil Rights Act of 1964 prohibits employers from discriminating against employees and applicants for employment on the bases of race, color, religion, national origin, and sex (which includes sexual orientation and gender identity). Title VII applies to employers with fifteen or more employees and requires that all employees or applicants for employment be treated equally with respect to the aforementioned protected grounds.

13. International human rights stakeholders have acknowledged the need for independent national human rights institutions, such as equality bodies, ombudspersons, or human rights commissions, in order to implement equal treatment legislation. For instance, the Paris Principles, adopted in 1993 by the UN General Assembly, encourage states to establish a national structure in charge of promoting and protecting human rights. Consistent with these stances, the European Union and the Council of Europe have developed Equinet, the European Network for Equality Bodies, which plays a critical role in coordinating, supporting, and offering legal interpretation and implementation guidance for equality bodies across thirty-six different countries in Europe, including all EU member countries.

14. By combining textual data analysis and the results of a correspondence study, Ian Burn, Patrick Button, Luis Felipe Munguia Corella, and David Neumark confirm that agist stereotypes in the language used in job ads are associated with hiring discrimination against older workers. See Burn et al., "Older Workers Need Not Apply?

Ageist Language in Job Ads and Age Discrimination in Hiring," *Journal of Labor Economics* 40, no. 3 (2022): 613–667.

15. This interpretation was endorsed by two rulings of the Court of Justice of the European Union: in the *Feryn* case (2008), in which a Belgian employer declared in a press interview that he would not recruit applicants of Moroccan origin, and in the *Accept* case (2013), in which the leader of a Romanian football club stated that the club would not hire a homosexual footballer.

16. *Equal Employment Opportunity Commission v. Abercrombie & Fitch Stores,* 575 U.S. 768 (2015).

17. In the UK, for instance, in 2022–2023 there were only three hundred discrimination cases in which compensation was awarded by employment tribunals. See https://www.gov.uk/government/statistics/tribunal-statistics-quarterly-april-to-june-2023/tribunal-statistics-quarterly-april-to-june-2023.

18. Ringelheim, "The Burden of Proof in Antidiscrimination Proceedings."

19. On situation testing, see Isabelle Rorive, "Proving Discrimination Cases: The Role of Situation Testing" (MPG and the Centre for Equal Rights, 2009).

20. In 2007, Froul Louzai, a Frenchman of North African origin, filed an application with the labor courts against Airbus France for "racial discrimination in hiring." Louzai had carried out two mission contracts at Airbus France between 2000 and 2001 and two others between January 2005 and September 2006 as a numerical control operator. When he applied for a permanent job, two less experienced candidates were chosen. In 2010, the social chamber of the Court of Appeal of Toulouse ordered Airbus to pay €10,000 in damages to the plaintiff, after the French equality body had demonstrated that individuals with North African–sounding first names and last names were almost never hired on an open-ended contract. This finding of discrimination was confirmed later by the Court of Cassation. For further details, see https://juridique.defenseurdesdroits.fr/doc_num.php?explnum_id=7550.

21. In France, for instance, this strategy, also called the "comparison panel method," was first developed in the 1990s to prove discrimination based on trade union membership. It was subsequently applied in cases of sex discrimination and, to a lesser extent, in cases of ethnic discrimination. This method has been recognized by the Court of Cassation and the Council of State as a valid approach to infer a presumption of discrimination. See Court of Cassation, Social Chamber, P+B Fluchère, *Dick and CFDT v SNCF,* no. 1027, March 28, 2000; Council of State, no. 16–102017, October 16, 2017.

22. Judgment of July 21, 2011, *Patrick Kelly v National University of Ireland* (University College, Dublin), C-104/10, ECLI:EU:C:2011:506. Judgment of April 19, 2012, *Galina Meister v. Speech Design Carrier Systems GmbH,* C-415/10, ECLI:EU:C:2012:217.

23. In medieval times, "group litigations" appear to have been quite common in England. These lawsuits involved groups of people, usually based on existing societal structures (villages, towns, parishes, and guilds), either suing or being sued in actions at common law.

24. Owen M. Fiss, "The Political Theory of the Class Action," *Washington & Lee Law Review* 53 (1996): 21.

25. Another shortcoming of class action lawsuits is that they do not easily apply to small and medium-size businesses, where hiring and promotion are rarely on a large enough scale to warrant their implementation. Yes, these businesses account for the vast majority of employers. Furthermore, at least regarding discrimination in hiring, it can be difficult to find rejected candidates and convince them to engage in litigation whose outcome is uncertain.

26. Robert H. Klonoff, "The Decline of Class Actions," *Washington University Law Review* 90, no. 3 (2013): 729–838.

27. European Union Agency for Fundamental Rights, "Being Black in the EU: Experiences of People of African Descent," Vienna, October 25, 2023.

28. David Neumark, "Strengthen Age Discrimination Protections to Help Confront the Challenge of Population Aging," *Economic Studies at Brookings* (2020). Several papers have analyzed the impact of disability antidiscrimination laws on the hiring of disabled people in the United States. However, they do not constitute a clean test of whether antidiscrimination laws generate negative unintended effects since disability discrimination protections in the United States lead to raising the cost not only of terminating disabled workers but also of hiring them. The law indeed requires employers to offer adequate facilities for disabled people (e.g., by enabling wheelchair access, purchasing special equipment for disabled employees, restructuring jobs to permit disabled employees to work part-time or from home, etc.). For more information, see Daron Acemoglu and Joshua D. Angrist, "Consequences of Employment Protection? The Case of the Americans with Disabilities Act," *Journal of Political Economy* 109, no. 5 (2001): 915–957; and D. Neumark, J. Song, and P. Button, "Does Protecting Older Workers from Discrimination Make It Harder to Get Hired? Evidence from Disability Discrimination Laws," *Research on Aging* 39, no. 1 (2016): 29–63.

29. See D. Neumark and W. Stock, "Age Discrimination Laws and Labor Market Efficiency," *Journal of Political Economy* 107, no. 5 (1999): 1081–1125; S. Adams, "Age Discrimination Legislation and the Employment of Older Workers," *Labour Economics* 11, no. 2 (2004): 219–241; D. Neumark and J. Song, "Do Stronger Age Discrimination Laws Make Social Security Reforms More Effective?," *Journal of Public Economics* 108 (2013): 1–16; D. Neumark and P. Button, "Did Age Discrimination Protections Help Older Workers Weather the Great Recession?," *Journal of Policy Analysis and Management* 33, no. 3 (2014): 566–601; and D. Neumark et al. (2019),

"Do State Laws Protecting Older Workers from Discrimination Reduce Age Discrimination in Hiring? Evidence from a Field Experiment," *Journal of Law and Economics* 62, no. 2 (2019): 373–402. Recently, Scott Delhommer found consistent results in the case of sexual orientation antidiscrimination laws in the United States. See Scott Delhommer, "Effect of State and Local Sexual Orientation Anti-Discrimination Laws on Labor Market Differentials" (June 16, 2020), https://ssrn.com/abstract=3625193 or http://dx.doi.org/10.2139/ssrn.3625193.

30. See J. Lahey, "State Age Protection Laws and the Age Discrimination in Employment Act," *Journal of Law and Economics* 51, no. 3 (2008): 433–460; and Neumark and Button, "Did Age Discrimination Protections Help Older Workers Weather the Great Recession?"

31. For further evidence that increasing the costs of terminating protected workers reduces their hiring, see Luc Behaghel, Bruno Crépon, and Béatrice Sédillot, "The Perverse Effects of Partial Employment Protection Reform: The Case of French Older Workers," *Journal of Public Economics* 92, nos. 3–4 (2008): 696–721.

## Chapter 11

1. Frank Dobbin and Alexandra Kalev, "Why Diversity Training Doesn't Work: The Challenge for Industry and Academia," *Anthropology Now* 10, no. 2 (2018): 48–55.

2. For the United States, see Lincoln Quillian, Devah Pager, Ole Hexel, and Arnfinn Midtbøen, "Meta-Analysis of Field Experiments Shows No Change in Racial Discrimination in Hiring over Time," *Proceedings of the National Academy of Sciences of the United States of America (PNAS)* 114, no. 41 (2017): 10870–10875. For the UK, see Anthony F. Heath and Valentina Di Stasio, "Racial Discrimination in Britain, 1969–2017: A Meta-Analysis of Field Experiments on Racial Discrimination in the British Labour Market," *British Journal of Sociology* 70, no. 5 (2019): 1774–1798. France is an exception among Canada, Germany, the Netherlands, the United Kingdom and the United States, since racial and ethnic discrimination in hiring declined, although from very high to "merely" high levels, as analyzed by Lincoln Quillian and John J. Lee, "Trends in Racial and Ethnic Discrimination in Hiring in Six Western Countries," *Proceedings of the National Academy of Sciences of the United States of America (PNAS)* 120, no. 6 (2023).

3. Marie-Anne Valfort, "Do Antidiscrimination Policies Work?," *IZA World of Labor* (2025).

4. As Denis Maguain reminds us, "Positive discrimination emerged from the movement for universal civil rights in the United States in the mid-1960s. . . . In 1961, Democratic President John Kennedy first used the expression 'affirmative action' in a decree stipulating that federal governments should ensure that firms applying for government contracts were treated on an equal footing with regard to 'race, colour, religion, sex or national origin.' . . . The Democrat Lyndon Johnson and then the

Republican Richard Nixon extended and clarified by decree the preferential policy that the federal government was to follow regarding the recruitment of public servants and the allocation of public procurement and subsidies. This culminated in 1972 with the 'affirmative action' law requiring administrations, public institutions and service providers working for the government to set up preferential programs for racial/ethnic minorities. The methods for moving towards greater equality of opportunity were specified in the form of targets to be attained in terms of minority participation in relation to their relative demographic availability." Denis Maguain, "Discrimination positive: Un bilan des expériences américaines et européennes," *Revue française d'économie* 21, no. 2 (2006): 147–193.

5. OECD, *Sickness, Disability and Work: Breaking the Barriers* (Paris: OECD Publishing, 2010).

6. Michael Fuchs, "Quota Systems for Disabled Persons: Parameters, Aspects, Effectivity" (Vienna: European Centre for social Welfare Policy and Research, 2014).

7. There are three official classifications of the population in India: (1) "General class," denoting castes whose members are on average ahead of other Indians economically and socially; (2) "Other Backward Classes," denoting castes that are educationally or socially disadvantaged; and (3) "Scheduled Castes and Scheduled Tribes," denoting castes long seen as being at the bottom of the caste system and hence subjected to the practice of untouchability before its legal abolition in 1950 (untouchability imposed various social restrictions on these castes, from their inability to touch other castes to their denial to use the same water source or even live in the same area).

8. Nina Smith, "Gender Quotas on Boards of Directors," *IZA World of Labor* 7 (2018). The proposal was adopted by the European Parliament by a large majority in 2013, but it took the Council of the European Union nearly ten years to reach a qualified majority vote. For an update on the situation, see https://www.europarl.europa.eu/legislative-train/theme-area-of-justice-and-fundamental-rights/file-gender-balance-on-boards.

9. F. M. Horwitz and H. Jain, "An Assessment of Employment Equity and Broad Based Black Economic Empowerment in South Africa," *Equality, Diversity and Inclusion: An International Journal* 30, no. 4 (2011): 297–317.

10. Stéphane Carcillo and Marie-Anne Valfort, "Combating Discrimination in the Labour Market" (French Council of Economic Analysis, 2020). In Canada, the use of job candidates' racial/ethnic origin as a criterion for granting eligibility to a hiring subsidy is more explicit. The PRIIME (Employment Integration Program for Immigrants and Visible Minorities) scheme pays a subsidy to employers for hiring people who have been granted permanent residence in the preceding five years or who belong to a visible minority born in Canada or the United States. Visible minorities in Canada are defined in the Employment Equity Act as "persons, other than Aboriginal peoples, who are non-Caucasian in race or non-white in colour." The

visible minority population consists mainly of the following groups: South Asian, Chinese, Black, Filipino, Latin American, Arab, Southeast Asian, West Asian, Korean, and Japanese. Source: Statistics Canada, "Visible Minority of Person," https://www23.statcan.gc.ca/imdb/p3Var.pl?Function=DEC&Id=45152, last updated March 25, 2021; accepted August 25, 2021.

11. Stijn Baert, "Wage Subsidies and Hiring Chances for the Disabled: Some Causal Evidence," *European Journal of Health Economics* 17 (2016): 71–86.

12. On subsidies boosting employment, see David Card, Jochen Kluve, and Andrea Weber, "What Works? A Meta-Analysis of Recent Active Labor Market Program Evaluations," *Journal of the European Economic Association* 16, no. 3 (2018): 894–931, and Pierre Cahuc, Stéphane Carcillo, and Thomas Le Barbanchon, "The Effectiveness of Hiring Credits," *Review of Economic Studies* 86, no. 2 (March 2019): 593–626.

13. Sylvain Chareyron, Laetitia Challe, Yannick L'Horty, and Pascale Petit, "Can Subsidies Paid Directly to Employers Reduce Residential Discrimination in Employment? An Assessment Based on Serial Field Experiments," *Urban Studies* 9, no. 6 (2022): 1202–1218.

14. More precisely, whether it is measured a few months before or one year after this scheme's implementation, the callback rate of applicants of North African origin is about one-third the callback rate of applicants of French origin, irrespective of where these applicants reside.

15. Baert, "Wage Subsidies and Hiring Chances for the Disabled."

16. Rafael Lalive, Jean-Philippe Wuellrich, and Josef Zweimüller, "Do Financial Incentives Affect Firms' Demand for Disabled Workers?," *Journal of the European Economic Association* 11, no. 1 (2013): 25–58.

17. John J. Donohue and James Heckman, "Continuous Versus Episodic Change: The Impact of Civil Rights Policy on the Economic Status of Blacks," *Journal of Economic Literature*,29. no. 4 (1991): 1603–1643.

18. Axana Dalle, Elsy Verhofstadt, and Stijn Baert, "The Subsidy Trap: Explaining the Unsatisfactory Effectiveness of Hiring Subsidies for the Senior Unemployed," *Journal of Economic Behavior & Organization* 227 (2024).

19. For a review, see Bernhard Boockmann, "The Effects of Wage Subsidies for Older Workers," *IZA World of Labor* 189 (2015). For more recent evidence, see Sam Desiere and Bart Cockx, "How Effective Are Hiring Subsidies to Reduce Long-Term Unemployment among Prime-Aged Jobseekers? Evidence from Belgium," *IZA Journal of Labor Policy* 12, no. 1 (2022)

20. Compared to their previous version, the new "free jobs" are more attractive and less restrictive. They are linked to a hiring bonus of €15,000 over three years (against €5,000 overall). In addition, the eligibility of the job seeker depends only

on proof of address, whereas previously, to be hired, the applicant had to be under the age of thirty, had to have been looking for work for at least a year, and had to have lived for at least six months in a sensitive urban area. That said, despite efforts to alleviate them, regulatory constraints associated with the new scheme are still significant. To benefit from the hiring subsidy, employers must send a detailed file with information on the company, the employee, and the employment contract to the Public Employment Service (PES), accompanied by the eligibility certificate of the selected candidate (provided by the PES) and proof of his or her address. The application form and instructions are six pages long and require a careful reading. The employer or his or her representative must certify on their honor that the information declared is accurate. The procedure exposes the company to controls by the PES and the tax authorities. The employer must also send proof of the employee's presence every six months.

21. Recruitment by simulation involves identifying, in the analysis of jobs posted by companies, the various skills needed to carry out the work, and then formulating procedures for assessing to what extent job applicants possess these skills.

22. Harry Holzer and David Neumark, "Assessing Affirmative Action," *Journal of Economic Literature* 38, no. 3 (2000): 483–568; Harry Holzer and David Neumark, "What Does Affirmative Action Do?," *Industrial and Labor Relations Review* 53, no. 2 (2000): 240–271.

23. Conrad Miller, "The Persistent Effect of Temporary Affirmative Action," *American Economic Journal: Applied Economics* 9, no. 3 (2017): 152–190.

24. Madeline E. Heilman, Caryn J. Block, and Peter Stathatos, "The Affirmative Action Stigma of Incompetence: Effects of Performance Information Ambiguity," *Academy of Management Journal* 40, no. 3 (1997): 603–625.

25. On majority group opposition to such policies, see Loukas Balafoutas, Brent J. Davis, and Matthias Sutter, "Affirmative Action or Just Discrimination? A Study on the Endogenous Emergence of Quotas," *Journal of Economic Behavior & Organization* 127 (2016): 87–98. On retaliation, see Lea M. Petters and Marina Schröder, "Negative Side Effects of Affirmative Action: How Quotas Lead to Distortions in Performance Evaluation," *European Economic Review* 130 (2020). On the resulting productivity losses, see Edwin Ip, Andreas Leibbrandt, and Joseph Vecci, "How Do Gender Quotas Affect Workplace Relationships? Complementary Evidence from a Representative Survey and Labor Market Experiments," *Management Science* 66, no. 2 (2020).

26. Lori Beaman, Raghabendra Chattopadhyay, Esther Duflo, Rohini Pande, and Petia Topalova, "Powerful Women: Does Exposure Reduce Bias?," *Quarterly Journal of Economics* 124, no. 4 (2009): 497–1540.

27. Lata Gangadharan, Tarun Jain, Pushkar Maitra, and Joseph Vecci, "Social Identity and Governance: The Behavioral Response to Female Leaders," *European Economic Review* 90 (2016): 302–325.

28. Victoire Girard, "Stabbed in the Back? Mandated Political Representation and Murders," *Social Choice and Welfare* 56 (2020): 595–634.

29. Lincoln Quillian, Devah Pager, Ole Hexel, and Arnfinn H. Midtbøen. 2017. "Meta-Analysis of Field Experiments Shows No Change in Racial Discrimination in Hiring over Time," *Proceedings of the National Academy of Sciences of the United States of America (PNAS)* 114, no. 41 (2017): 10870–10875.

30. Marianne Bertrand, Sandra E. Black, Sissel Jensen, and Adriana Lleras-Muney, "Breaking the Glass Ceiling? The Effect of Board Quotas on Female Labour Market Outcomes in Norway," *Review of Economic Studies* 86, no. 1 (2018): 191–239.

31. Claudia Goldin and Cecilia Rouse, "Orchestrating Impartiality: The Impact of 'Blind' Auditions on Female Musicians," *American Economic Review* 90, no. 4 (2000): 715–741.

32. Mitchell Hoffman, Lisa B. Kahn, and Danielle Li, "Discretion in Hiring," *Quarterly Journal of Economics* 133, no. 2 (2018): 765–800.

33. That said, the impact of introducing the job test on the average quality of hired workers is positive: cohorts of workers hired with job testing have substantially longer tenures than cohorts of workers hired without testing. Not surprisingly, the outcome of the job test allows acquiring better information about whether a worker has the rights skills or will be a good fit, compared to résumés or job interviews without job testing.

34. David Neumark, "Age Discrimination in Hiring: Evidence from Age-Blind vs. Non-Age-Blind Hiring Procedures," *Journal of Human Resources* 57, no. 4 (2022).

35. Luc Behaghel, Bruno Crépon, and Thomas Le Barbanchon, "Unintended Effects of Anonymous Résumés," *American Economic Journal: Applied Economics* 7, no. 3 (2015): 1–27.

36. Dobbin Franck and Alexandra Kalev, *Getting to Diversity: What Works and What Doesn't* (Cambridge, MA: Harvard University Press, 2022).

37. Sonia K. Kang, K. A. DeCelles, A. Tilcsik, and S. Jun, "Whitened Résumés: Race and Self-Presentation in the Labor Market," *Administrative Science Quarterly* 61, no. 3 (2016).

38. OECD, *All Hands In* (Paris: OECD Publishing, 2020).

39. C. Kaiser et al., "Presumed Fair: Ironic Effects of Organizational Diversity Structures," *Journal of Personality and Social Psychology* 104, no. 3 (2013): 504–519.

40. L. Edelman et al., "When Organizations Rule: Judicial Deference to Institutionalized Employment Structures," *American Journal of Sociology* 117, no. 3 (2011): 888–954.

41. T. Dover, B. Major, and C. Kaiser, "Diversity Initiatives, Status, and System-Justifying Beliefs: When and How Diversity Efforts De-legitimize Discrimination

Claims," *Group Processes & Intergroup Relations* 20, no. 10 (2003): 1–9. On women's reduced ability to detect sexist practices, see L. Brady et al., "It's Fair for Us: Diversity Structures Cause Women to Legitimize Discrimination," *Journal of Experimental Social Psychology* 57 (2015): 100–110.

42. Joseph Price and Justin Wolfers, "Racial Discrimination among NBA Referees," *Quarterly Journal of Economics* 125, no. 4 (2010): 1859–1887.

43. Devin Pope, Joseph Price, and Justin Wolfers, "Awareness Reduces Racial Bias," *Management Science* 64, no. 11 (2018): 4967–5460.

44. Anne Boring and Arnaud Philippe, "Reducing Discrimination in the Field: Evidence from an Awareness Raising Intervention Targeting Gender Biases in Student Evaluations of Teaching," *Journal of Public Economics,* 2021, 193.

45. OECD, *Reporting Gender Pay Gaps in OECD Countries: Guidance for Pay Transparency Implementation, Monitoring and Reform* (Paris: OECD Publishing, 2023). See also OECD, *Pay Transparency Tools to Close the Gender Wage Gap* (Paris: OECD Publishing, 2021).

46. Approval of the Pay Transparency Directive followed a formal agreement on the directive that the European Parliament and the Council of the European Union reached in December 2022. See https://ec.europa.eu/commission/presscorner/detail/en/IP_22_7739.

47. Insofar as the main purpose of pay reporting is to measure the wage of men and women in a comparable work situation, it is important that the concept of equal pay for work of equal value be defined in national laws as entailing that men and women be paid the same amount in two situations: (1) if they do identical or similar jobs and (2) but also if they do completely different work that can be shown to be of equal value, when based on objective criteria. The latter point is important to help correct for the historical undervaluation of jobs and sectors that have typically been considered "women's work." In Spain for instance, the Supreme Court found that, although housekeepers and bartenders in the same hotel were not doing the same job, it was not justified that housekeepers (mostly women) were underpaid relative to bartenders (mostly men) since these jobs were related to work of equal value (Spanish Supreme Court No. 2328/2013). For operationalization purposes, it is important that the legal framework endorse the creation of a gender-neutral job classification system, devised according to objective work-related characteristics, that would be applicable to all employers. Such a job classification system should not factor in the characteristics of workers most likely to hold a given job, such as their gender, but should focus instead on the objective characteristics necessary to perform the job.

48. It is worth stressing that, following this change, female candidates did not receive fewer bids from employers than men did, suggesting they faced little penalty for demanding wages comparable to those asked by men. For more information, see Nina Roussille, "The Role of the Ask Gap in Gender Pay Inequality," *Quarterly Journal of Economics* (forthcoming).

49. That said, in some countries or jurisdictions where racial and ethnic self-identification is routinely collected by national statistical offices and other stakeholders, pay transparency reporting by employers extends to visible minorities. For example, in Canada, federally regulated employers are required to report pay gaps across racial and ethnic groups. Similarly, several U.S. states have recently taken steps in this direction. Massachusetts, for instance, passed legislation on July 31, 2024, imposing new pay data reporting requirements on employers with 100 or more employees. Under this law, covered employers must submit annual reports detailing pay data by race, ethnicity, sex, and job category.

50. OECD, *The Economic Case for More Gender Equality in Estonia* (Paris: OECD Publishing, 2022).

51. Institut des Politiques Publiques, *Évaluation de l'Index de l'égalité professionnelle,* Rapport IPP no. 42 (Paris: IPP, 2023).

52. Thomas Piketty, *Mesurer le racisme, vaincre les discriminations* (Paris: Seuil Libelle, 2022).

53. For a comprehensive analysis of visible minorities in OECD countries, including how they are identified in register-based and survey data, and recommendations for enhancing data collection on these groups, see OECD, "Strengthening the Evidence Base for Racial/Ethnic Disadvantage in OECD Countries" (forthcoming in 2025).

54. DARES (Direction de l'Animation de la Recherche, des Études et des Statistiques), "Discrimination à l'embauche selon 'l'origine': Que nous apprend le testing auprès de grandes entreprises?," DARES Analyses 76 (2016).

55. Patrick Kline and Chris Walters, "Reasonable Doubt: Experimental Detection of Job-Level Employment Discrimination," *Econometrica* 89 (2021): 765–792.

56. Patrick Kline, Evan K. Rose, and Christopher R. Walters, "Systemic Discrimination among Large U.S. Employers," *Quarterly Journal of Economics* 137, no. 4 (2022): 1963–2036.

57. Patrick Kline, Evan K. Rose, and Christopher R Walters, "A Discrimination Report Card," *American Economic Review* 114, no. 8 (2024): 2472–2525.

58. Job boards are online sites where recruitment agencies and employers post advertisements for open job positions and where candidates can upload their CVs and contact information.

59. Dominik Hangartner, Daniel Kopp and Michael Siegenthaler, "Monitoring Hiring Discrimination through Online Recruitment Platforms," *Nature* 589 (2021): 572–576.

60. Jack Blundell, Emma Duchini, Stefania Simion, and Arthur Turrell, "Pay Transparency and Gender Equality," *American Economic Journal: Economic Policy* (forthcoming); Morten Bennedsen, Elena Simintzi, Margarita Tsoutsoura, and Daniel

Wolfenzon, "Do Firms Respond to Gender Pay Gap Transparency?," *Journal of Finance* 77, no. 4 (2022): 2051–2091.

61. Berson Clémence, Morgane Laouénan and Emmanuel Valat, "Outsourcing Recruitment as a Solution to Prevent Discrimination: A Correspondence Study," *Labour Economics* 64 (2020).

62. Dobbin Frank and Alexandra Kalev. "Why Diversity Programs Fail and What Works Better," *Harvard Business Review* 94 (2016): 52–60.

63. Patricia G. Devine, Patrick S. Forscher, Anthony J. Austin, and William T. L. Cox, "Long-Term Reduction in Implicit Race Bias: A Prejudice Habit-Breaking Intervention," *Journal of Experimental Social Psychology* 48, no. 6 (2012): 1267–1278.

64. Alex Lindsey, Eden King, Michelle Hebl, and Noah Levine, "The Impact of Method, Motivation, and Empathy on Diversity Training Effectiveness," *Journal of Business and Psychology* 30 (2015): 605–617.

65. Edward H. Chang, Katherine L. Milkman, Dena M Gromet, and Adam M. Grant, "The Mixed Effects of Online Diversity Training," *PNAS* 116, no. 16 (2019): 7778–7783.

66. In their book, *Getting to Diversity. What Works and What Doesn't*, Franck Dobbin and Alexandra Kalev even claim, based on a correlational analysis, that diversity training produces primarily negative outcomes for populations who are discriminated against because it alienates the dominant group by making them feel blamed, which can ultimately elicit backlash and exacerbate biases.

67. Marianne Bertrand, Dolly Chugh, and Sendhil Mullainathan, "Implicit Discrimination," *American Economic Review* 95, no. 2 (2005): 94–98.

68. Iris Bohnet, *What Works: Gender Equality by Design* (Cambridge, MA: Harvard University Press, 2016).

69. Richard A. DeVaul, Faith Jervey, James A. Chappell, Patricia Caver, Barbara Short, and Stephen O'Keefe, "Medical School Performance of Initially Rejected Students," *JAMA* 257, no. 1 (1987): 47–51.

70. Shai Danziger, Jonathan Levav, and Liora Avnaim-Pesso, "Extraneous Factors in Judicial Decisions," *Proceedings of the National Academy of Sciences of the United States of America (PNAS)* 108, no. 17 (2011): 6889–6892.

71. Hangartner, Kopp, and Siegenthaler. "Monitoring Hiring Discrimination through Online Recruitment Platforms."

72. Jeffrey A. Flory, Andreas Leibbrandt, Christina Rott, and Olga Stoddard, "Increasing Workplace Diversity: Evidence from a Recruiting Experiment at a Fortune 500 Company," *Journal of Human Resources* 56, no. 1 (2021): 73–92

73. OECD, *The Economic Case for More Gender Equality in Estonia.*

74. L. Rivera and A. Tilcsik, "Scaling Down Inequality: Rating Scales, Gender Bias, and the Architecture of Evaluation," *American Sociological Review* 84, no. 2 (2019): 248–274.

75. Relying on an experiment among men and women from nearly eighty countries (including the United States), a group of social psychologists has shown that men are more likely than are women to be seen as "brilliant." Interestingly, the study shows that, if anything, people explicitly say they associate women with brilliance. Yet implicit measures reveal a different story about the more automatic gender stereotypes that come to mind when thinking about brilliance. See Daniel Storagea, E. S. Tessa, B. Charlesworth, Mahzarin R. Banajib, and Andrei Cimpianc, "Adults and Children Implicitly Associate Brilliance with Men More Than Women," *Journal of Experimental Social Psychology,* 2020, doi: 10.1016/j.jesp.2020.104020.

76. B. Lucas et al., "A Longer Shortlist Increases the Consideration of Female Candidates in Male-Dominant Domains," *Nature Human Behaviour* 5/6 (2021): 736–742.

77. For a comprehensive discussion of the benefits and risks that artificial intelligence poses for labor markets, we refer to the 2023 edition of the OECD's *Employment Outlook*. Several principles are crucial when utilizing AI in the workplace, especially for decisions that have an impact on individual opportunities and rights. These include adapting workplace legislation to accommodate AI use, promoting the adoption of rigorous auditing and certification tools, endorsing a human-in-the-loop approach, and devising mechanisms to lucidly explain the rationale behind decisions powered by AI. See OECD, *Employment Outlook: Artificial Intelligence and the Labour Market* (Paris: OECD Publishing, 2023).

78. Mitchell Hoffman, Lisa B. Kahn, and Danielle Li. "Discretion in Hiring," *Quarterly Journal of Economics* 133, no. 2 (2018): 765–800.

79. Hilke Schellmann, *The Algorithm: How AI Can Hijack Your Career and Steal Your Future* (Hurst, 2024).

80. Leon Yin, Davey Alba, and Leonardo Nicoletti, "Open AI'S GPT Is a Recruiter's Dream Tool: Tests Show There's Racial Bias," Bloomberg, March 7, 2024.

81. Danielle Li, Lindsey R. Raymond, and Peter Bergman, "Hiring as Exploration," NBER Working Paper 27736, August 2020.

82. OECD, *Preparing Our Youth for an Inclusive and Sustainable World: The OECD PISA Global Competence Framework* (Paris: OECD Publishing, 2018).

83. According to David Broockman and Joshua Kalla, the nonjudgmental exchange of narratives is "a strategy where an individual attempts to persuade another person by providing to or eliciting from them narratives about relevant personal experiences while non-judgmentally listening to the views they express." This strategy builds on two approaches in the psychology literature, narrative persuasion and

high-quality listening. Previous research suggests that individuals are particularly receptive to persuasion through narratives as narratives are seen as less manipulative and thus as eliciting less counterarguing than direct argumentation. Furthermore, research in psychology indicates that nonjudgmental conversational contexts can diminish resistance to attitude change by lessening threats to one's self-identity. For more information, see Joshua Kalla and David E. Broockman, "Reducing Exclusionary Attitudes through Interpersonal Conversation: Evidence from Three Field Experiments," *American Political Science Review* 114, no. 2 (2020): 410–425.

84. For a literature review, see Elizabeth Levy Paluck, Roni Porat, Chelsey S. Clark, and Donald P. Green, "Prejudice Reduction: Progress and Challenges," *Annual Review of Psychology* 72 (2021): 533–560. See also Elizabeth Levy Paluck and Donald P. Green, "Prejudice Reduction: What Works? A Review and Assessment of Research and Practice," *Annual Review of Psychology* 60 (2009): 339–367.

85. Nilanjana Dasgupta and Anthony G. Greenwald, "On the Malleability of Automatic Attitudes: Combating Automatic Prejudice with Images of Admired and Disliked Individuals," *Journal of Personality and Social Psychology* 81, no. 5 (2001):. 800–814.

86. Oscar Barrera, Sergei Guriev, Emeric Henry, and Ekaterina Zhuravskaya, "Facts, Alternative Facts, and Fact Checking in Times of Post-Truth Politics," *Journal of Public Economics* 182 (2020): 104–123.

87. Andrew R. Todd, Galen V. Bodenhausen, Jennifer A. Richeson and Adam D. Galinsky, "Perspective Taking Combats Automatic Expressions of Racial Bias," *Journal of Personality and Social Psychology* 100, no. 6 (2011): 1027–1042.

88. Natalie R. Hall, Richard J. Crisp, and Mein-woei Suen, "Reducing Implicit Prejudice by Blurring Intergroup Boundaries," *Basic and Applied Social Psychology* 31, no. 3 (2009): 244–254.

89. OECD, *Fighting Homophobia and Transphobia in Schools: A Groundbreaking Impact Assessment* (Paris: OECD Publishing, 2023).

90. Luca Paolo Merlino, Max Friedrich Steinhardt, and Liam Wren-Lewis, "More Than Just Friends? School Peers and Adult Interracial Relationships," *Journal of Labor Economics* 37, no. 3 (2019): 663–713. In a subsequent paper using the same data, the authors show that, 20 years after exposure, white individuals who had more Black peers of the same gender in their grade tend to live in census tracts with higher proportions of Black residents. Further analysis suggests that this result is unlikely to be driven by economic opportunities or social networks; rather, the effect on residential choice appears to stem from a shift in preferences among white individuals. See Luca Paolo Merlino, Max Friedrich Steinhardt, and Liam Wren-Lewis, "The Long-Run Impact of Childhood Interracial Contact on Residential Segregation," *Journal of Public Economics* (2024). In collaboration with Philip Rosenbaum,

the authors extend their research in a new paper by applying their methodology to other countries. Specifically, they exploit quasi-random variation in the share of immigrant students across cohorts within Danish schools to examine whether inter-ethnic contact during childhood influences the hiring behavior of managers. Using administrative employer-employee data, they confirm that having more immigrant peers of the same gender in school leads Danish managers to hire more immigrants later in life. See Liam Wren-Lewis, Max Friedrich Steinhardt, Luca Paolo Merlino, and Philip Rosenbaum, "The Impact of Childhood Inter-ethnic Contact on Managers' Hiring Decisions," working paper (2024).

91. David Broockman and Joshua Kalla, "Durably Reducing Transphobia: A Field Experiment on Door-to-Door Canvassing," *Science* 352, no. 6282 (2016): 220–224.

92. On the approach urging the public not to discriminate, see Lisa Legault, Jennifer N. Gutsell, and Michael Inzlicht, "Ironic Effects of Antiprejudice Messages: How Motivational Interventions Can Reduce (but Also Increase) Prejudice," *Psychological Science* 22, no. 12 (2011): 1472–1477. On the humorous approach, see Aldert Vrij, Lucy Akehurst, and Beverley Smith, "Reducing Ethnic Prejudice: An Evaluation of Seven Recommended Principles for Incorporation in Public Campaigns," *Journal of Community & Applied Social Psychology* 13, no. 4 (2003): 284–299.

93. Another illustration of these approaches can be seen in the "Racism—Condemn or condone: There's no in-between" campaign launched in the UK in 1999. This campaign featured various posters similar to those in the Adia campaign. One of them showcased a close-up of a Black male's face with the word "Scared?" in bold red letters. This was followed by the caption "You should be. He's a dentist" in smaller white letters.

94. Abdelatif Er-rafiy and Markus Brauer, "Modifying Perceived Variability: Four Laboratory and Field Experiments Show the Effectiveness of a Ready-to-Be-Used Prejudice Intervention," *Journal of Applied Social Psychology* 43, no. 4 (2013): 840–853.

95. McConahay's modern racism scale, created in 1986 and subsequently translated and adapted to the French context by Michael Dambrun and Serge Guimond, is constructed from a list of statements regarding which interviewees are asked to state their degree of agreement/disagreement (e.g., "If the unemployment rate is high in France, it is because North Africans take jobs from the French"). See Michael Dambrun and Serge Guimond, "La théorie de la privation relative et l'hostilité envers les Nord-Africains," *Revue internationale de psychologie sociale* 14, no.1 (2001): 57–89; and John McConahay, "Modern Racism, Ambivalence, and the Modern Racism Scale," in *Prejudice, Discrimination and Racism*, ed. John F. Dovidio and Samuel L. Gaertner (New York: Academic Press, 1986), 91–126.

96. This line of research is informed by "psychic numbing," a phenomenon that resonates with the saying, "One man's death is a tragedy; a million deaths is a statistic." Rather than solely relying on statistics highlighting the pervasive

stigmatization, discrimination, and violence experienced by the outgroup, sharing personal testimonials and anecdotes often proves more effective in humanizing the issue. For more information on psychic numbing, see Daniel Västfjäll, Paul Slovic, Marcus Mayorga, and Ellen Peters, "Compassion Fade: Affect and Charity Are Greatest for a Single Child in Need," *PLOS ONE* 9, no. 6 (2014).

97. On the results in high-income countries, see Joshua L. Kalla and David E. Broockman, "Which Narrative Strategies Durably Reduce Prejudice? Evidence from Field and Survey Experiments Supporting the Efficacy of Perspective-Getting," *American Journal of Political Science* 67, no. 1 (2023): 185–204. On the results in low-income countries, see Nicole Audette, Jeremy Horowitz, and Kristin Michelitch, "Personal Narratives Reduce Negative Attitudes toward Refugees and Immigrant Outgroups: Evidence from Kenya," working paper (2021).

98. Audette, Horowitz, and Michelitch, "Personal Narratives Reduce Negative Attitudes toward Refugees and Immigrant Outgroups."

99. For Australia, Denmark, the UK, and the United States, see Maria Carmen Huerta, William Adema, Janeen Baxter, Wen-Jui Han, Metta Lausten, Rae Hyuck Lee, and Jane Waldfogel, "Fathers' Leave and Fathers' Involvement: Evidence from Four OECD Countries," *European Journal of Social Security* 16, no. 4 (2014): 308–347. For Canada, see A. Patnaik, "Reserving Time for Daddy: The Consequences of Fathers' Quotas," *Journal of Labor Economics* 37, no. 4 (2019): 1009–1059. For France, see A. Pailhé, A. Solaz, and M. Tô, "Can Daddies Learn to Care for Babies? The Effect of a Short Paternity Leave on the Division of Childcare and Housework," *Population Research and Policy Review* 43, no. 46 (2024). For Germany, see M. Tamm, "Fathers' Parental Leave-taking, Childcare Involvement and Labor Market Participation," *Labour Economics* 59 (2019): 184–197. For Spain, see G. Meil et al., "The Impact of Paternity Leave Compared to Unemployment on Child Care and Housework Distribution in Spain," *Journal of Family Issues,* 2021, 0192513X2110544. For Sweden, see A. Almqvist and A. Duvander, "Changes in Gender equality? Swedish Fathers' Parental Leave, Division of Childcare and Housework," *Journal of Family Studies* 20, no. 1 (2014): 19–27.

100. Farré, Lídia, Christina Felfe, Libertad Gonzalez and Patrick Schneider, "Changing Gender Norms across Generations: Evidence from a Paternity Leave Reform." IZA Discussion Paper no. 16341 (2023).

101. John Ekberg, Rickard Eriksson, and Guido Friebel, "Parental Leave: A Policy Evaluation of the Swedish 'Daddy-Month' Reform," *Journal of Public Economics* 97 (2013): 131–143.

102. Daniel Avdic and Arizo Karimi, "Modern Family? Paternity Leave and Marital Stability," *American Economic Journal: Applied Economics* 10, no. 4 (2018): 282–307.

103. Hélène Périvier and Grégory Verdugo, "Where Are the Fathers? The Effects of Earmarking Parental Leave on Fathers in France," *Industrial and Labor Relations Review* 77, no. 1 (2023).

104. Mathilde Émeriau, Jens Hainmueller, Dominik Hangartner, and David D. Laitin. "'Welcome to France': Can Mandatory Integration Contracts Foster Immigrant Integration?," *American Journal of Political Science* (forthcoming).

105. Alexia Lochmann, Hillel Rapoport, and Biagio Speciale, "The Effect of Language Training on Immigrants' Economic Integration: Empirical Evidence from France," *European Economic Review* 113 (2019): 265–296.

106. Alex Pont-Grau, Yu-Hsiang Lei, Joel Z. E. Lim, and Xing Xia, "The Effect of Language Training on Immigrants' Integration: Does the Duration of Training Matter?," *Journal of Economic Behavior & Organization* 212 (2023): 160–198.

107. Émeriau et al., "Welcome to France."

108. Thomas Liebig and Gilles Spielvogel, "Residential Segregation of Immigrants: Patterns, Drivers, Effects, and Policy Responses," in *International Migration Outlook 2021* (Paris: OECD Publishing, 2021).

109. Kirk Bansak et al., "Improving Refugee Integration through Data-Driven Algorithmic Assignment," *Science* 359, no. 6373 (2018).

## Chapter 12

1. For a more systematic review of these effects and ways of countering them, see Karla Hoff and James Walsh, "The Whys of Social Exclusion: Insights from Behavioral Economics," *The World Bank Research Observer* 33, no. 1 (2018): 1–33, and Marianne Bertrand and Esther Duflo, "Field Experiments on Discrimination," in *Handbook of Field Experiments*, vol. 1, ed. Abhijit V. Banerjee and Esther Duflo (North Holland: Elsevier, 2017), 309–393.

2. Holger Bonin, Thomas Dohmen, Armin Falk, David B. Huffman, and Uwe Sunde, "Cross-sectional Earnings Risk and Occupational Sorting: The Role of Risk Attitudes," *Labour Economics* 14, no. 6 (2007): 926–937.

3. Thomas Dohmen, Armin Falk, David B. Huffman, Jürgen Schupp, Uwe Sunde, and Gert Wagner, "Individual Risk Attitudes: Measurement, Determinants and Behavioral Consequences," *Journal of the European Economic Association* 9, no. 3 (2011): 522–550.

4. Muriel Niederle and Lise Vesterlund, "Do Women Shy Away from Competition? Do Men Compete Too Much?," *Quarterly Journal of Economics* 122, no. 3 (2007): 1067–1101.

5. Evren Örs, Frédéric Palomino, and Eloïc Peyrache, "Performance Gender Gap: Does Competition Matter?," *Journal of Labor Economics* 31, no. 3 (2013): 443–499.

6. Marcus Dittrich, Andreas Knabe. and Kristina Leipold, "Gender Differences in Experimental Wage Negotiations," *Economic Inquiry* 52, no. 2 (2014): 862–873.

7. Andreas Leibbrandt and John A. List, "Do Women Avoid Salary Negotiations? Evidence from a Large-Scale Natural Field Experiment," *Management Science* 61, no. 9 (2015): 2016–2024.

8. Alison L. Booth and Patrick Nolen, "Gender Differences in Risk Behaviour: Does Nurture Matter?," *Economic Journal* 122, no. 558 (2012): F56–F78.

9. Claude M. Steele and Joshua Aronson, "Stereotype Threat and the Intellectual Test Performance of African Americans," *Journal of Personality and Social Psychology* 69, no. 5 (1995): 797–811; Claude M. Steele and Joshua Aronson, "Stereotype Threat and the Test Performance of Academically Successful African Americans," in *The Black-White Test Score Gap*, ed. Christopher Jencks and Meredith Phillips (Washington, DC: Brookings Institution Press, 1998), 401–427. While most research identifying stereotype threat effects on Black students have been undertaken in predominantly white institutions (as in the article previously mentioned), a recent study failed to detect such effects on student performance in an historically Black institution with a racially more diverse faculty, suggesting the importance of the environment: see Mackenzie Alston, William A. Darity, Catherine C. Eckel, Lawrence McNeil, and Rhonda Sharpe, "The Effect of Stereotypes on Black College Test Scores at a Historically Black University," *Journal of Economic Behavior & Organization* 194(C) (2022): 408–424.

10. Robert Rosenthal and Lenore Jacobson, "Pygmalion in the Classroom," *Urban Review* 3, no. 1 (1968): 16–20.

11. See, for instance, in the case of the Netherlands, Reyn van Ewijk, "Same Work, Lower Grade? Student Ethnicity and Teachers' Subjective Assessments," *Economics of Education Review*30, no. 5 (2011): 1045–1058.

12. Lee Jussim and Kent D. Harber, "Teacher Expectations and Self-Fulfilling Prophecies: Knowns and Unknowns, Resolved and Unresolved Controversies," *Personality and Social Psychology Review* 9, no. 2 (2005): 131–155.

13. Dov Eden and Abraham B. Shani, "Pygmalion Goes to Boot Camp: Expectancy, Leadership, and Trainee Performance," *Journal of Applied Psychology* 67, no. 2 (1982): 194–199.

14. Elisha Y. Babad, Jacinto Inbar and Robert Rosenthal, "Pygmalion, Galatea, and the Golem: Investigations of Biased and Unbiased Teachers," *Journal of Educational Psychology*, 74 (4), 1982, p. 459–474.

15. Victor Lavy and Edith Sand, "On The Origins of Gender Human Capital Gaps: Short- and Long-Term Consequences of Teachers' Stereotypical Biases," *Journal of Public Economics* 167 (2018): 263–279.

16. Michela Carlana, "Implicit Stereotypes: Evidence from Teachers' Gender Bias," *Quarterly Journal of Economics* 134, no. 3 (2019): 1163–1224.

17. Stephen J. Ceci, Donna K. Ginther, Shulamit Kahn, and Wendy M. Williams, "Women in Academic Science: A Changing Landscape," *Psychological Science in the Public Interest* 15, no. 3 (2014): 75–141.

18. Alberto Alesina, Michela Carlana, Eliana La Ferrara, and Paolo Pinotti, "Revealing Stereotypes: Evidence from Immigrants in Schools," *American Economic Review* 114, no. 7 (2024): 1916–48.

19. Nina Guyon and Elise Huillery, "Biased Aspirations and Social Inequality at School: Evidence from French Teenagers (with Nina Guyon)," *Economic Journal* 131, no. 2 (2021): 745–796.

20. Albert Bandura, *Self-Efficacy: The Exercise of Control* (Basingstoke: Macmillan, 1997).

21. J. B. Grossman and J. E. Rhodes, "The Test of Time: Predictors and Effects of Duration in Youth Mentoring Programs," *American Journal of Community Psychology* 30 (2002): 199–206.

22. D. L. DuBois, B. E. Holloway, J. C. Valentine, and H. Cooper, "Effectiveness of Mentoring Programs for Youth: A Meta-Analytic Review," *American Journal of Community Psychology* 30, no. 2 (2002): 157–197; J. E. Rhodes, "Improving Youth Mentoring Interventions through Research-Based Practice," *American Journal of Community Psychology* 41 (2008): 35–42.

23. David J. De Wit, David L. DuBois, Gizem Erdem, Simon Larose, and Ellen L. Lipman, "Predictors of Mentoring Relationship Quality: Investigation from the Perspectives of Youth and Parent Participants in Big Brothers Big Sisters of Canada One-to-One Mentoring Programs," *Journal of Community Psychology* 48 (2020): 192–208.

24. Thomas S. Dee, "A Teacher Like Me: Does Race, Ethnicity, or Gender Matter?," *American Economic Review* 95, no. 2 (2005): 158–165; S. E. Carrell, M. E. Page, and J. E. West, "Sex and Science: How Professor Gender Perpetuates the Gender Gap," *Quarterly Journal of Economics* 125, no. 3 (2010): 1101–1144; and J. Lim and J. Meer, "The Impact of Teacher-Student Gender Matches: Random Assignment Evidence from South Korea," *Journal of Human Resources* 52, no. 4 (2017): 979–997.

25. See, for instance, E. Lawner, D. Quinn, G. Camacho, B. Johnson, and B. Pan-Weisz, "Ingroup Role Models and Underrepresented Students' Performance and Interest in STEM: A Meta-Analysis of Lab and Field Studies," *Social Psychology of Education* 22 (2019): 1169–1195; J. R. Gladstone and A. Cimpian, "Which Role Models Are Effective for Which Students? A Systematic Review and Four Recommendations for Maximizing the Effectiveness of Role Models in STEM," *International Journal of STEM Education* 8 (2021): 59.

26. T. Breda, J. Grenet, M. Monnet, and C. Van Effenterre, "How Effective Are Female Role Models in Steering Girls towards STEM? Evidence from French High Schools," *Economic Journal* 133, no. 653 (2023): 1773–1809.

27. Eliana La Ferrara, Alberto Chong, and Suzanne Duryea, "Soap Operas and Fertility: Evidence from Brazil," *American Economic Journal: Applied Economics* 4, no. 4 (2012): 1–31.

28. Sarah C. Gomillion and Traci A. Giuliano, "The Influence of Media Role Models on Gay, Lesbian, and Bisexual Identity," *Journal of Homosexuality* 58, no. 3 (2011): 330–354.

29. Ellen Riggle, Alan Ellis, and Anne Crawford, "The Impact of 'Media Contact' on Attitudes toward Gay Men," *Journal of Homosexuality* 31 (1996): 55–69.

30. GLAAD and P&G, *LGBTQ Inclusion in Advertising & Media* (2020), https://www.glaad.org/inclusion. In the absence of any random or quasi-random assignment of non-LGBTIQ+ people to films, TV shows, or ads showing LGBTIQ+ people, this survey merely provides descriptive evidence and cannot establish a causal relationship between exposure and acceptance. For instance, one cannot exclude that the non-LGBTIQ+ people who are more comfortable with homosexuality are also those spontaneously more often exposed to and welcoming of media content showing LGBTIQ+ people.

31. David S. Yeager et al., "Teaching a Lay Theory before College Narrows Achievement Gaps at Scale," *Proceedings of the National Academy of Sciences of the United States of America (PNAS)* 113, no. 24 (2016).

32. Geoffrey L. Cohen, Julio Garcia, Nancy Apfel, and Allison Master, "Reducing the Racial Achievement Gap: A Social- Psychological Intervention," *Science* 313, no. 5791 (2006): 1307–1310.

33. Geoffrey L. Cohen, Julio Garcia, Valerie Purdie-Vaughns, Nancy Apfel, and Patricia Brzustoski, "Recursive Processes in Self-Affirmation: Intervening to Close the Minority Achievement Gap," *Science* 324, no. 5925 (2009): 400–403.

34. Joshua Aronson, Carrie B. Fried and Catherine Good, "Reducing the Effects of Stereotype Threat on African American College Students by Shaping Theories of Intelligence," *Journal of Experimental Social Psychology* 38, no. 2 (2002): 113–125.

35. David Paunesku, Gregory M. Walton, Carissa Romero, Eric N. Smith, David S. Yeager and Carol S. Dweck, "Mind-Set Interventions Are a Scalable Treatment for Academic Underachievement," *Psychological Science*, 26, no. 6 (2015): 784–793.

36. D. S. Yeager, P. Hanselman, G. M. Walton, et al., "A National Experiment Reveals Where a Growth Mindset Improves Achievement," *Nature* 573 (2019): 364–369.

37. Elise Huillery, Adrien Bouguen, Axelle Charpentier, Yann Algan, and Coralie Chevallier, "The Role of Mindset in Education: A Large-Scale Field Experiment in Disadvantaged Schools," *Economic Journal* (forthcoming).

38. Sule Alan, Teodora Boneva, and Seda Ertac, "Ever Failed, Try Again, Succeed Better: Results from a Randomized Educational Intervention on Grit," *Quarterly Journal of Economics* 134, no. 3 (2019): 1121–116.

39. Eric P. Bettinger and Rachel Baker, "The Effects of Student Coaching: An Evaluation of a Randomized Experiment in Student Advising," *Educational Evaluation and Policy Analysis* 36, no. 1 (2014): 3–19.

40. Angela L. Duckworth, Teri Kirby, Anton Gollwitzer, and Gabriele Oettingen, "From Fantasy to Action: Mental Contrasting with Implementation Intentions (MCII) Improves Academic Performance in Children," *Social Psychological and Personality Science* 4, no. 6 (2013): 745–753.

41. Flavio Cunha and James J. Heckman, "The Evolution of Inequality, Heterogeneity and Uncertainty in Labor Earnings in the U.S. Economy," NBER Working Paper 13526 (Cambridge, MA: National Bureau of Economic Research, 2007). See also Flavio Cunha, and James Heckman, "The Technology of Skill Formation," *American Economic Review* 97, no. 2 (2007): 31–47.

42. For an evaluation of the Peery Pre-school Project, see James J. Heckman, Song Hyeok Moon, Rodrigo Pinto, Peter A. Savalyev, and Adam Q. Yavitz, "The Rate of Return to the Highscope Perry Preschool Program," *Journal of Public Economics* 94, nos. 1–2 (2010): 114–128.

43. Marianne Bitler, Hilary Hoynes, and Thurston Domina, "Experimental Evidence on Distributional Effects of Head Start," NBER Working Paper 20434 (Cambridge, MA: National Bureau of Economic Research, 2014).

44. See Bitler, Hoynes, and Domina, "Experimental Evidence on Distributional Effects of Head Start," and Janet Currie and Duncan Thomas, "Does Head Start Make a Difference?," *American Economic Review* 85, no. 3 (1995): 341–364.

45. K. Lee, "The Effects of Children's Age at Entering Head Start on Their Short- and Long-Term Developmental Outcomes," *Social Service Review* 82, no. 4 (2008): 663–702.

46. A. Krueger, "Economic Considerations and Class Size," *Economic Journal* 113, no. 485 (2003); A. Krueger and D. Whitmore, "The Effect of Attending a Small Class in the Early Grades on College-Test Taking and Middle School Test Results: Evidence from Project STAR," *Economic Journal* 111, no. 468 (2001).

47. R. Chetty, J. Friedman, N. Hilger, E. Saez, D. Schanzenbach, and D. Yagan, "How Does Your Kindergarten Classroom Affect Your Earnings? Evidence from Project STAR," *Quarterly Journal of Economics* 76, no. 4 (2011).

48. T. Piketty and M. Valdenaire, "L'impact de la taille des classes sur la réussite scolaire dans les écoles, collèges et lycées français: Estimations à partir du panel primaire 1997 et du panel secondaire 1995," *Les Dossiers de l'Education Nationale* no. 173 (Paris: MENDEP, 2006).

49. P. Fredriksson, B. Öckert, and H. Oosterbeek, "Long-Term Effects of Class Size," *Quarterly Journal of Economics* 128, no. 1 (2013).

50. Peter Fredriksson, Björn Öckert, and Hessel Oosterbeek, "Parental Responses to Public Investments in Children: Evidence from a Maximum Class Size Rule," *Journal of Human Resources* 51, no. 4 (2016): 832–868.

51. Adrien Bouguen, Julien Grenet, and Marc Gurgand, "La taille des classes influence-t-elle la réussite scolaire?," Note IPP no. 28 (Paris: Institut des Politiques Publiques, 2018).

52. Shira K. Mattera, Robin Jacob, Cullen MacDowell, and Pamela A. Morris, *Long-Term Effects of Enhanced Early Childhood Math Instruction: The Impacts of Making Pre-K Count and High 5s on Third-Grade Outcomes* (New York: MDRC, 2021). See http://www.mdrc.org/project/making-pre-k-count#design-site-data-sources.

53. The program has also been introduced in the UK, Canada, Mexico, Australia, and Israel.

54. See http://www.successforall.org and G. Borman, R. E. Slavin, A. Cheung, A. Chamberlain, N. A. Madden, and B. Chambers, "Final Reading Outcomes of the National Randomized Field Trial of Success for All," *American Educational Research Journal* 44, no. 3 (2007): 701–731.

55. See T. R. Guskey and T. D. Pigott, "Research on Group-Based Mastery Learning Programs: A Meta-Analysis," *Journal of Educational Research* 81, no. 4 (1988): 197–216.

56. OECD, *Effective Teacher Policies: Insights from PISA* (Paris: OECD Publishing, 2018).

57. Roland G. Fryer and Will Dobbie, "Getting Beneath the Veil of Effective Schools: Evidence from New York City," *American Economic Journal: Applied Economics* 5, no. 4 (2013): 28–60.

58. Roland G. Fryer and Will Dobbie, "Are High Quality Schools Enough to Close the Achievement Gap? Evidence from a Social Experiment in Harlem," *American Economic Journal: Applied Economics* 3, no. 3 (2011): 158–187. For the impact on math, reading, and writing skills, see Atila Abdulkadiroğlu, Joshua Angrist, Susan Dynarski, Thomas Kane, and Parag Pathak, "Accountability and Flexibility in Public Schools: Evidence from Boston's Charters and Pilots," *Quarterly Journal of Economics* 126, no. 2 (2011): 699–748.

59. Joshua Angrist, Sarah Cohodes, Susan Dynarski, Parag Pathak, and Christopher Walters, "Stand and Deliver: Effects of Boston's Charter High Schools on College Preparation, Entry, and Choice," *Journal of Labor Economics* 34, no. 2 (2016): 275–318.

60. Joshua Angrist, Susan Dynarski, Thomas Kane, Parag Pathak and Christopher Walters, "Who Benefits from KIPP?," *Journal of Policy Analysis and Management* 31, no. 4 (2012): 837–860.

61. Roland G. Fryer and Will Dobbie, "The Medium-Term Impacts of High-Achieving Charter Schools," *Journal of Political Economy* 123, no. 5 (2015): 985–1037.

62. Christina Clark Tuttle, Kevin Booker, Philip Gleason, Gregory Chojnacki, Virginia Knechtel, Thomas Coen, Ira Nichols-Barrer, and Lisbeth Goble, *Understanding the Effect of KIPP as It Scales: Volume I. Impacts on Achievement and Other Outcomes* (Princeton, NJ: Mathematica Policy Research, 2015).

63. Alicia Demers, Ira Nichols-Barrer, Elisa Steele, Maria Bartlett, and Philip Gleason, *Long-Term Impacts of KIPP Middle and High Schools on College Enrollment, Persistence, and Attainment (Final Report)* (Princeton, NJ: Mathematica Policy Research, 2023).

64. Will Dobbie and Roland Fryer, "Charter Schools and Labor Market Outcomes," *Journal of Labor Economics* 38, no. 4 (2020).

65. Christopher R. Walters, "The Demand for Effective Charter Schools," *Journal of Political Economy* 126, no. 6 (2018): 2179–2223.

66. Michael Gilraine, Uros Petronijevic, and John D. Singleton, "Horizontal Differentiation and the Policy Effect of Charter Schools," *American Economic Journal: Economic Policy* 13, no. 3 (2021): 239–276.

67. A. Eyles, C. Hupkau, and S. Machin, "Academies, Charter and Free Schools: Do New School Types Deliver Better Outcomes?," *Economic Policy* (2016): 453–501.

68. For Sweden, evidence of such segregation in line with the development of Free schools is provided by Anders Böhlmark, Helena Holmlund, and Mikael Lindahl, *Skolsegregation och skolval*, IFAU Report 2015:5. In the case of France, where about 18 percent of pupils are enrolled in publicly subsidized private schools, see Constance Frohly, "Does School Choice Increase Social Segregation? Evidence from Private Schools Opening in France between 2005 and 2019," mimeo (2022); P. Givord, M. Guillerm, O. Monso, and F. Murat, "La ségrégation sociale entre les collèges," *Education et formations* 91 (2016): 53–76; and Youssef Souidi, "School Segregation: Is It All about Residential Sorting? Evidence from a Nationwide School System," mimeo (2023).

69. Since 2001, the Paris-based Sciences Po university has been practicing a form of positive discrimination for young people from some one hundred high schools located in priority education zones. In 2017, there were 158 such admissions.

70. Thomas J. Espenshade and Chang Y. Chung, "The Opportunity Cost of Admission Preferences at Elite Universities," *Social Science Quarterly* 86, no. 2 (2005): 293–305.

71. Caroline M. Hoxby and Christopher Avery, "The Missing 'One-Offs': The Hidden Supply of High-Achieving, Low-Income Students," *Brookings Papers on Economic Activity,* Spring 2013, 1–61.

72. Caroline Hoxby and Sarah Turner, "What High-Achieving Low-Income Students Know about College," *American Economic Review* 105, no. 5 (2015): 514–517.

73. Peter Arcidiacono, Esteban M. Aucejo, and Ken Spenner, "What Happens after Enrollment? An Analysis of the Time Path of Racial Differences in GPA and Major Choice," *IZA Journal of Labor Economics* 1 (2012).

74. The impact on human capital investment is not settled, though. See the debate on the effects of Proposition 209 in California, which, following its enactment in 1998, prohibited state governmental institutions from considering race, sex, or ethnicity, specifically in the areas of public employment, public contracting, and public education: R. Caldwell Jr., "The Effects of University Affirmative Action Policies on the Human Capital Development of Minority Children: Do Expectations Matter?," Working Paper Series in Theoretical and Applied Economics, University of Kansas, Department of Economics (2010); K. Antonovics and B. Backes, "The Effect of Banning Affirmative Action on Human Capital Accumulation Prior to College Entry," *IZA Journal of Labor Economics* 3, no. 5 (2014).

75. Peter Arcidiacono and Michael Lovenheim, "Affirmative Action and the Quality-Fit Trade-Off," *Journal of Economic Literature* 54, no. 1 (2016): 3–51.

## Conclusion

1. Barack Obama, "Nelson Mandela Annual Lecture 2018: Obama's Full Speech," Nelson Mandela Foundation, July 18, 2018.

2. Ipsos survey for the Foot Ensemble association, May 17, 2018.

# Index